August 5, 1997

To David,

with admiration

for a theological fellow traveler.

Peace!

Charles Marsh

RECLAIMING
DIETRICH BONHOEFFER

RECLAIMING DIETRICH BONHOEFFER

The Promise of His Theology

CHARLES MARSH

New York   Oxford
OXFORD UNIVERSITY PRESS
1994

Oxford University Press

Oxford   New York   Toronto
Delhi   Bombay   Calcutta   Madras   Karachi
Kuala Lumpur   Singapore   Hong Kong   Tokyo
Nairobi   Dar es Salaam   Cape Town
Melbourne   Auckland   Madrid

and associated companies in
Berlin   Ibadan

Copyright © 1994 by Charles Marsh

Published by Oxford University Press, Inc.
200 Madison Avenue, New York, New York 10016

Library of Congress Cataloging-in-Publication Data
Marsh, Charles, 1958–
Reclaiming Dietrich Bonhoeffer :
the promise of his theology /
Charles Marsh.
p.   cm.   Includes bibliographical references and index. ISBN 0-19-508723-2
1. Bonhoeffer, Dietrich, 1906–1945.
2. Theology, Doctrinal—History—20th century.
I. Title.
BX4827.B57M35   1994   230'.044' 092—dc20   93-30806

1 3 5 7 9 8 6 4 2

Printed in the United States of America
on acid-free paper

To Karen

PREFACE

This book offers a new way of reading the Christian theologian
Dietrich Bonhoeffer—one not previously developed in detail by theologians. I understand Bonhoeffer's theology as an account of the continuities of God's identity, as well as human identities, socially and
personally considered, in Jesus Christ. In this context, I argue that
Bonhoeffer's christological description of life with others offers a
compelling and unexpectedly rich alternative to post-Kantian models of selfhood—to conceptions of the self as the center of all relations to others. By evaluating his writings against the background of
modern German philosophy, I show that Bonhoeffer, while working
within the circumference of Karl Barth's theology, provides both a
powerful critique and an innovative redescription of the tradition of
transcendental subjectivity. As such, I wish to reclaim Bonhoeffer's
theology for contemporary theological inquiry.

But the success of reclaiming Bonhoeffer's theology requires several demanding and interconnected tasks. First, we must reckon with
the theological complexity of his relationship with Karl Barth. While
most interpretations of the relationship tend to impose overly sim-
plistic and reductionistic schemes to this matter—that is, Lutheran
versus Reformed, *theologia crucis* versus *theologia gloriae*, *finitum
capax infiniti* versus *finitum non capax infiniti*, theologian of divine
promeity versus theologian of divine aseity—each of which has an
indisputably important role in accounting for the differences but is
not singly the basic difference, I wish to attend to the conversation
between Bonhoeffer and Barth in a way that preserves its intricacy
and narrative drama.

As early as his habilitation thesis, *Act and Being*, Bonhoeffer was
concerned with the problem of divine and human continuities in
Barth's theology. In particular, he wished to preserve the four conti-

nuities of (1) God in himself (*a se*), (2) God in relation to the world
(*ad extra*), (3) human community, or the continuity of the self and
its others, and (4) human subjectivity in itself, from the impression-
isms of a dialectical actualism. Barth's distinction between the primary and secondary objectivity of revelation, driven by the trinitarian
logic of his advanced dogmatic reflections, provided Bonhoeffer with
the theological framework within which to think these continuities
in reference to their christological coherence.

What does the distinction involve? Barth's purpose was to stress
the priority of God's aseity over his promeity, though not with the
intention of intruding a dichotomy between God in himself and God
in his revelation but rather to emphasize the priority of God's identity over all other identities, to stress that human and worldly pres-
ences are meaningful only in relation to the primary identity of God's
trinitarian self-relation, in short, to say that before all else is, God is
God. If objectivity is ascribed to God (as must be done when speaking about God as the source of all reality and of Jesus Christ as the
witness of God to humanity), then we must distinguish between God
in his triune life as such (in his primary objectivity) and God as he
comes to us in the revelation of Jesus Christ (in his secondary objectivity). As Barth writes, "In His triune life as such, objectivity, and
with it knowledge, is divine reality before creaturely objectivity
and knowledge exist. We call this the primary objectivity of God, and
distinguish from it the secondary, i.e., the objectivity which He has
for us too in His revelation, in which He gives Himself to be known
by us as He knows Himself. It is distinguished from the primary
objectivity, not by a lesser degree of truth, but by its particular form
suitable for us, the creature."[1] In both cases, God is *objective for us*;
however, only in the immanent trinitarian self-relation is it possible
to say that God's objectivity is primary, that it is originarily self-
identical to who God is in himself.

In my view, the way to make more meaningful Bonhoeffer's conversation with Barth is to see his thought as a rigorous exploration of
the secondary objectivity of revelation, keenly attentive to the inner
christological sense of worldliness, though by no means discounting
the magnificent story of God's aseity told by him. Bonhoeffer wants
to interpret all reality as part of the rich tapestry of God's promeity.
Yet importantly—for I think this is the missing link between conventional views of the relationship and one that promises new
avenues for reflection—Bonhoeffer pursues the inquiry of the secondary objectivity of revelation within the presupposition of Barth's narration of God's primary trinitarian self-identity. The failure of even

the most sympathetic interpreters to situate Bonhoeffer's christo-centric, "christomorphic,"[2] or "christocratic"[3] theology in a deeper trinitarian ground has the ironic effect of eviscerating Bonhoeffer of much of his theological sophistication and power. Indeed, christology and sociality are intimately connected in Bonhoeffer's theology, yet when deracinated from the primary context of the identity of God's self-relation, christology and sociality become at once mutually totalizing and theologically ambiguous. On the one hand, categories derived from human sociality tend to usurp the priority of christology; on the other hand, christology bereft of trinitarian reflection tends to compress theological and social realities into its own exclusive reason.

I claim that Bonhoeffer's investigation of the secondary objectivity of revelation must be interpreted such that it always presupposes the primary objectivity of God's trinitarian identity. Whatever differences of emphasis and background inform the complex interactions of the two theologians, Bonhoeffer's theology is possible only in view of Barth's revolution in theological method. Apropos of this indebtedness, Hans Frei once remarked that the daunting prolixity of Barth's oeuvre, the "lengthy, even leisurely unfolding" of his theological universe, was utterly indispensable.[4] Frei says, "For he was restating or re-using a language that had once been accustomed talk, both in first-order use in ordinary or real life, and in second-order technical theological reflection, but had now for a long time, perhaps more than 250 years, been receding from natural familiarity, certainly in theological discourse."[5] Barth's massive recreation of "a universe of discourse," with its peculiar principles and rules, signs and significations, with its own logic and internal rhythm, is the very condition of the possibility of Bonhoeffer's theological pilgrimage. Moreover, the animating center of Barth's revolution was not human crisis, dialectical negation, or political subversion, but the celebration of God's triune mystery. I understand Bonhoeffer's theology to be fully meaningful only in view of his attentiveness to this mystery. Therefore, while it is undoubtedly true, as virtually all Bonhoeffer scholars agree, that his description of selfhood must be understood in the context of community, it is equally necessary to hold that his description of community must be understood in the context of the trinitarian identity of God's being God.

The second task of reclaiming Bonhoeffer's theology requires a consideration of his thought in the framework of its larger intellectual milieu. My attention herein will focus on Bonhoeffer's use of philosophy. Despite the prominence of philosophical concerns in much of Bonhoeffer's writings, precious little scholarly attention has been given to this facet of his thought.[6] Yet the problem is more serious than a paucity of critical secondary literature. Bonhoeffer genuinely loved to read philosophy, and the effects of scholarship which write this interest out of the picture through theological revisionism, interpretive legerdemain, or mere omission create distorted presentations of the man himself. For example, Bonhoeffer spent his first two university terms at the University of Tübingen in the academic year 1923–1924 engrossed in the study of philosophy. He participated in Karl Groos's seminars in Logic, the History of Contemporary Philosophy, and Kant's First Critique.[7] A glance at Bonhoeffer's course register at the University of Berlin, where he transferred the following year, illustrates his decision to work with many of finest theological minds in contemporary Europe, that is, Reinhold Seeberg, Karl Holl, Adolf Deissmann, and Adolf von Harnack, but it also confirms his continued interest in philosophy. He read epistemology with Heinrich Maier and "Ideengeschichte der Logik" with the *Privatdozent* Rieffert. Additionally, he attended lectures on psychology and "Gestalt-theorie" by the eminent Berlin psychologists Max Wertheimer and Wolfgang Köhler.[8] When Bonhoeffer returned to Berlin in early 1929 from his year as a curate in Barcelona, he became a "voluntary assistant" for Seeberg's successor, Wilhelm Lütgert, a specialist in German idealism and author of the multivolume work *Die Religion des deutschen Idealismus und ihr Ende*. Bonhoeffer's philosophical interests are especially evident in his doctoral dissertation, *Sanctorum Communio* (1927), and his habilitation thesis, *Act and Being* (1930), both containing sustained discussions of seminal figures from modern German philosophy, but they are also found in numerous lectures, essays, and occasional pieces written during his years as a lecturer at Berlin.[9]

Importantly, Bonhoeffer did not abandon his interest in philosophy after he decided to leave the Berlin faculty in 1933 in response to the increasing demands of the church crisis. *The Cost of Discipleship*, *Life Together*, and *Ethics* form a kind of trilogy in which the triadic shape of Bonhoeffer's theology—christology, community, and selfhood—are explicated by a complex theological grammar. This grammar has too often been construed as pietistic and naive (at least in reference to the first two books). In fact, these texts offer important subtextual discussions with Bonhoeffer's philosophical conversation partners on the issues of divine and human identity. The time is propitious for these discussions to be reconstructed and in turn integrated into the interpretation of Bonhoeffer's theology, not simply for the scholarly purpose of locating and clarifying philosophical influences but in order to show that much of the subtextual material illuminates (perhaps surprisingly) the sophistication, complexity, and continuity of his thought. Further, the allusive and evocative power of the *Letters and Papers from Prison* compels the reader to position Bonhoeffer in a broad range of intellectual interests and concerns. As I intend to show, by considering Bonhoeffer with reference to his philosophical and extratheological concerns, a new understanding of his thought begins to emerge: one more conceptually and intellectually nuanced than hitherto imagined, one of a theologian who read deeply and eclectically, who crafted deliberately cunning and shrewd arguments against the tradition of transcendental subjectivity, a Bonhoeffer whose profession of Jesus Christ as Lord united a disorienting confessional simplicity with an elaborate texture of biblical, philosophical, and political thematics.

The third task of reappraising, or reinvigorating, Bonhoeffer's theology is to show how both the previously mentioned tasks are brought into the service of his thinking about the new social ontology of Christ's presence in the world. "Christ existing as community," "Christ the center," "Christ as the real," and "Jesus as the one for other"—in all these formulations Bonhoeffer is trying to give expression not only to a theological manner of understanding God's promeity (his being for the world) but also to the way in which humanity in general and the individual self in particular become reconfigured *in Christ*, that is, in the life of discipleship and of obedience to Jesus Christ. Bonhoeffer was convinced that the assertion of the self-constitutive subject endemic to the modern identity has invidious consequences for the project of conceiving christology, community, and selfhood. Theologically, it tends to compromise revelation's prevenient alterity. Imbricated in social experience, it tends to consume the other into some form of univocal self-sameness. Throughout the course of his writings, Bonhoeffer tried to demonstrate how a christological description of human togetherness could affirm the integrity of the self and the other—both the divine and human other—within the unity of God's identity. Bonhoeffer's understanding of the concreteness of revelation in human togetherness can only be fully understood when it is seen as a theological response to the aporias of his philosophical tradition within the context of Barth's new linguistic world.

Thus, to restate, I consider Bonhoeffer's theology to be an account of the continuities of God's identity, as well as human identities, socially and personally considered, in Jesus Christ. However, to probe whether and how this is the case will involve studying not primary and secondary objectivity *in general* but rather the *particularities* of this objectivity with regard to (1) philosophy (chapters 2 and 3), (2) Christology (chapters 4 and 5), (3) community (Chapter 6), and (4) selfhood or anthropology (Chapter 7). I hope to show that there is still much to be claimed from the promise of Bonhoeffer's theological legacy.

Baltimore   C. M.
August 1993

ACKNOWLEDGMENTS

I take pleasure in thanking the friends, colleagues, and institutions that made this book possible. Merold Westphal and the participants of an NEH Summer Workshop at Fordham University provided a stimulating environment for reading and arguing Hegel, even during the dog days of July in the Bronx. I owe a great deal to various members of the English Language Section of the International Bonhoeffer Society whose commitment to careful scholarship and responsible action is a standard for my own work; in particular, to Clifford Green, Wayne Floyd, Geffrey Kelly, John Godsey, Robin Lovin, and Larry Rasmussen. Without hours of conversation with my colleague and friend Jim Buckley, this book would have never been written. It is both astonishing and humbling that he is always willing to use his extraordinary knowledge of Christian theology in service to others. I am indebted to my editor at Oxford University Press, Cynthia Read, for her enthusiastic support, intellectual insight, and all-around good sense. Of course, there are numerous people who have shaped this book in an indirect though meaningful way and to whom gratitude is due: among these are David Klemm, William Desmond, Robert Scharlemann, Nan Toler, and my parents, Robert and Myra Toler Marsh.

A sabbatical leave to write this book was supported by the J. Mack Robinson Foundation and the generous patronage of W. Lee Burge, John and Marion Ellis, and Joy Roberts. The Deutsche Akademische Austauschdienst gave me the opportunity to complete the book at the University of Heidelberg. Wolfgang Huber did more than his share to make my stay in Heidelberg not only productive but fun: he was truly the perfect host. Eberhard and Renate Bethge gladly opened their home in Villiprott to yet another scholar eager to talk to Bonhoeffer's best friend and niece. Their contribution to both Bonhoeffer scholarship and contemporary theology is incalculable. I thank Peter Macek, of Charles University in Prague, Czechoslovakia, for his interest in my work and for the opportunity to lecture on Bonhoeffer and Barth to an exciting group of students. I also owe a special thanks to the community of the Baptist Theological Seminary in Rüschlikon, Switzerland, for offering me, time and again, a refuge of rest and rejuvenation.

Finally, I am exceedingly grateful to my wife, Karen Wright Marsh, whose love and comradery are the ground under my feet, and to our sons, Henry and Will, whose playful irreverence is my greatest delight.

An earlier and substantively different version of Chapter 5 was first published as "Human Community and Divine Presence: Bonhoeffer's Theological Critique of Hegel," in the *Scottish Journal of Theology* (Winter 1992). An earlier version of Chapter 6 initially appeared under the title "Bonhoeffer on Heidegger and Togetherness," in *Modern Theology* (July 1992). Portions of Chapter 7 were originally published under the title "The Overabundant Self and the Transcendental Tradition: Bonhoeffer Against the Self-Reflective Subject," in the *Journal of the American Academy of Religion* (Fall 1992). Thanks to the publishers and editors of these journals for permission to reprint sections of my articles. Scripture quotations are from the New International Version, copyright © 1978, by the New York International Bible Society.

CONTENTS

III The Self for Others

I

The Context
of Reclamation

1

Barth and Bonhoeffer on the Worldliness of Revelation

The Biographical Context

Bonhoeffer discovered Karl Barth's theology sometime between his visit to Rome in the winter of 1924 and the beginning of work on *Sanctorum Communio* in the summer months of 1925.[1] Bonhoeffer sounds very much the student of the Berlin school in his journal entry of August 1924: "I have a very interesting book, Max Weber's *Sociology of Religion.* . . . After Weber I also propose to read Troeltsch's *The Social Teachings of the Christian Churches* and to finish off Husserl—and, if I have time, to tackle Schleiermacher thoroughly."[2] However, in May and June of 1925 the tone of his journal entries and letters dramatically changed. He began reading works by Barth and by many of the other so-called dialectical theologians and, as Bethge says, an " 'entirely new' note crept in."[3] Bonhoeffer became such an admirer of Barth's *The Word of God and the Word of Man* that he implored his mother to read it (which she read alongside Troeltsch, in whom her son had by now lost interest) and also presented a copy of the book as a gift to his god-father, Hans von Hase. During several attacks of the flu in the winter 1924–1925, Bonhoeffer spent most of his time reading Barth and Ibsen intermittently.[4]

Two important situations inspired Bonhoeffer's interest in Barth. The first was his friendship with his cousin Hans-Christoph von Hase, who after hearing Barth's lectures at Göttingen, decided to abandon his major in mathematics and transfer to the theology faculty. Bonhoeffer borrowed von Hase's notes, which had been meticulously transcribed by hand under the heading "Karl Barth, dictated notes on 'Instruction on the Christian Religion.'"

The second was the controversy between Barth and Adolf von Harnack that waged as early as 1920 in numerous theological symposia and in the pages of the influential *Christliche Welt*. According to Harnack, theology ought to be about the business of redressing the positivization of Christianity by means of the historical-critical task of separating dogma from kerygma. Harnack liked to recite the phrase from the classical Latin dramatist Terence, *homo sum, nihil humanum a me alienum puto*, and reformulate it to read, *homo sum, nihil historicum a me alienum puto*.[5] The man Jesus gave birth to a religion that has both a historical and a human-ethical factor. For Harnack, the historical forms of the religion of Jesus are at the same time the bearers of the truth of Jesus: In these forms the essence of religion continually displays and amplifies itself. Harnack describes the essence of religion as the simplicity of trust and love, based on a notion of the Gospel "being something so simple, so divine, and therefore *so truly human*, as to be most certain of being understood when it is left entirely free, and also as to produce essentially the same experiences and convictions in individual souls."[6] Barth would have very few kind words to say about this description.

Nowhere is the conflict better illustrated than at the Aarau Students' Conference of April 1920, where Barth delivered the paper "Biblical Questions, Insights, and Vistas." In the presence of Harnack, Barth unleashed a full-scale attack on what he considered the central convictions of the liberal-historical school. "Jesus simply has nothing to do with religion. The meaning of his life is the actuality of that which is not actually present in my religion—the actuality of the unapproachable, the unreachable, the incomprehensible, the realization of the possibility, which is not a matter of speculation: 'Behold I make all things new!'"[7] In opposition to Harnack and the liberals, Barth called singular attention to the transcendent Word of God which is actively invading the world in judgment and crisis. He said, "The affirmation of God, man, and the world given in the New Testament is based exclusively upon the possibility of a new order absolutely beyond human thought; and therefore, as prerequisite to that order, there must come a crisis that denies all human thought."[8]

Harnack knew exactly what was going on, and he did not like it. The next day he told Barth to keep his idea of God to himself and not "make it an 'export article.'"[9] Later in an open letter to the "Despisers of Scholarly Theology" on 11 January 1923, Harnack challenged Barth to step out from behind the smoke screen of his dialectical rendering of revelation and honestly face the demands of the academy. However, Barth had no interest in the fashions of the *universitas litterarum*. As he put it, "We are not outside, as it were, but inside."[10] In other words, theology's business is primarily that of discerning its own inner logic and meaning. It must approach with caution and skepticism any method that borrows its concept, categories, and models from alien—outside—vocabularies.

Although Bonhoeffer had certainly followed this debate from Berlin, it was not until he read *The Epistle to the Romans* and *The Word of God and the Word of Man* in the summer of 1925 that this "export article" was received with great purchase. Bethge explains that Bonhoeffer began now for the first time to take real joy in his work—"it was like a liberation."[11] In Barth he discovered a freedom and confidence that suited the independence and restlessness of his own intellectual temperament. "Rearguard actions and apologias were scorned, and inconsistencies were left unreconciled."[12]

During Bonhoeffer's Sloan postdoctorate at Union Seminary in 1930–1931 he actively promoted Barth's theology to an American theological audience he considered thoroughly lightweight (all religion and ethics, he said).[13] Considering the fact that fellow students once broke out in laughter at quotations from Luther's *De Servo Arbitrio*, Bonhoeffer clearly had his work cut out for him. He delivered an almost hagiographic account of Barth in a seminar presentation at Union, "The Theology of Crisis," which began appropriately, "I confess that I do not see any other possible way for you to get into real contact with Barth's thinking than by forgetting, at least for this one hour, everything you have learnt before."[14] With Barth, Bonhoeffer says, we do not simply have one more weary solution to the "problem of God," but "we stand in the tradition of Paul, Luther, Kierkegaard—in the tradition of genuine Christian thinking."[15] In fact, to strengthen his case before the Americans, Bonhoeffer seemed perfectly content to lay aside his own sharp polemic with Barth on the issue of the continuity of revelation, which he had recently put forth in *Act and Being*, and instead to emphasize the importance of Barth's theological revolution. He writes, "But now the Christian message comes. . . . [God] breaks into the circle of man, not as a new idea. . . . But in concreteness as judgment and forgiveness of sin, the promise of eschatological salvation."[16]

Bonhoeffer did not meet Barth personally until he returned to Germany from New York in the summer of 1931 and visited his seminar at Bonn. After a long conversation together at dinner on the evening of July 23, he wrote excitedly that "Barth is even better than his books."[17] "He has a frankness, a willingness to listen to criticism, and at the same time such an intensity of concentration on the subject, which can be discussed proudly or modestly, dogmatically or tentatively, and is certainly not primarily directed to the service of his own theology."[18] Nevertheless, Bonhoeffer always considered himself a "theological illegitimate" among what he called the "genuine initiates" at Bonn, and he felt excluded from the inner circle of Barth's students, who at times seemed sycophantic and smug. In maladroit terms, he once described the scene to Erwin Sutz: "No Negro is allowed to pass for white; his finger-nails and the soles of his feet are carefully scrutinized."[19]

Bonhoeffer and Barth exchanged letters until the last days in prison. In 1933, when Bonhoeffer had taken residence in the London vicarage of the Reformed Church of Saint Paul, Barth wrote an urgent letter insisting that Dietrich get back to Berlin on the next ship (or, at the latest, the one after that), for this was no time for retreat and introspection. In reply, Bonhoeffer admits that his move to London was motivated by a desire to "go into the wilderness for a while and simply do pastoral work, with as few demands as possible,"[20] since he "simply did not any longer feel up to . . . questions and demands."[21] He expresses concern for disappointing Barth by going away. "It also occurs to me that I have let you down personally by going away. Perhaps you will not understand that. But it is a very great reality to me."[22] Yet he quietly insists that his actions, though confusing to Barth and perhaps not fully clear to himself, were appropriate. Bonhoeffer did return to Germany, though many ships later in the spring of 1935.

The final correspondence took place during the years in which Bonhoeffer worked for the counterintelligence agency (the *Abwehr*) as a political conspirator against Hitler. In this last letter, dated 17 May 1942, Bonhoeffer beseeches Barth to put to rest any suspicion of his new freedom to travel outside Nazi Germany, no longer surreptitiously but now with an official passport.[23] He writes, "In a time when so much must rest simply on personal trust, then *everything* is really over when distrust arises. . . . Let me just add this: it would be unbearably painful for me if the admittedly difficult effort to continue our solidarity were to end in inner alienation. And why should I conceal my belief that, at least in the eastern part of Germany, there are few who have declared their loyalty to you as often as I have tried in recent years."[24] Bonhoeffer hopes that the course of action he has taken—indisputably his own—will become clear to Barth, and, if not, that their trust in each other will suffice to assuage his apprehensions of the situation. He admired Barth until the end as the theologian who showed him the way to Christian freedom, and thus as a kind of mentor or parent, challenging, praising, and provoking him—prodding him along the way of his uncertain pilgrimage.

John Godsey is correct to say that "almost everything Bonhoeffer wrote was written with Barth in mind."[25] Yet Bonhoeffer never shied away from offering sharp criticisms of Barth and the Barthians, and, in this manner, he always felt himself to be something of an anomaly[26]—though, of course, no description is more fitting of Barth himself.

Theological Analysis

Significantly more complicated than the biographical sketch of Bonhoeffer and Barth's interactions is an analysis of Bonhoeffer's theological relationship to Barth. There are five parts to the analysis which I provide in this chapter. First, I introduce the theological issues at stake in their relationship by reconstructing Bonhoeffer's critique of Barth in *Act and Being*, an extremely important text which has not been given the attention it deserves in the scholarly literature. Second, I turn to Barth's *Church Dogmatics* II/1 in order to show the extent to which many of Bonhoeffer's early concerns about Barth's theology are resolved in his axiom "God's being is in God's act." Third, I discuss Bonhoeffer's fragmentary comments from prison concerning Barth's developing dogmatic system and provide a new angle on the "positivism of revelation" charge. Fourth, I review Barth's epistolary response to Bonhoeffer's posthumously published prison writings and also evaluate the positive influence of Bonhoeffer in his conception of "secular parables" and "worldly lights." Finally, although Barth for obvious chronological reasons always has the last word in this conversation, I allow Bonhoeffer to speak from the grave, as it were, regarding not only the issue of secular parables but also the final totality of Barth's dogmatic system.[27]

Discontinuity in Dialectical Theology

Bonhoeffer's habilitation dissertation, *Act and Being*, was accepted at the University of Berlin on 18 July 1930 and was published in 1931. In this important treatise, Bonhoeffer confronts directly the issue of whether revelation should be understood in terms of act (God is the one who always acts) or being (God is the one who is), or whether there is not a way of overcoming this historical impasse. He says, "[My] whole project represents an attempt to unify the aims of true transcendentalism and true ontology within an 'ecclesiastical thought'" ("in einem 'kirchlichen Denken'").[28] This unity is not the result of a mere allocation of those elements amenable to his work—a picking and choosing of favorable concepts—but is an attempt to get beyond the conceptual aporias of the transcendental tradition, to search for a theological form of thinking which will emancipate theology from "the ultimate concealed premises of metaphysics."[29]

Bonhoeffer attempts to rethink the relationship of the themes of act and being in the interpretation of God's self-witness to the world.[30] Therefore, in the critiques of transcendental and ontological thought in the first section of the book, he argues that revelation cannot be reduced to either a transcendental or an ontological description, or to act and being, but is a reality prior to both. As that reality prior to the split of transcendence and immanence, revelation is its own donor, its own knowing, and its own being, unique to the concreteness of "Christ existing as community." Hans-Richard Reuter explains, "Bonhoeffer intends to make the thematic of act and being fruitful in a new way for the interpretation of an actuality—this time non-metaphysically conceived. He finds this actuality in the self-binding of God to the historical revelation in Jesus Christ and from this perspective he fought constantly against the predominance of the category of 'possibility' in theology as a late birth of the nominalistic *potentia Dei absoluta.*"[31]

Bonhoeffer surveys two contemporary strategies for overcoming the theological appropriation of the transcendental-idealist reduction of God to an aspect or object of experience. First, there is Friedrich Brunstäd's proposal in *Die Idee der Religion* to systematically rethink the relation of the transcendental I and the being of God in terms of the correlation of the idea of the unconditional personality and the experience of God. This way claims that the experience of God is the self-experience of the transcendental I, which is itself the grounding for all other experiences. As Brunstäd states the agenda, "The ultimate, true reality is that which is attested in our self-activity, our I-hood."[32] God does not stand over against the I as a possible object of experience but behind the I. Kant's transcendental unity of apperception—the ultimate subjective condition of the possibility of any knowledge which is however itself no object of knowledge—is appropriated for theological purposes. Thus, in Brunstäd's view, the experience of God resides in the experience of the unity of the I. Religion is true because it constitutes the ground of all possible truth in the experience of the "unconditional-synthetic unity of the I."[33] As a result, I can never say "I" without, by coimplication, saying "God," although I have no relation to God in an existential sense, since the unconditional ego is always different than the I who I am in my facticity.

The second possible way of recovery from the metaphysical tradition also borrows from the Kantian theme of the nonobjectivity of God but toward a different end. Here the "purely transcendental thesis" is appropriated. God is understood as infinitely different (or infinite difference), transcendent of any object, so that every attempt to point to God is mitigated by the qualification "not-God." God is inaccessible to the act of reflection. He *is* in the pure execution of his knowing act but remains transcendent of every attempt to grasp him in reflection.[34]

Bonhoeffer finds both positions inadequate. However, the latter position is explored in greater depth since it characterizes much of what he finds problematic in Barth's theology. According to Bonhoeffer in *Act and Being*, if God is in revelation strictly as act, then the question arises of how one can speak of divine and human continuity. More to the point, on the basis of divine actualism and dialectical negation, he says, how one can speak of the continuities of (1) God in himself (*a se*); (2) God in relation to the world (*ad extra*); (3) human community, or the continuity of the self and its others; and (4) human subjectivity in itself? Does not talk of the self's own continuity become impossible? Does not talk of the continuity of human community meet its end? Does not talk of God's real self-giving to the world in grace collapse in light of God's coming to the world in crisis? And does not talk of God's inner continuity (in being) become meaningless since God is always coming to the world (in acting)? Bonhoeffer explores these levels of continuity in his critique.

In Barth's early theology, passionate testimony is given to the glory and majesty of the God who remains free and unconditional in relation to everything that is given and conditional.[35] Barth says, "Without prejudice to and yet without dependence upon His relationship to what is event, act and life outside Him, God is in Himself free event, free act and free life."[36] Since God is the one who is pure act, God encounters humankind as act; thus all reflection on the event (*actus reflectus*) has already fallen away from the purity of the act itself. Barth's dramatic emphasis on the freedom of God—"Being completely different, it is the *krisis* of all power, that by which all power is measured."[37]—admits the conclusion that God is bound by nothing, not even, as Bonhoeffer says, "by the manipulable 'entity' of his 'historical' Word."[38] Revelation's paradox is its exploding into time and history without becoming part of time and history; its eternal contradictoriness. The event of revelation, despite the fact that Barth employs temporal terms to describe it, cannot be conceived as truly temporal. For the prevenient act of God, which is always "beginning at the beginning," is at all times free, and free in a way that disallows any inference from one act to the next. Although Barth understands this emphasis as an attempt to translate the transcendental concept of act into terms which are historical (*geschichtlich*),[39] nonetheless, his attempt (Bonhoeffer argues) is bound to failure for the reason that no historical moment can be *capax infiniti*. That is, because there is no "being of the revealed or the revealer in the world,"[40] there is no continuity that perdures between the acts of revelation. God's act in revelation has no material or temporal extension, no history as such, no place in the world as its concrete expression. God is free, never subject to the control of human interests.

Barth's theological *tour de force* in the dialectical literature, which Bonhoeffer read admiringly, is the delineation of God as the one who is *always subject*. This orientation reverses Kant's skepticism about the presence of God in experience by the ironic means of beating him at his own game. For in *The Critique of Pure Reason* Kant argued with devastating effect that the God of traditional theism was conceptually inadequate. The crux of his well-known argument was based on demonstrating the unbridgeable difference between that totality of all possible experiential properties called the world and the inference that the being of God is in some way the being of the world writ large. Kant argued that this disjunctive inference represents a permanent (and unsurpassable) theological problem—most of the classical theistic arguments for the existence of God are based on this fallacious inference. Yet the more theologically troubling of Kant's critique is the consequence of God's unknowability. God (or the *idea of God*) has no objective place in the concreteness of spatiotemporal experience; therefore, theological statements run aground in antinomous thinking. (Conversely, the appeal to atheism is equally untenable, since no incontrovertible statement regarding the being of God, world or soul, can be attained.)

Of course, Kant's critical philosophy does not divest the idea of God of an essential truthfulness. That God cannot be located in experience by reason in its pure employment does not rule out the alternative possibility that there is a truthfulness about the idea of God that appears in the course of practical reason. Although the idea of God is unknowable, and in its hypostasized form an "illusion"

(*Schein*), it nonetheless continues to assert a regulative function in our experience. Kant's response is to show that God is that postulate, itself not identical with nature, which makes possible "the exact coincidence" of happiness with morality. God is the idea by and through which we are morally regulated. However, despite the regulative role of the divine idea in practical reason, the decisive consequence of Kant's inquiry is that God is absent from the world of phenomenal reality. Since our epistemic faculties are delimited with respect to what is empirically real, God must be construed in every case as wholly other than experience.

Against this conclusion, Barth's strategy for reckoning with Kant's critique resembles the method certain idealist philosophers had used with some measure of success. For example, in his *Wissenschaftslehre*, Fichte responded to Kant by showing that the science of knowing is not only a "critical" but an "absolute" system. Reason is not only legislative (providing forms and connection in which real objects must appear if they are to be objects of experience) but creative (producing the objects of experience); and the world of sense is not only appearance (*Erscheinung*: phenomenal in contrast to noumenal) but also illusion (*Schein*). In this way, the explicit structure of the science of logic illustrates the unifying concern of idealist philosophy to demonstrate the *subjective* constitution of the world.

Barth tries to resolve the quandary of God's absence in experience by thinking of God as the divine subject who creates the world through his own knowing. If God cannot be an object of knowledge (Kant's claim), then God must be the knowing subject itself (Barth's claim). The absoluteness of the creative I (Fichte) is reconceived by Barth in terms of the subjectivity of God's creative Word—as the one whose knowing the world is both its *Erscheinung* and *Schein*. In fact, Barth emphasizes repeatedly that the Cartesian epigram *cogito ergo sum* should be reversed for theological reasons by the formula (coined by Franz von Bäder) *cogitor ergo sum*.[41] "That God speaks, that we, known by Him, see ourselves and the world in His light, is something strange, peculiar, new."[42] God is not known in the world, rather God's knowing is the very creative origin of the world itself.

Nonetheless, Bonhoeffer sees this response as a pyrrhic victory of sorts. Although a way is found to contest the claim that the world is bereft of God (insofar as God as divine subject comes into the world in gracious and revealing acts), the reversal of terms from the untenable notion of God as object in the world to the idea of God as knowing subject of the world fails to resolve the problem of God's inner continuity or the continuity of God's relation to the world. If the world comes into existence by the creative, knowing acts of God, and indeed its existence depends on God's continuing to act in time, then we are still left without a way to conceive the being of God and the being of the world between the acts of divine knowing. There is no full appreciation of the divine I who has come in the being of concrete worldliness itself (in the being of the person Jesus Christ).

Bonhoeffer attempts to counter the problem by insisting that the divine subjective act is the being of revelation in community. "Christ existing as community" is the concretization of God's knowing act in time and history. He says, "[Revelation] must be thought of as enjoying a mode of being which embraces both entity and non-entity, while at the same time 'suspending' within itself man's intention of it.'"[43] God's freedom has bound itself into the personal communion, and it is precisely through this binding that God's freedom is most clearly testified—"that God should bind himself to humankind."[44] Therefore, the Christian community is "God's final revelation."[45] In the being of Christ as community, God *is* "in the *act* of understanding himself."[46]

Barth's dialectical actualism also affects the continuities of human subjectivity and community in that a wedge is driven between the continuity of the new existence of faith and that of the whole I. Bonhoeffer claims that Barth is unable to make the new I in faith coherent as the total, historical I; he is unable to conceive the new being of the person as continuous in part with the old. As a result, not only individual subjectivity but genuine community, the latter of which is based on (among other things) the internal or inner coherence of individuals, is forfeited.[47] Barth's conception of the new being of the person in faith terminates in a final collapse of the whole or total I.

Is this a fair criticism? A satisfactory answer requires further probing of Barth's early theology. In the *Epistle to the Romans* Barth describes the new I in faith in terms of the following paradox: as "the non-being of the first world which is the being of the second, just as the second has its basis-of-being ('Seinsgrund') in the non-being of the first."[48] The meaning of the new I is understood in terms of the negation of the former I—of the not-I of the I "in Adam." Barth says, "[Jesus] Christ is the new man, standing beyond all piety, beyond all human possibility. He is the dissolution of the man of this world in his totality."[49] Personal continuity can only be spoken of as faith ordained by the divine act of God. "[By] faith we are what we are not."[50] The new I as the I that is wholly other than the old I can only be expressed as *what I am not*, and is thus conceived in strict eschatological terms. "Projected into the midst of human life," writes Barth, "the new man seems no more than a void, his 'passionate motions of eternity' . . . are invisible."[51]

Bonhoeffer concedes that this "heavenly double" ("himmlischer Doppelgänger") circumvents the problems of the experience-oriented theologies of the nineteenth century, but it does so at the expense of the historicity and continuity of the person. Although Barth certainly recognizes the necessity to think the total, historical I inclusively with the I as *überzeitlich*, his concepts of grace, freedom, and contingency have been so sharply defined (as Bonhoeffer says "over-determined" or *überbestimmt*) before even approaching the total, historical person that he can no longer think the historical-temporal character of the new I.[52] The I of faith becomes theologically schizophrenic, for the new I is the not-I, and thus *not* only the cancellation of the old I but also the instantiation of the impossible I. The seemingly insurmountable difficulty arises of how the I in faith can still be connected to the not-I unless there were not two separate acts of faith—one of the I and one of the not-I.[53] The I and not-I, in Barth's dialectical scheme, involve themselves in an infinite play of internegation.

How does Bonhoeffer propose to solve these problems? First, he concludes that conceptions of revelation configured strictly in terms of the act of God's freedom short-circuit the full reality of the world and splinter selfhood and community into discrete events of divine decision. The four previously mentioned relationships remain discontinuous: (1) God in himself (*a se*); (2) God in relation to the world (*ad extra*); (3) human community, or the continuity of the self and its others; and (4) human subjectivity in itself. Bonhoeffer then contests the priority of revelational actualism as the proper starting place of theology. He cuts right to the heart of the matter in his own disarmingly simple proposal: "In revelation it is a question less of God's freedom on the far side from us, i.e., his eternal isolation and aseity, than of his stepping-out-of-himself in his *given* Word . . . and his freedom as it is most strongly attested in his having freely bound himself to historical humanity."[54] The event of revelation does not coerce a distinction between God's identity and God's presence; Christ as community demonstrates the refiguration of both. What it means for God to be God is that Jesus Christ is the source of life together. God's being is in God's becoming for us in Jesus Christ; God's aseity is interpreted by God's promeity. Furthermore, God's freely binding himself to the world in concrete community manifests the positive location of the continuities of human subjectivity and intersociality. This glad news neither denies trinitarian immanence nor sells out to experiential economy; on the contrary, it attests to the equiprimordiality of God's promeity and aseity, or more precisely, to the fact that God's aseity is interpreted by his promeity. "God is not free of man or from humankind, but for humankind"[55] ("Gott ist frei nicht vom Menschen, sondern für den Menschen").

Perhaps as a way of guarding against the idea that the world is necessary for God, or that the world extends or amplifies God's creative power, Barth emphasizes that God's freely willed relation to the world is contained within God's relation to himself, for "nothing can accrue to Him from Himself which He had not or was not already."[56] But for Bonhoeffer "Christ existing as community" is the way God shows himself as one whose freedom is in his binding, because God in Jesus Christ is one who really steps out of himself into the world, without losing himself or relinquishing his identity. Unlike Barth, Bonhoeffer is willing to risk the thought that God and humanity together in Jesus Christ is a greater conception than God alone in himself; God and the world in unity is a greater conception than God *a se.* The world reconciled to God in Jesus Christ *does* add something to God that God did not have before. Through and in Jesus Christ, one can think of God as one who discovers unprecedented delight in the world which he created and reconciled to himself. Bonhoeffer's suggestion resonates with the mystery of the Pauline description: "And God raised us up with Christ and seated us with him in the heavenly realms in Christ Jesus, in order that in the coming ages he might show the incomparable riches of his grace, expressed in his kindness to us in Christ Jesus" (Eph. 2:7). Of course, this is not the world's own achievement but a demonstration of God's desire that the fellowship he enjoys in trinitarian community gain expression in the luminescence of his mysterious, worldly, and communal otherness. God *is* a present God, accessible, in fact *habbar*, in concrete community.

Thus, revelation is located neither in a novel occurrence of the past, in an event which has no direct connection with my old or new existence, nor in the always free and nonobjective divine acts.[57] Rather, the being of revelation is the "being of the community of persons, constituted and embraced by the person of Christ."[58] Revelation happens within and as the personal communion.

In this way, Bonhoeffer in *Act and Being* considers Barth's dialectical conception of God inadequate. If revelation is nonobjective and actualistic, the result is that God always remains subject and eludes every attempt to be conceptually grasped.[59] Such an account admirably accents certain doxological themes—God's sovereignty over all things, his prevenience in grace—yet in Bonhoeffer's estimate this view does not sufficiently characterize genuine Christian theological reflection. For if we are really speaking of revelation, then we must mean that in God's becoming manifest to humankind, he also takes shape in the concreteness of human community. As Hans Urs von Balthasar says in his own polemic with Karl Barth: "When we say that 'the Word was made flesh,' we are saying two things. We are talking about a being (or a particular nature), and we are talking about an event (or a part of history). . . . The concept of nature obtains equal status with the concept of actuality."[60] Attending to the worldliness of revelation necessitates amending one's talk about act with talk about the reality which is the source of both being and act; with talk about "that which was from the beginning, which we have heard, which we have seen with our eyes, which we have looked at and our hands have touched" (I John 1:1).

"God's Being Is in God's Act"

That Barth would have acknowledged the validity of Bonhoeffer's criticisms of his dialectical writings seems likely, given what we know of Barth's own later discontent with this stage of his thought. But what is certain is that he would have denied the applicability of these criticisms to his theology after 1931. For Barth's understanding of the relation of God and world changes in critical ways from the second edition of the *Epistle to the Romans* (1922) to *Fides Quaerens Intellectum* (1931) and the *Church Dogmatics* (for our purposes the first four parts, 1932–1942). In *Church Dogmatics* II/1 Barth is able to absorb much of the force of Bonhoeffer's criticism and to respond in a persuasive way with his reflection on the axiom "God's being is in God's act." Even though Bonhoeffer was not unaware of the change under way in Barth's theology,[61] he seems to lack due appreciation for the significance of this change.

In *Fides Quaerens Intellectum* (1931), Barth discovered in his study of Anselm's *Proslogion* a bridge from his early rhetoric of the paradox of revelation to the idea that there is already contained in the words of faith an understanding of the God who is revealed in the story of Jesus Christ. What Barth is seeking in his meditation on Anselm is *not* a definition of the being of God. "That than which nothing greater can be conceived" is rather a naming of God in the form of a rule of thinking, a noetic rule which leads to an ontic conclusion about the reality of God. According to Barth, Anselm discovers that there is a revelation of God contained in the ordinary words

of the formula—"that than which nothing greater can be conceived."
These words are a revelation of God in the sense that only through
their meaning can one encounter the reality of what is meant by the
name of God. The primary theological task is not, then, a matter of
inferring the existence of God from some entity like the ecclesial
institution or the verbally inspired biblical texts; rather, it is a matter of recognizing that in the words of this formula is opened up a
way to think-after God's own thoughts through the self-giving of God
in language.

Theology turns out to be an enterprise of *nachdenken*, a thinking afterward, of what has been thought before. Thinking theologically means to rethink the meaning of those words in which God's
story is inscribed. Thinking theologically means to rethink the content that is there as something which has been pre-thought and given
us to think by God himself. Thinking theologically is the work of
thinking-after, not as speculative thinking, metaphysical thinking,
or reflection on one's belief but as a retracing of the line of thought
that is contained in those words of the church whose meaning represents an encounter with the reality of God revealed in Jesus Christ.

The significance of Anselm for Barth cannot be overemphasized.
In the earlier period, God is present only in a momentary, paradoxical way. As we saw, Barth inscribes a theological expressionism in
which God, who is always bursting into time without touching time,
recedes into nonobjectivity. He says, "So new, so unheard of, so unexpected in this world is the power of God unto salvation, that it can
appear among us, be received and understood by us, only as contradiction."[62] The effect of God's acting into time is that of a "crater
made at the percussion point of an exploding shell, the void by which
the point on the line of intersection makes itself known in the concrete world of history."[63] The divine Thou is always an encountering
Thou, and to this extent, all theological propositions are grounded in
the requirement of saying *not-God* when one speaks of God and *not-
I* when speaking of the I in faith. The reality of God in the dialectical
period would be like the spark that jumps between the gap of two
electrically charged poles; the spark jumps the gap, but as soon as it
does so it is gone.[64] It is important that after the study on Anselm
one finds in Barth an objectification in human language of that same
reality that dialectically jumps the gap between the positive and the
negative. This objectification is the meaning contained in the language which is the narrating of the word *God*, an objectification
grounded in the *analogia fidei*.[65]

In this context, Barth's axiom "God's being is in his act" is monumentally important. His discovery of Anselm led to the recognition that ontological language—concepts of being—need no longer be dismissed in the theological task. In revelation, God who is the active subject as Father, Son, and Holy Spirit takes up humanity into the event of his self-disclosure as "secondary, subsequent spirits."[66] In revelation, Barth says, we are not speaking only of an event "which takes place on high, in the mystery of the divine Trinity. . . . But we are now speaking of the revelation of this event on high and therefore of our participation in it."[67] We are not speaking of the radical transcendence of dialectical theology but of the God who comes into the world in the self-witness of Jesus Christ. Of course, Barth does not take this as suggestive of humanity's deification.[68] Rather, God's acting in Jesus Christ to reconcile the world to himself—to take up humanity into himself—is the act of humanity's salvation. And it is precisely the event of humanity's salvation that invokes the question of God's being, for now "we have to inquire after the *ground* of the taking up of man into the event of God's being."[69]

In advancing the axiom "God's being is in his act," Barth is not conceding anything to a general ontological description of divine being, that is, he is not advancing the *analogia entis*, that notion that claims one can discover not only God's existence but also certain meaningful propositions about God's nature by reflection on worldly or creational structures. Barth finds nothing in his reading of Anselm to warrant the conclusion that there can be reliable speaking about God on the basis of some normative concept of being. Ontological statements have as their anterior requirement the God who acts in love and freedom. However, with this in mind Barth does not shrink from using the language of being within the movement of God's prevenient acting—as long as all concepts of being are measured against the God who is in his acts.[70] Thus, God's being is not a deposit in the being of creation but is primordially specific to his trinitarian self-relations as Father, Son, and Holy Spirit; herein are the paradigmatic acts of God's freedom. As Barth says, "We are in fact interpreting the being of God when we describe it as God's reality, as 'God's being in act,' namely, in the act of His revelation, in which the being of God declares His reality; not only His reality for us—certainly that—but at the same time His own, inner, proper reality, behind which and above which there is no other."[71] In his inner-trinitarian relationality, God is *already* for us, and so the promeity of God must be positioned theologically within his everlasting aseity.

Importantly, God's actuality is not divorced from other actualities, nor is God's history disconnected from our history. Barth's point is that our history is a predicate of God's history.[72] What then is the act illustrative of God's history? The particularity of the divine event is the particularity of the being of the person of Jesus Christ. "We speak of an action, of a deed, when we speak of the being of God as a happening. Indeed the peak of all happening in revelation . . . consists in the fact that God speaks as an I, and is heard by the thou who is addressed. The whole content of the happening consists in the fact that the Word of God became flesh and that His Spirit is poured out upon all flesh."[73] In other words, the proposition "God is God" (not to be taken as simple tautology) can only be parsed through the determination of the act of God's revelation.[74] God's decision is thus a decision *for both God and humanity.* God does not will to be God just for himself or to dwell alone with himself: "He wills as God to be for us and with us, who are not God."[75] Consequently, God's being in act is expressed nowhere more decisively than in God's love toward humanity.

A question arises here—one which Bonhoeffer will ask in his prison criticisms—regarding the consequences of Barth's response for thinking about the relation between God and the world. Perhaps as a way of guarding against the idea that the world is necessary for God, or that the world extends or amplifies God's creative power, Barth emphasizes that God's freely enacted relation to the world is contained originally within God's relation to himself. He says, "What new thing can the world offer, lend or be to Him, when the ground of the novelty of its existence, and of all the novelties in its essence, is in Himself, and would be so no less even if there were no world."[76] Barth resists all speculation about God's evolutionary development or "the world come of age" by holding that God's relation to the world is a modification or extension of God's self-relation—"nothing can accrue to Him from Himself which He had not or was not already."[77] In its very reality, a reality which is nevertheless distinct from God, "it is always upheld by God, [so] that it never falls out of His hands in this reality and autonomy."[78] Yet the world as *opera Dei ad extra* is, it seems, contained with the *opera Dei ad intra.* Although creation is thereby different than God, that difference is finally reduced to the identity of trinitarian perfection. The difference of the world must be understood as internal to the self-containment of divine freedom, for not even difference can demonstrate a quality that God does not already possess in himself. Thus, one might be tempted to say of Barth that in waging war against the idea that God is *part of the world*, he ends up advocating the nearly opposite idea that *the world is in God.*

However, to be fair, Barth's purpose in this reflection is to emphasize God's sovereignty over all finite reality; he does not wish to deny the world's autonomy. Only through the clearest affirmation of God's absoluteness can that which is not God be recognized. In this way, Barth claims that act and being are not conflicting descriptions within the thought of God's absolute freedom. "It is just the absoluteness of God properly understood which can signify not only His freedom to transcend all that is other than Himself, but also His freedom to be immanent within it, and at such a depth of immanence as simply does not exist in the fellowship between other beings."[79] Moreover, the particularity of the event of God is not exhausted by his dialectical transcendence, but "must always be understood with equal strictness as immanence."[80] Therefore, God can be free in diverse and novel ways while remaining faithful to his own originary, revelatory intention. Through the act of divine freedom God pledges himself "in a certain way to the world" according to his own standpoint "in correspondence with His divine being, as He determines and wills in His freedom."[81]

What is of utmost importance about Barth's claim is that the miraculous freedom that informs and shapes the presence of God in the world has its norm and its law in Jesus Christ. The fulfilled union of divine and human in Jesus Christ is the condition of the possibility—"the possibility of all other possibilities"—of the divine immanence as well as the resplendence of creation itself. That God is free means that God is able to indwell the created order "in the most varied ways according to its varying characteristics."[82] Lest this be falsely construed as an insinuation of natural theology, Barth further argues that whatever sparks of deity we discern in creation are constitutive of God's direct intention—his *actus directus*—with regard to the creature, not the sufficiency to speak reliably about God on the basis of the immanent.[83] The world is able to be the world because God became human, that is, because God gave himself to the world that was already his as his creation without becoming identical to the world. "[God] himself is the Son who is the basic truth of that which is other than God."[84] Of course, it cannot be forgotten that as other, Jesus Christ is really God himself. Otherness is primordially an innertrinitarian quality, which God did not need the world to demonstrate. Barth says, "Before all worlds, in His Son He has otherness in Himself from eternity to eternity."[85] Creation and worldliness belong to God alone as the natural expression of him *ad extra*. Through the self-relatedness of God we have "the quintessence of all possible relationship and fellowship generally and as such."[86] So in the transcendent freedom of God thus expressed we see "the archetype and the norm of all the possible ways in which He expresses His freedom in this relationship and fellowship."[87]

What then has been achieved in *Church Dogmatics* II/1 by way of answering the critical questions posed by Bonhoeffer in *Act and Being*? I think two principal concerns. First, the reality of God is no longer conceived in dialectical suspension from the world. The event of God is not deracinated from the being of the world, but brings the latter into itself. Second, Barth has taken seriously the problem—endemic to dialectical theology—of the continuities of (1) God in himself (*a se*); (2) God in relation to the world (*ad extra*); (3) human community, or the continuity of the self and its others; and (4) human subjectivity in itself. To the extent that continuities (2), (3), and (4) are determined within the context of continuity (1), that is, to the extent that all relationships outside of God are secured solely on the basis of the internal relationality of the trinitarian God, Barth gives a compelling response to Bonhoeffer's objections. However, as we will see next in the prison writings, Bonhoeffer, though in agreement with Barth on the issue of the prevenience of God in knowledge, experience, and salvation, remained uneasy in his later prison writings about certain aspects of Barth's understanding of the relation between the identity of God and the being of the world.

Church Dogma: "Like It or Lump It"

However persuasive Barth's extended reflection on "God's being in God's act" might be, Bonhoeffer continued to think through the implications of Barth's emerging dogmatic system in light of the problem of the relation of God and world. In a letter from Tegel prison written 5 May 1944, Bonhoeffer conjectures that Barth, after showing that the act of revelation generates the veritable implosion of human religious pretensions, failed to capitalize on the implications of this epochal breakthrough, and instead recapitulated to the development of positive doctrine. In effect, Barth says to the believer, here is the virgin birth, the Trinity, the Resurrection, and all the rest— "Like it or lump it" ("Friss Vogel, oder stirb").[88] Bonhoeffer claims that this positivism of revelation makes faith all too easy for itself, by in fact setting up "a law of faith" which "mutilates what is—by Christ's incarnation!—a gift for us."[89] The language of the church replaces religion as the sole presupposition of faith; the world—and everything not the church—goes unaccounted for. He writes, "In the place of religion there now stands the church—that is in itself biblical—but the world is in some degree made to depend on itself and left to its own devices, and that's the mistake."[90] The rich worldly texture of revelation is not given full recognition.

What does Bonhoeffer have in mind in this charge? The reader should be initially warned that inasmuch as Bonhoeffer's prison criticisms of Barth are speculative in nature, so any analysis of these later texts will be similarly disposed. Notwithstanding this reservation, I take Bonhoeffer to mean that Barth's critique of religion (energetically executed in the dialectical literature)[91] gives way to the development of an ecclesial-theological architectonic that has the effect of collapsing world history into salvation history and sociopolitical struggle into church struggle. The distance between Word and world is resolved on the side of the Word—and this in the overwhelming of world by Word. When Bonhoeffer says misleadingly that the world is given over to its "own devices," he does not mean that the world is enabled to attain a relative autonomy in view of revelation (as Bonhoeffer himself proposes in the prison writings in contradistinction to Barth). Rather, he thinks that Barth's revelational monism occludes a way of apprehending the world in its distinctive autonomy, with its own logic and meaning. Bonhoeffer assumes that he differs from Barth in having a profound interest not only in the reality of the church but in both the worldliness of the world and the worldliness of revelation. Indeed, in the May 5 letter Bonhoeffer expresses his desire to reinterpret "in a 'worldly sense' " (that is to say, in the sense of both the Hebrew Scriptures and of the Fourth Gospel), the concepts of repentance, faith, justification, rebirth, and sanctification.[92] Thus, Bonhoeffer's allegation that the world is "in some degree made to depend on itself" ought not to obscure his larger point that for Barth the world is ultimately depleted by revelation.

What concerns Bonhoeffer is that Barth overdetermines the relationship of God to world (of eternity to time, grace to creation, primary to secondary objectivity); worldly experience is not able to be grasped in its full concreteness, in terms proportionate to the situation itself. He thinks Barth is inclined to read *the situation*—whether that is the particular political, social, or intellectual *sitz-im-Leben*—through the principal theme of God's sovereign word, seemingly at the expense of a *theologia crucis*, and with a sublime and alarming confidence (in his quickness to declare victory) in God's dominion over human suffering and crisis. Repression's drive toward meaninglessness (as one such case), the particularity and absolute mass of its distortions, seems somehow lost in the overriding theological optimism.[93]

In contrast to Barth, Bonhoeffer wants to account for the inner rhythm of the world's worldliness in a more nuanced, more indig-

enously atuned way. Bonhoeffer holds that there need be no decision
between God or the world, for as he says in the ethics texts, "Whoever professes to believe in the reality of Jesus Christ, as the revelation of God, must in the same breath profess his faith in both the reality of God and the reality of the world; for in Christ he finds God
and the world reconciled."[94] To be sure, in this he is in basic agreement with Barth. However, Bonhoeffer stretches his point in a way
that would make Barth uncomfortable. The reconciliation of God and
the world in Jesus Christ demonstrates that God's reality can be
thought only in the context of the world even as the world gains its
integrity only in the context of recapitulation in Christ; the
Christian's concrete existence in the world divides him neither from
Christ nor from the world. "Belonging wholly to Christ, he stands at
the same time wholly in the world."[95] In Christ it is discovered that
the autonomy and a-theism of the world are not concealed, but rather
revealed, and "exposed to an unexpected light."[96] Those who are in
Christ find themselves unexpectedly entangled in all the telluric
complexity of genuine worldliness.

Consequently, Bonhoeffer avows the church's need to form measured and empirical perspectives on "secular problems as well as [on]
particular earthly conditions." For example, "there are . . . certain eco-
nomic or social attitudes and conditions which are a hindrance to faith
in Christ and which consequently destroy the true character of man
in the world."[97] These must be subject to detailed narratives and critical analyses, informed with maximum precision by the texture of
particular situations. According to Bonhoeffer, this task is a direct
extension of confessing Christ as mediator and reconciler of God and
world, and is not to be considered subordinate to the practice of theology itself. The implication is undeniable that Barth's developing
dogmatic theology suppresses the need to formulate nuanced, autonomous, and systematic accounts of the natural and social orders.

But we must call Bonhoeffer's critique into question at this point.
For the rejoinder should be made that Barth in no way abdicates responsibility for the world in his celebration of "God's being in his act."
Indeed, Barth emphasizes in *Church Dogmatics* II/1 that God in his
opus ad extra does really encounter his created other in a reciprocity
of relationship.[98] He adds even more, "Man is determined, called and
enabled by God's revelation to put this reciprocity into practice."[99]
Barth's concern is rather in keeping in view the fundamental difference between Creator and creature, particularly since it is a difference which is also *not* a difference.

In addition to *Church Dogmatics* II/1 there is further textual evidence to support Barth's defense that he has sufficiently, indeed abundantly, answered Bonhoeffer's objections. Earlier, in *Church Dogmatics* I/2 (1940), he had conceived the relation of "God's time" and "our time" in reference to the *act* of God "in the breaking in of new time into the midst of the old."[100] Since this breaking in is not yet complete, and revelation is not yet redemption,[101] the kingdom of God must be understood in the element of its "at-handness." As a result, there occurs a parallelism between fulfilled time and general, worldly time, converging at the place of Jesus Christ who illustrates that God's time is really "the time God has for us."[102] According to Barth, this convergence, considered alongside the fact that Christ has not yet come "in the glory of his Father" (Matt. 16:27), bears witness to the good news that "our time is conserved," not exhausted in God. The revelation of Jesus Christ did not happen as completed time, as the annulment of our time, but proleptically "as the announcement of the end of all things *in* [our] time itself."[103] He says, "The grace and mercy of God, which become effective in that He has time for us, i.e., His own time for us, answer to that long-suffering of God whereby He leaves us time, and our time at that, to adopt an attitude to this condescension, time, that is, to believe and repent."[104] Our time is conserved—as the time of expectation, as the time which hangs in the balance between the already and the not yet.

The world must be understood, and indeed can only be understood, from the perspective of God's own relation to himself, just as worldliness can only be understood from the perspective of the church. In this manner, the relation of the church to the world is theologically analogous to the relation of God to the world, for, as Barth says, "[It] is impossible to be absolutely outside the Church."[105] Every person is gathered up into the church by the fact that he or she resides in the space between the Ascension and the Parousia. No one can escape this demarcation, just as no one can escape the salvation event of Jesus Christ that casts its light over every reality.[106] Barth is always unwilling to allow talk of Christ's presence to take precedence over talk of Christ's identity,[107] so he consistently restrains talk about autonomy with talk about God's prior acting in revelation. As Eberhard Jüngel explains, "The coming in which God's being is, is God himself. But this coming has been thought in its completion only when it is grasped as source, arrival and future. . . . And thus, in the unity of origin and goal, God is the one who is coming. . . . As love, God's being is in coming."[108]

What shall we then make of Bonhoeffer's prison criticisms of Barth? It seems to me that the evocative sense of his comments is that Barth's God overwhelms the world in the passion of eternal coming, albeit not as divine emptying or self-negating kenosis but in filling and overfilling the world in the gracious event of Jesus Christ. Loving himself so much (perhaps even too much), God overwhelms the world and annuls its autonomy; there can be no possession we call our own, no *novitas mundi*. In the unending event of God's coming into and overcoming the world, the world's freedom to be *in its otherness to God* is crushed. As Hans-Richard Reuter says, "While Bonhoeffer intends in a theology of mystery to put in play human forms of thought in order to protect the *mysterium*, he sees Barth in his theology of revelation as primarily occupied with the attempt to make the human logos into a moment of the self-explication of the divine logos."[109] The world is made to lie still, and silently let God be God. "Indeed, grace is all-embracing, *totalitarian*."[110]

The sense of Bonhoeffer's criticism has a further implication. Nowhere more clearly do we see Barth struggling to get beyond the nineteenth century and all the while remaining within its firm grasp; for while rejecting the priority of the self-reflective human subject in knowledge of self, world, and God, he emphasizes instead the preeminence of the self-reflective divine subject, a notion still deeply ingrained in the transcendental tradition's conceptual repertoire. Barth wants to avert the primary theological aporia of the nineteenth century that God is in and over the world only in "a higher degree of the movement which we know well enough as our own,"[111] but he so greatly overstates his protest that in avoiding the assimilation of God into the world, the world turns out to be consumed by grace. He writes, "The fact that God's being is event, the event of God's act, necessarily (if, when we speak of it, we turn our eyes solely on His revelation) means that it is His own conscious, willed and executed decision. It is His own decision, and therefore independent of the decisions by which we validate our existence. It is His executed decision—executed once for all in eternity, and anew in every second of our time, and therefore in such a way that it confronts what is not divine being as a self-contained, self-containing spirit."[112] Decision and act are proper to God; God decides to reveal himself for himself in his act alone, because it is only in his act that God is who he is. Every proposition concerning what God is, and every explanation of how God is, must state and explain both what and how he is in his act and decision.

Contrarily, Bonhoeffer wants to understand the conjunction between the human religious act and the divine act of belief without assigning them to two different spheres or suppressing the subjectivity of God or the worldly effect of revelation.[113] By no means does he wish to soften the totality of grace; rather, he wants to hold the two thoughts of God's prevenience in revelation and the world's freedom to be other than God in an unsystematic unity.

I read Bonhoeffer's point in the following way. The assertion that God's coming to the world means "for the latter that it can never *have* itself"[114] (Barth) is a shortsighted attempt to displace the presumption of the self-constitution of the world by the reciprocal turn to the enactment of otherness (qua God in Jesus Christ) as the absolute ground of worldliness. Barth's view puts divine self-possession in opposition to human self-possession and assumes that one must choose one or the other. Self or divine possession, theological presumption or faithfulness to the first commandment—no other options seem available. Why is this the case? Bonhoeffer might suggest that Barth's attempt rests on the mistake of equating self-constitution with self-having (or self-relation) and, as a result, fails to recognize that the will to world-constitution and mastery is different than the relative autonomy of self or world (self-having or relation). For *in Christ*, one need not divest the self of its worldly, experiential depths; one need not accentuate sheer extrinsicality and alterity; one need not say, "we must look away from ourselves to him, if we are to know the truth of our existence."[115] Such descriptive excess ignores the psychic, spiritual and aesthetic thickness of selfhood; and as a result, it unnaturally bifurcates natural experience from divine identity. Overturning the absolute claims of the world to have or to be itself (being) through the actualistic description of the coming of the divine other (act) fails to reckon with the possibility of an attainable union of both act and being. Bonhoeffer seeks precisely a union which will preserve genuine self-relation even while affirming the otherness and prevenience of grace; a union which will grant the world its freedom to be other than God (from the standpoint of revelation) and at the same time depict that very autonomy as an instantiation of revelation (from the standpoint of belief).

However, it might be the case that the critical conjectures I have made on Bonhoeffer's behalf are themselves resolved in part or in full in Barth's subsequent writings. I will turn next to his final responses to Bonhoeffer.

Overcoming the "Positivism of Revelation"

Barth tried to sort out the various loose ends of Bonhoeffer's criticisms in two letters written years after Bonhoeffer's death. The first was

addressed to P. W. Herrenbrück on 21 December 1952. In the letter
Barth is both vexed and perplexed by the "enigmatic utterances" of the
letters. He characterizes Bonhoeffer as "an impulsive, visionary thinker
who was suddenly seized by an idea which he gave a lively form, and
then after a time he called a halt (one never knew whether it was final
or temporary) with some provisional last point or other."[116] Barth denies
ever holding up certain doctrines as indispensable aspects of Christian
theology and ponders what the hard-core Calvinist crowd in Holland
would think of his portrayal as a revelational positivist. He is disappointed, but not at all surprised, that Bonhoeffer in prison could only
recall the *Church Dogmatics* indistinctly and impressionistically. The
aphoristic style of Bonhoeffer's criticisms betrays absentmindedness
and distraction more than prophetic insight—he was in prison, for
heaven's sake. Readers are misled who think that he has something
"tangible" in mind. Try as one may, there is simply no way to get a
"deeper meaning" beneath these impulsive conundrums. Yet despite
the tone of incredulity and mild reprimand, Barth concludes his letter
to Herrenbrück on a generous note: "The hope remains that in heaven
at least he has not reported about me to *all* the angels (including the
church fathers, etc.) with just this expression."[117]

The second response comes in a letter to Eberhard Bethge congratu-
lating him on the occasion of the completed biography of Dietrich
Bonhoeffer in 1967. Barth's attitude toward Bonhoeffer is paternalis-
tic; he appears the gentle but judicious father chiding the imprudent
child. He restates his earlier opinion that the prison letters are from
start to finish concealed in impenetrable mystery. And he asks, "What
is 'world come of age'? What does 'non-religious intepretation' mean?
What am I to understand by the 'positivism of revelation' which he
applied to me?"[118] Then in an *ad hominem* shift, Barth suggests that
the real source of confusion stems from Bonhoeffer himself. "But to
this day I do not know what Bonhoeffer himself meant and planned
with it all, and very softly I venture to doubt whether theological sys-
tematics (I include his *Ethics*) was his real strength. Might he not later
have simply dropped all those catchy phrases?"[119] Barth construes
Bonhoeffer's prison criticisms, and the whole of the prison writings,
as an assortment of incomplete, sometimes whimsical, fragments
toward an indeterminate end. Speculation concerning the nature and
meaning of the end is muddled from the start.

I think Barth is uncharacteristically mean-spirited in these epistolary assessments. In the prison texts Bonhoeffer is not just tossing
off ideas as they impressionistically appear before him (nor does he
pass the hours in Tegel coining catchy phrases); rather, he is address-

ing a conflict in Barth's theology which he had begun to detect as early as *Act and Being*, namely, the tension between revelation and temporality. In the prison writings, just as in numerous other texts not written under such duress, Bonhoeffer tried to ameliorate this tension in his task of thinking through the meaning of modernity in light of the God who had reconciled the world to himself in Jesus Christ— of providing a christological interpretation of worldliness per se. As the driving force behind theological discussions of the worldliness and secularity, Bonhoeffer must be recognized, at the same time, as a primary inspiration of Barth's treatment of these themes in his discussion of "secular parables" in *Church Dogmatics* IV/3. I wish to summarize the significance of this concept for the ongoing conversation between Barth and Bonhoeffer. I will then conclude the chapter with a final comment on Bonhoeffer's own project in view of the totality of Barth's system.

Barth's concept of "secular parables" is intended to answer the question of how certain "worldly lights," ostensibly not associated with Jesus Christ, can nonetheless become signs of redemption and in their relative autonomy bespeak God's redemptive goodness. Again, Barth is not making any concession to natural theology here; as he says, "nothing could be further from our minds than to attribute to the human creature as such a capacity to know God and the one true Word of God, or to reproduce true words corresponding to this knowledge."[120] Jesus Christ remains the sole criterion of truth, even in those special cases in which secular realities are empowered to become "children to Abraham."[121] Worldly, non-Christian (or even anti-Christian) experience is taken up into the lordship of Jesus Christ, quite apart from its own capability, and thereby empowered to witness to him.[122]

Thus, the efficacy of secular parables works only on the absolute basis of the priority of Jesus Christ, so that there is no way from the "other words" to the Word, but only from the Word to other words.[123] George Hunsinger nicely describes the relationship in terms of three concentric spheres. The innermost sphere is the Bible and the church, which is surrounded by two distinct outer spheres, respectively, the sphere of those whose secularism is "mixed and relative" and that of those whose secularism is "pure and absolute."[124] All three have as their center Jesus Christ; none lacks connectedness to this center. As Barth states,

> If with the prophets and apostles we have our starting-point at His resurrection and therefore at His revelation as the One who was and is and will be; if we recognize and confess Him as the One who was and is and will be, then we recognize and confess that not we alone, nor the com-

munity which, following the prophets and apostles, believes in Him and loves Him and hopes in Him, but *de iure* all men and all creation derive from His cross, from the reconciliation accomplished in Him, and are ordained to be the theater of His glory and therefore the recipients and bearers of His Word.[125]

Hence, those who find themselves in the inner sphere must be attentive to "the voice of the Good Shepherd" in all places of the world. While humanity may deny God, God never denies humanity.[126] The fact that the person in the outermost sphere might be closed to the Gospel does not change the fact that the Gospel is open for him and that the Gospel is the center of the truth in which he unknowingly lives. Barth says, "[In] the world reconciled by God in Jesus Christ there is no secular sphere abandoned by Him or withdrawn from His control, even where from the human standpoint it seems to approximate most dangerously to the pure and absolute form of utter godlessness."[127]

Barth's discussion of "secular parables" reflects an important aspect of his developed doctrine of creation, that the created order continually presents itself to humankind with a certain inner teleology. In creation and preservation God not only declares himself but also arouses and stimulates the cosmos "to a spontaneous work of ordering and fashioning" which corresponds to the specific way in which *it is*.[128] There is an inner richness—a mystery—in creation, which always and everywhere witnesses to the divine mystery within which "it is concealed." Although creation does not contain its own ground, it is not for this reason meaningless, or even without self-relation. That is to say, its self-relation is not self-grounded but grounded in God, for "[in] the Word spoken in disclosure of the divine mystery, there is also disclosed what the creature itself cannot disclose as its truth, namely, that it is creature, the creature of God, but no more."[129]

Therefore, since God is with us, as the good news of the Christian message announces, then that presupposes that humanity in its difference from God *is able to be humanity in its integrity and difference*, and hence is able to live in the time that is its own and to act in the uniqueness of its own act.[130] "If the fact that God is with us is a report about the being and life and act of God, then from the very outset it stands in a relationship to our own being and life and acts."[131] It then seems that Barth has achieved that double thought—held together in asymmetrical unity—of revelation as the event in which God's prevenient grace is enacted in Jesus Christ which at the same time enables humanity to be humanity. Barth calls this unity the "common history" of God and humanity, the history "which God wills to share us."[132] The divine being, life, and act "take place" alongside and with ours, and it is only because the divine takes place that ours has meaning and reality.[133] Significantly, the asymmetrical unity of the priority of revelation and the integrity of the world is not self-contained in the divine life but signifies the real communion of God with his other—indeed, "the togetherness of God and man."[134]

Barth answers most of Bonhoeffer's concerns in a manner that is magnificent in breadth and detail. In Jesus Christ, the world is preserved in its otherness even as it is taken up into the history of God; worldliness is not enervated but is energized in God's redemptive event. In the togetherness of God and humanity, Barth envisions a union which preserves both genuine self-relation and openness to otherness, a union which allows the world the freedom to be other than God within the totality of revelation. In the end Barth can say, without impugning the being and integrity of the world, that humankind is what *it is* only *in God*.

The Basic Difference Reconsidered

What, then, is the difference between Bonhoeffer and Barth? In what way is Bonhoeffer's project distinguished from Barth's? Certainly the case could be made (I have only here suggested the possibility) that even as Bonhoeffer's theological pilgrimage was called into being by Barth, so Barth in turn was compelled to rethink and occasionally revise his own ideas in reading Bonhoeffer.[135] At least on one matter, that of discipleship, Barth was tempted to simply reproduce passages in the *Church Dogmatics* from *Nachfolge* in an extended quotation.[136] Even so, for present purposes we must attend specifically to Bonhoeffer, to the objections he raises to Barth and to Barth's response, and ask what Bonhoeffer might say in the final analysis about his theological relationship to Barth, and whether there are lingering concerns that should be pursued in greater detail.

John Godsey offers one explanation of the basic distinction between Barth and Bonhoeffer. Godsey argues that for Bonhoeffer, knowledge of God, which is always based in its foundation on Christ, cannot be attained apart from complete immersion in the joys, sufferings, and splendor of everyday life, where one encounters Christ in the other.[137] On the other hand, knowledge of God for Barth "involves cognitive acknowledgment of a *fait accompli*, namely, the predetermination of human destiny in the works and ways of the same Christ."[138] According to Godsey, this difference amplifies diverging ways of receiving and engaging worldliness. He says, "For Bonhoeffer, Christ, as the incarnate, crucified and risen One . . . leads his follow- ers into the very midst of precisely this world."[139] Christ encounters us in the very depths of worldliness.

However, surely our analysis of the *Church Dogmatics* (particu- larly volumes 2 and following) shows this explanation to be incom- plete. Bonhoeffer would not claim, as I am sure Godsey agrees, that Christ is found in the other in some sort of self-evidential a priori experience. In agreement with Barth, Bonhoeffer holds that the com- munion of God and humankind is not an anthropological given but is constitutive of God's prior acting in revelation. God alone animates all sacramental encounter. One does not find Christ in the joys and sufferings of the world by virtue of one's own capacity, but only on the basis of the fait accompli of reconciliation.

Godsey further reduces the basic difference to Barth's emphasis on the divinity of Jesus Christ and Bonhoeffer's focus on the hiddenness of God in the humiliation of the cross. Barth's theology is a *theologia gloriae*, a great celebration of God's gracious action in Jesus Christ,[140] "a theology of the glory of the new man actualized and introduced in the crucified Jesus Christ who triumphs as the Crucified."[141] In con- trast, Bonhoeffer's theology, Godsey says, is "quite evidently" a *theologia crucis* which ensures "the *costliness* of God's grace in Christ."[142] Godsey cites for evidence a passage from *Christ the Cen- ter*: "We have seen the exalted one, only as the crucified; the sinless one, only as the guilt-laden; the risen one, only as the humiliated.[143]

The problem with this claim has important consequences for our task. Bonhoeffer's christology is shaped not solely by Luther's theme of God's condescension and passion but also (for example) by Irenaeus's notion of "recapitulation," in which the whole of creation is conceived to be re-constituted ("gathered together, included and comprised")[144] in Christ. Christ descends to the humiliation of a criminal's death, but he is resurrected as the inaugurator and guar- antor of a new, redeemed humanity. Nowhere is this more clearly expressed than in the essay from the ethics texts, "Christ, Reality and Good": "[The] whole reality of the world is already drawn in into Christ and bound together in Him, and the movement of history con- sists solely in divergence and convergence in relation to this cen- ter."[145] But just as Bonhoeffer does not emphasize the humiliation of God at the expense of his exaltation; neither does Barth emphasize the splendor of grace at the expense of humanity of God. As early as *Church Dogmatics* I/2, Barth drew attention to the "sacramental character" of oppressed and downtrodden people whose suffering is a palpable sign of the suffering of Jesus Christ who has taken on their suffering in his flesh.[146] In fact, he construes faith itself as "a political attitude, decisively determined by the fact that we are made responsible to all who are poor and wretched in our eyes, that we are summoned on our part to espouse the cause of those who suffer wrong."[147] Surely Barth is careful not to mistake social realities for the gospel, nor to conflate social action and faith; nonetheless, Godsey's explanation (and similar ones) does not seem to fully appreciate the breadth and depth of either theologian's christological scope.

In my view the way to make sense of Bonhoeffer's theological relationship to Barth is to distinguish, as does Barth, between the primary and secondary objectivity of God. The purpose of this distinction is to stress the priority of God's aseity over his promeity, not in order to forge a dichotomy between God in himself and God in his revelation but simply to say that before all else is, God is God. If objectivity is ascribed to God (as we must do when speaking about God as the absolute source of all reality, and of Jesus Christ as the decisive source of knowledge of God), then we must distinguish between God in his triune life as such (in his primary objectivity) and God as he comes to us in revelation (in his secondary objectivity). "In His triune life as such, objectivity, and with it knowledge, is divine reality before creaturely objectivity and knowledge exist. We call this the primary objectivity of God, and distinguish from it the secondary, i.e., the objectivity which He has for us too in His revelation, in which He gives Himself to be known by us as He knows Himself. It is distinguished from the primary objectivity, not by a lesser degree of truth, but by its particular form suitable for us, the creature."[148] God is immediately objective to Himself, but only mediately objective to us.[149] Thus, humanity never comes before and to God directly, but always "clothed under the sign and veil of other objects different from Himself."[150] This is not to say that the secondary objectivity of God is unreliable, that God is true only in himself and illusory in his promeity (a kind of nominalist anxiety); rather, secondary objectivity is "fully true," for its correspondence and basis are grounded in God's primary objectivity. Barth says, "For first to Himself, and then in His revelation to us, He is nothing but what He is in Himself."[151]

Importantly, in both cases of primary and secondary objectivity, God is *objective for us*, but only in the immanent trinitarian self-relation can we say that God's objectivity is primary, that it is originally self-identical to who God is in Himself. "[The] primary objectivity of God to Himself is reality in His eternal being as the

Father, the Son and the Holy Spirit. As the triune God, God is first and foremost objective to Himself."[152] God does become objective to us, but in confirming His divine nature in the event of revelation, God must be known as "the One who first of all and apart from us is objective to Himself."[153] Barth states that any compromise of God's trinitarian priority leads to the fateful confusion of God's presence (in the world) and God's identity (in himself), a result of which is the emergence of the notion of general anthropological knowledge of God and a compromise of Christ's uniqueness.

Thus, the way to make more intelligible the conversation between Bonhoeffer and Barth is to see the drift of Bonhoeffer's thought as a continuous wandering along the various paths of the secondary objectivity of revelation, attentive with an intensity not found in Barth to the inner rhythms of worldliness but by no means disregarding the majestic narrative of God's aseity inscribed by him. Bonhoeffer wants to plumb the depths of the meaning of God's promeity; to understand the earth, its riches, delights, and sorrows, in all its christic grandeur. In a sense this is where Bonhoeffer begins and where he ends, in the fascination with the mystery of worldliness, particularly embodied in the mystery of human sociality. His preoccupation with the concreteness of revelation is part and parcel of this fascination.

I think it is important to stress at the outset that although I am positioning Bonhoeffer within a loose Barthian framework, I am not disclaiming important differences between the two theologians. The designation of Bonhoeffer as a Barthian purely and simply, besides being an unproductive line of inquiry, ignores a couple of subtle, but powerful, distinctions, which may in the course of my account stretch the bonds between the two to a point of tension.[154]

The first is Bonhoeffer's preoccupation with (what he calls) the "Antaean"—the indefatigable love of the earth—and his concomitant interest in shaping a description of community and selfhood that is rooted firmly in the earth even as it is primordially grounded in God's self-revelation in Jesus Christ. He says, "A glimpse of eternity is revealed only through the depths of our earth. The one who would leave the earth, who would depart from the present distress, loses the power which still holds him by eternal, mysterious forces. That is the Christian's song of earth and her distress."[155] This cannot be written off as unpurged romantic blather or as adolescent jingoism, for faith's earthiness, its this-wordliness, remains central to Bonhoeffer's thinking, and is even reintroduced directly in some of the final prison writings.

The second distinction is rhetorical. Barth's vast system, whether understood as a conceptual whole (a logical series of inferences stemming from a governing premise) or as a concert of recurring motifs, approximates a total theological universe that is at once secure and inhabitable. Every proposition is a glint of God's great Yes. On the other hand, Bonhoeffer's discourse is a broken one, fragmented by time, contingency, and death. There are fractures in his thought, unrepaired by logic, refracted in the uneven texture of his literature. Bonhoeffer did not lack confidence; his confidence lacked the leisure of solitude and time (the writer's greatest, perhaps only, commodity). System was subverted, yet again, by the untalliable particularity of life, even though his life retained coherence and his thought continuity.

Do these distinctions graduate into larger theological issues? Whether at some point early or late Bonhoeffer leaves the circumference of Barth's thought and ends up in altogether new territory is a question I can answer only at the conclusion of the book.

2

Karl Barth on Philosophy

Worldliness and Philosophy

Nowhere is Bonhoeffer's interest in the worldly texture of revelation better illustrated than in the way he employs philosophical sources in the practice of theology. While utterly convinced that revelation establishes its own criteria of truth and knowledge, Bonhoeffer nonetheless treats philosophy with a principled respect and with the conviction that certain themes can be taken into the service of thinking about the new social ontology of the living Christ. Bonhoeffer's understanding of philosophy sets the general context within which I develop the specific discussions of christology (chapters 4 and 5), community (Chapter 6), and selfhood (Chapter 7). His approach, which I will introduce in the next chapter and then apply to his various conversation partners in the second part of the book, stands in contrast to Barth's ambivalence toward the use of philosophy.

I do not wish to parrot the conventional wisdom that portrays Barth as antiphilosophical, as unleashing a monolithic iconoclasm against all areas of human culture.[1] The nature of philosophy is kaleidoscopic; Barth realizes that. He also recognizes that philosophical notions often make their way into the material of theology. As he says, "If we open our mouths, we find ourselves in the province of philosophy."[2] Indeed, it would be "grotesque comedy" to assume that while others have succumbed to certain philosophical influences, one has oneself consistently stuck to the facts and spoken the brute truth.[3] In such cases where one finds oneself speaking philosophically, Tertullianesque rage is not necessarily in order. Barth even pauses at times to provide what seem to be criteria for assessing the theological validity of a philosophical idea. Even so, his overall position on philosophy is what might be called "benign neglect."[4]

In this chapter I will explore a number of Barth's texts (some of which are lesser-known works) which offer helpful material for understanding his view of philosophy.

Barth's *ad hoc* Reflections on the Meaning and Use of Philosophy

Theology as the Crisis of the Sciences: "The Word of God and the Task of Theology"

Philosophy or philosophical anthropology is not the accoutrement of theology. Barth's thinking during his dialectical period begins with the realization that theology as a discipline is tied up with the structure of paradox. There is a "pathos of distance" or a "diastasis" between God and the world; thus, the purpose of theology is to use every conceivable rhetorical device to articulate humankind's inability to fathom the righteous and incomprehensible God.[5] Dialectical theology must labor always to prevent the obscuring of that paradox, while realizing that its labor can never become a technique. As Barth says, "There is no *way* which leads to this event."[6] The theologian takes refuge in dialectical thinking—like the weary parishioner going to church—in hopes of hearing the word of God. If philosophy happens to find its way into the theologian's expectant discourse, which it inevitably does, this simply attests to the propensity of human speech to accommodate principles of logic constitutive of the cultural fabric of a particular vocabulary. This inevitability does not betray a theological need.

In the 1922 essay "Das Wort Gottes als Aufgabe der Theologie" (The Word of God and the Ministry), Barth places the problem of theology within the broader context of the problem of the human sciences—in the context of what Kant calls the "conflict of the faculties," Husserl the crisis of European sciences, and Kuhn the clashing of scientific paradigms. "Theology is an omen, a sign," Barth says, "that all is not well, even in the *universitas litterarum*."[7] Theology must not appeal to concepts borrowed from nontheological sciences, either for justification or for material appropriation, for the other sciences are themselves tottering on the brink of a radical skepticism—if not a pervading nihilism. The incomprehensibility of theology's own subject matter is symptomatic of the uncertainty built into the presuppositions of all the sciences. Even though the programmatic needs of the other disciplines are often ostensibly met (research agendas are satisfied, experiments verified, and so forth), they feel a certain uneasiness about themselves in the presence of the theologian. All too often theology habitates in the academy as a sign of the insecurity of any science. Knowing well that there is a "minus sign" standing in front of its parenthesis, theology reminds every science that it need be confessedly uncertain of itself, "uncertain not simply of this point or that, but of its *fundamental* and ultimate *presupposition.*"[8] As Barth says, "The hushed voice with which that sign is ordinarily spoken of betrays the secret that it is the nail from which the whole science hangs; it is the question mark that must be added to the otherwise structurally perfect logic."[9] This minus sign, the agitating thought of a radical otherness evading all human grasping, the terrible reminder of the ruptures in our self-sufficiency like glimpses of a perfect negativity—like glimpses of the abyss—is really the "ultimate fact" of each of the sciences, evidence that "the so-called academic cosmos is an eddy of scattered leaves whirling over a bottomless pit."[10]

Because a question mark is the "ultimate fact of each of the sciences," academe is left to fret over its fate with an anxious conscience and tolerates theology within its walls only because it is (secretly) glad that some one is willing to "talk aloud and distinctly about the undemonstrable Fact upon which all other facts depend."[11] Paradoxically, it is only when theology risks a word about this outrageous and unspeakable thought (God!) that its place in the academy is demarcated. Barth says, "Only when a *theological* faculty undertakes to say, or at least points out the need for saying, what the others *rebus sic stantibus* dare not say, or dare not say out loud, only when it keeps reminding them that a chaos, though wonderful, is not therefore a cosmos, only when it is a question mark and an exclamation point on the farthest rim of scientific possibility—or rather, contradistinction to the philosophical faculty, beyond the farthest rim—only then is there a *reason* for it."[12] Religious questions and anthropological descriptions of human longing after deity, however noble or inspiring, however new or remarkable, are just "questions like all other questions." They ultimately give way to that entrenched theological method since Kant of finding unclaimed and uninhabited niches to be staked out and then inhabited, at least until such niches prove to be crude stopgaps. As Bonhoeffer suggested, stopgaps are like slopes where religious hypotheses precariously rest until avalanches of scientists and poets, engineers and novelists, sweep them away in grand narratives the theologians can most often never match. Thus, only when he speaks, in a moment of unguarded audacity, of the transcendent Word who is both divine and human, and speaks of the Word in the company of Kierkegaard, Calvin, Luther, Paul, and Jeremiah, is the theologian doing what he ought to be doing. According to Barth, the notion of a venerable theological science nestled cozily in the *universitatis litterarum* obscures the scandalous claims of faith. Theology's fundamental presupposition—the righteous incomprehensible God—is the crisis of all other presuppositions; thus all sciences totter on the brink of a radical skepticism. Theology not only illustrates this crisis but enacts it as well.

The Case of Schleiermacher

In *The Humanity of God* (1956) Barth dated the collapse of his confidence in liberal theology to a certain "black day" in early August 1914 when ninety-three German professors and writers proclaimed their support of the war policy of Wilhelm II. With the feeling that an epoch had played itself out, Barth observed his theological mentors joining the ranks of these intellectuals. It became clear to him that, at least for his own thinking, a theological kinship with the nineteenth century was no longer possible. He recalls, "In despair over what this indicated about the signs of the time I suddenly realized that I could not any longer follow either their ethics and dogmatics or their understanding of the Bible and of history."[13] This bleak (though inaccurate)[14] memory signified for Barth the *historical* marker of the end of liberal theology.

The *theological* marker involves a slightly different matter. According to Barth, most troublesome about the legacy of the theology of the nineteenth century was its tendency to become the mirror of culture such that very little could be accomplished by way of "a new and positive understanding of Christian truth and truths in themselves."[15] Barth says, "We miss a certain carefree and joyful confidence in the self-validation of the basic concerns of theology, a trust that the most honest commerce with the world might best be assured when the theologians, unheeding the favors or disfavors of this world, confronted it with the results of theological research carried out for its own sake."[16] Nineteenth-century theologians, excluding "anomalies" like Kierkegaard and the Blumhardts, tried to demonstrate the content and possibility of faith by hooking up with some paradigmatic Weltanschauung. As a result, the Christian *religion* gained preeminence over the Christian *message*, for the principal theological task became that of locating an external point of reference that would lend legitimacy to the content of faith.

In his 1923–1924 lectures at the University of Göttingen, Barth gave a critique of the nineteenth century with specific reference to Schleiermacher's analysis of the religious self-consciousness. Barth's main point is well worth repeating.

In *The Christian Faith* Schleiermacher describes piety or religion as a modification of the feeling of absolute dependence wherein God is named the "Whence" or the co-determinant of this feeling. Absolute dependence stems from the universal propensity for self-consciousness, which accompanies all human activity as "the consciousness that the whole of our spontaneous activity comes from a source outside of us."[17] To feel oneself absolutely dependent and to be conscious of being in relation to God are one and the same. Thus, the feeling of absolute dependence expresses "the unity of the self for which not even the sum of the world's influences upon the individual can account."[18] This aboriginal synthesis, which Schleiermacher discusses in the introduction of *The Christian Faith*, generates the methodological principle that shapes the subsequent formation of doctrine.

One of the most intriguing implications of Barth's critique is that Schleiermacher's identification of the "Whence" of feelings of absolute dependence as God and the naming of God as the co-determinant of these feelings appears altogether arbitrary, unwarranted by the psychological priority of religious feeling. The "Whence" might just as easily, and perhaps more convincingly, be correlated with other descriptions of ultimacy familiar to modernity, such as psychoanalysis, Marxism, and nationalism. Although Schleiermacher himself names the "Whence" God, there is nothing about the nature of the case that sanctions this denomination. As Barths says, "[Schleiermacher] introduces the absolute here [as the 'Whence'] and in so doing he can posit the feeling of absolute dependence where he ought only to have put a question mark."[19] The naming of God to fill the void between feelings of dependence and descriptions of ultimacy amounts to a theological contrivance, albeit conditioned by an intellectual milieu that gives it an ostensible logic. Nonetheless, by beginning with a general cognitive and affective model, Schleiermacher proceeds, across increasingly shaky ground, to the conclusion of the reality of God.

Furthermore, even though the system of doctrine has a putative communal orientation, the introduction endangers the integrity of doctrine by portraying theological talk as a second-order discourse based on *individual* religious experience. As such, the relation between the introduction and the system of doctrine is itself arbitrary, like the relation between theology and any cultural or philosophical attachment. Schleiermacher's procedure impedes not only divine freedom but the basic human capacity (itself animated by freedom) of being *encountered by* God. According to Barth, there *is* a void between experience and God, but it *is unnameable*; only God can come to us in the vast emptiness where all desire and feeling run aground.

Schleiermacher sets in motion the slow march toward Feuerbach's impasse, where God is totally present in, and thus identical to, the infinite quality (of kindness or cruelty) of the human species. Barth says stop, there is no experience that will lead to God, no place baptized in smiles of divine certainty, untrammeled by even the theologian's bewildered way. Why not just stick to theology, Barth asks, and in the long haul the poets and philosophers will probably like you better for it.

The Debate with Bultmann

In a letter of 8 June 1928, Rudolf Bultmann put in writing his first reactions to Barth's recent *Prolegomena zur christlichen Dogmatik: Die Lehre vom Wort Gottes*, a text in which Barth attempts to develop a systematic expression of his thought in categories which were derived, in part, from phenomenological and existentialist philosophy. What is interesting about the letter is that even in Barth's few early ventures to (quite deliberately) appropriate philosophical sources in dogmatics, Bultmann actually sees the momentum of Barth's work as antiphilosophical. "It seems to me," he says, "that you are guided by a concern that theology should achieve emancipation from philosophy."[20] Bultmann criticizes Barth for ignoring philosophy ("[You] have failed to enter into (latent but radical) debate with modern philosophy and naively adopted the older ontology from patristic and scholastic dogmatics")[21] and chides him for "a lack of clarity and sobriety" and for his "sovereign scorn" of contemporary phenomenological issues. Bultmann further advances the charge that Barth's ambivalence towards philosophy has the effect only of recapitulating to an antiquated metaphysics. He says, "Now if the critical work of philosophy, which is ongoing, and which is being done today with renewed awareness and radicalness, is ignored, the result is that dogmatics works with the uncritically adopted concepts of an older ontology."[22] If dogmatics is a science, then it must address the question of appropriate concepts and models,[23] otherwise it forages among antiquarian notions for its conceptual material and makes itself irrelevant. Likewise the church, which needs to be cognizant of "the thoughts that live today behind our educated people and in our papers,"[24] is rendered a disservice in Barth's methodological myopia.

Four days later Barth replied in writing to Bultmann. He begins by doubting that his response will ease Bultmann's worries, for what has been demanded of him is a complete transformation of the "intellectual habitus" in which he dwells, and it involves "ultimately the wish that the wild and crooked tree that I appear to be in your eyes . . . should be given a more pleasing shape by an upright pole placed alongside it."[25] Bultmann has his Heidegger, while Barth hesitates to move outside the totality of God's revealing Word. What Bultmann wants of him is just not his cup of tea. Barth adds, "It is also a fact that I have come to abhor profoundly the spectacle of theology constantly trying above all to adjust to the philosophy of its age, thereby neglecting its own theme."[26] Moreover, Barth never agreed in the first place with Harnack's thesis that the Platonic and Aristotelian elements of orthodoxy obviate the meaning of the gospel, and thus the adoption of an "older terminology" into his own theological vocabulary—if in fact this is what he does—does not mean solidifying his case with the underlying philosophy.[27]

Finally, Barth concedes his ambivalence toward philosophy. Perhaps this does signify a "decisive characteristic" of his thought. So what? He is more at home in the kind of authorial freedom of his *Epistle to the Romans* and *Christliche Dogmatik*, namely, that of appropriating terms, images, and categories "without considering the problem of a preestablished harmony between the matter itself and these particular concepts, because my hands were already full in trying to *say* something very special."[28] He admits the "gypsylike" quality of this approach but questions the importance of spending the rest of his life "acquiring an unambiguous terminology from the phenomenologists."[29] His understanding of the relationship of theology to philosophy is purposefully cavalier; no wonder that it might seem dilettantish. Be that as it may, Barth's primary responsibility is "to hear . . . the voice of the church and the Bible, and to let this voice be heard, even if in so doing, for want of anything better, I have to think somewhat in Aristotelian terms."[30] Although Bultmann's preoccupation with a philosophical point of contact might prove useful in thinking about certain secondary matters, Barth relinquishes the task of dealing with Scheler, the Gundolfians, and "all the philosophers" to Bultmann, Gogarten, and company. Theology really must be done as if nothing else happened.[31]

"Fate and Idea in Theology"

In February and March 1929 Barth gave a series of lectures in the *Hochschulinstitut* in Dortmund under the title "Fate and Idea in Theology." In the lectures he discussed the relation of theology to both realist and idealist streams of the philosophical tradition.

The distinction between realism and idealism, or "fate" and "idea" as he refers to the terms in the address, represents the binary oppositions of Western metaphysics, those basic contradictions between reality and truth, nature and spirit, the objective and non-objective, and being and thinking. Barth says, "To designate these boundaries as 'fate and idea' is to imply that not only our act of thinking but also our act of living (which also involves thinking) is determined in a two-fold way. . . . We live our fate or destiny, yet we also live our project or idea."[32] Barth chooses fate and idea because he thinks the other "conceptual pairs" express this situation only theoretically. Theology must ask how these oppositions are related to one another, and it must ask about their priority and of the possibility of a higher synthesis.

In the Dortmund lectures Barth considers the meaning of theology as *Wissenschaft*. Theology's task as a scientific undertaking is that of the second-order, reflective discipline of the church which speaks about God as the theme of the church's first-order language and proclamation. Since in "the empty space" above the churches and the confessions there is no theology,[33] the confessing community is both the context of the theological science and the condition of the possibility of theology. Thinking about God anyway other than *cum ira et studio* might give way to "the problem of God as such," but it would not yield a reflection grounded in the God of the Christian proclamation.[34] Theology is the science that has God as its object only to the extent that it has God as its subject.[35]

Theology and Fate

Knowledge of God particular to the concept of fate involves the belief that what is true is derived from that which is experienced and from so-called existing reality. Theological inquiry in this paradigm consists of a threefold development. First, the assertion is made that "God is," for where there is being, there must be God. Second, the inference arises that "God is being itself." "God is" introduces the correlative task of thinking about God and thinking about being.[36] Third, the conclusion follows that since God is being itself, everything that exists participates in God, and further, everything that exists, exists because it participates in God. As such, thought shaped by the priority of fate yields the *analogia entis*. Barth says, "It is thus the case that we stand in relation to God by virtue of the fact that we ourselves *are* and that things outside of us *are*. . . . *Analogia entis* means the dissimilarity and similarity to God which I myself have as knower and the thing outside me has as the known."[37] Barth detects the realist position not only in its classical Thomistic setting but also in Schleiermacher's definition of piety as feelings of absolute dependence (as well as in Erich Schäder's "theocentric theology" and its conception of the "God of our consciousness").

But are these descriptions not in fact valid inasmuch as God in the event of revelation makes himself to be an object of human experience?[38] If God has revealed himself in the world, does not human experience participate in revelation? Barth asks, "What is revelation if not God's making himself accessible to our experience, if not God's giving over of himself to that objective-subjective *similitudo* of himself, if not God's letting himself be found within and without. . . . What does revelation mean if not that God is our fate?"[39]

His answer cuts to the heart of his rejection of realism as a legitimate theological framework. The attempt to understand God as *Wirklichkeit*, as actuality or reality, demonstrates the desire to connect the concept of fate to worldly experience and to construe God as *causa prima, ens realissimum*, and *actus purus*—as "the reality of all reality."[40] Where realism regulates theological thought, God is construed as a reality (albeit more powerful and sublime) alongside other realities—as just another being, albeit the highest, perfect being. Barth's counters with the claim, now familiar, that theology cannot be done except on the basis of the Word of God, which "does not confirm and reinforce the naive confidence that it is possible for human beings to experience God."[41] The Word presents a radically new truth.

The Concept of Idea

Whereas the notion of fate posits a correlation or analogy between beings and being, the concept of idea (or idealism) offers a correlation between thinking and truth or between the being of thinking and the truth of being. Whereas a theology interpreted by realism conceives God as *ens realissimum*, a theology governed by the concept of idea gives rise to the meaning of God as the nongiven and unconditional.

Barth recognizes that no "serious" theology is completely lacking in some element of idealism, for "wherever the concept of God is taken seriously, God's givenness must not only be distinguished, but fundamentally distinguished, from all other being."[42] To the extent that idealist vocabularies most often enforce God's nongivenness, they serve as reminders of the relativity and inadequacy of all human words about God, and thus an "antidote to all demonology." Only a "dilettantish idealism" would maintain that God is something less than the Unconditional itself.

But, of course, idealism presents serious problems to be reckoned with, the most immediate of which is christological in nature: the novelty of God's self-witness in Jesus of Nazareth and the freedom of God in this event are compromised. For in and through Jesus Christ one beholds the inauguration of a qualitatively new fellowship with God, which the movement of Idea or Spirit (*Geist*) can neither anticipate nor contain. Therefore, Barth reiterates that theology "belongs just as little to the humanities as to the sciences,"[43] attentive as it is to the singular reality of "the Word dwelling in inapproachable light." Theology neither produces nor articulates this Word; "it bears witness to it."[44]

The Consequences of Philosophy

Barth's critical purpose in the Dortmund lectures is not to deny the role of reason in theology, despite rumors to the contrary,[45] but to show that any thinking about God must be "directed, guided and ordered by something superior to itself, something that has no part in its antithesis."[46] That something, "the Word dwelling in inapproachable light," does not elicit the response of passivity or arrogance but of obedience. For the theologian works faithfully only when he or she heeds the call to obey and follow after; only then does the theologian evidence that humility of thought bowed by the severe confession that "we know ourselves only in relation to something outside ourselves."[47] The truth of theology can be recognized only as the truth that is spoken to us in Jesus Christ.

What are the consequences of this view of revelation for understanding the relationship between theology and philosophy? Before answering this question, Barth draws some important conclusions about the nature and structure of philosophical reasoning on the basis of his analysis of fate and idea.

Philosophy is plagued by an incorrigible drive toward synthesis. Even if it settles for something less than the encyclopedic systems of Thomas or Hegel, even if it maintains a critical and self-critical posture, philosophical thinking would still aspire to say an "ultimately definitive word," and it would reckon that word to be "potentially utterable."[48] The philosopher whose thought remains "conscious of its [dialectical] limits as philosophy, as reflection on the reality and truth of human existence, at whose limits the idea of God can emerge only as a question,"[49] the philosopher who does not confuse and identify his synthesis with God will encounter no resistance by the Christian theologian. Nonetheless, theology cannot couple with this peculiar dialectic, for "the art of theology cannot be the art of synthesis."[50] A theological assertion might incline toward realism or idealism, "but as theology it has neither the *primum* nor the *secundum* as an overarching *tertium*. It has no *tertium* at all—neither to propose and promote, nor to suggest, nor even to approximate."[51] The dialectic of theology is a dialectic of sustained tension, a dialectic without immanent synthesis, reflecting the crisis of the Word of God in human thought and existence.[52]

Undoubtedly, the tools of theology are nothing more or less than "ordinary human thought and speech," with their own laws, structures, possibilities, and limitations. Theology always offers itself as human knowledge; it can never make the truth of its claim directly visible, not to mention verifiable. Having no "divinely unambiguous categories" at its disposal, theology can never just speak the brute truth. Even though the theologian is unable to prove to the philosopher with "final triumphant clarity" that he means something completely different when he speaks of God (which seems most often the case), a genuine speaking about God *as* God's own bespeaking remains the aim of the theological science. Barth says, "Thinking and speaking humanly, all too humanly, yet nevertheless letting God's Word be said—that is the task of theology."[53] To be sure, the great temptation of the theologian is to become what he so often aspires to be, a philosopher. "Theology stands under the insufferable pressure of a situation where it can speak only humanly and where this occurs so much better in philosophy."[54] However, if the difference between theology and philosophy seems to be slight, "it is nevertheless an abyss."[55] For while the theologian's inevitable use of philosophical sources and concepts may on occasion suggest some type of correlation, in truth he or she must be solely attentive to God's Word. The theologian uses, or misuses, philosophy only as an unavoidable consequence of this attentiveness.

The First Commandment of Theology

On 10 March 1933 Barth delivered the lecture "The First Commandment as an Axiom of Theology" in Copenhagen on his first trip to Denmark. In many ways the piece anticipates and explicates the *Barmen Confession,* which he wrote the following year on behalf of the Confessing Church as a declaration against the German Christian heresy. While I have no intention of separating "The First Commandment" from the dynamic of its historical environment, it is important that we take note of the implications of the Denmark address for understanding the relationship between theology and philosophy.

"Thou shalt have no other gods before me." This axiom is the decisive command for theology, although "it can neither be proven nor is it in need of proof."[56] Barth distinguishes the theological axiom from a general axiom. "Whatever 'axiom' means here must be determined by the matter which it designates . . . irrespective of the general sense of that concept. . . . We say 'axiom' because, in this concept, an opportunity to try to say just what the concept in its general use could *not* say—namely, what this absolutely fundamental and foundational presupposition of theology is all about."[57] The distinction between a general axiom and a theological axiom approximates the difference between philosophy and theology. A general axiom (*axioma*) is accessible to any human being who reasons according to certain rules and guidelines, and thus has universal human accessibility. A general axiom "waits somewhere in the sphere of the human, to be discovered and valued by human beings."[58] In reference to a general axiom, I assert myself in some manner *as human being*— "There I am lord."[59] However, before the theological axiom of the first commandment, I acknowledge myself to be *the object of a presupposition*—"Here I have a lord."[60] Specific to "the divine sphere," that is, to the freedom of God in the event of Jesus Christ, the first commandment is entirely self-involving, prompting either obedience or disobedience for the person so involved.

The theme of lordship emerges in this 1933 lecture as the definitive criterion for theological thinking. The theological axiom is not some formal method but the most basic claim of soteriology. Understanding the practice of theology is indistinguishable from responding to the question "Who do you call Lord?" Barth says, "I think and speak with theological responsibility when I know myself to be responsible to that commandment in what I think and speak as a theologian; when I perceive that responsibility as a responsibility to an authority above which there is no appeal, because it is itself the last and highest, the absolutely decisive authority. 'You shall have no other gods before me!'"[61] The one who is obedient to the theological axiom is also the one who dwells within the *regnum gratiae*. Thus, an axiom that purports to be abstractly derivable in creation, whatever else it may be, is not the commandment of God, for the axiom of theology is unique to the revelation of God in Jesus Christ. This axiom compels "the emergence of *one* god, the *deus ecclesiae* out of the multiplicity of gods."[62] As Barth says, "God reveals all other gods as nothings."[63] The "heart" of theology, then, is its humility before the first commandment.

Nonetheless, Barth realizes that even though theology must be solely obedient to the lordship of Jesus Christ, it still engages other, external realities. He is not denying that the "and" can sometimes be theologically significant. Barth's point is that theology does not *need* external realities in order to be about its distinctive work.

Two criteria must inform the theologian's conversation with nontheological sources. First, in cases where theology is aware of its responsibility to the first commandment and yet includes the "and" in its discourse, it will speak of the "and" only for the sake of revelation. Barth thinks that certain contemporary Protestant theologians—Hirsch, Althaus, Gogarten, and Brunner—obscure through their preoccupation with "points of contact" the clarity with which the Protestant reformers brought "that other authority" into line with the lordship of Christ. Theology proclaims the freedom of God as the sole authority over all creation and history. It does not need modernity's various appendages, for example, the eighteenth century's "revelation and reason," Schleiermacher's "revelation and the religious self-consciousness," Ritschl's "revelation and the ethos of culture," Troeltsch's "revelation and the history of religion," and the 1930s emerging notion of "revelation and creation."[64] To avoid turning the "and" into the "end," one must interpret those other realities according to revelation and not the other way around. "Theology will not try to illuminate the heavens with a searchlight mounted on earth, but will try to see and understand earth in light of heaven."[65]

Second, in the times when theology speaks of the "outside," it must do so without admixing the "alien" vocabulary with its own inner sense. There should be no interchange between the "down here" and the "up there" of grace. Barth says, "[The theologian] will *not* consider an apology for other concerns over against the concern of the church. He will not consider, therefore, another task of theology."[66] Anything less than faithfulness to the axiom of theology results in compromising the integrity of the gospel.

"Philosophy and Theology"

The essay "Philosophy and Theology," written in 1960 as a contribution to the Festschrift for his brother Heinrich (a philosopher at Basel), expands the conversation between the theologian and the philosopher without abandoning the theological criterion of the earlier texts. What is new here is the claim that theology and philosophy are preoccupied with the same single truth. According to Barth, there is a definite overlap between the subject matter of philosophy and theology inasmuch as both attempt to understand the source of "the real," its nature and significance. The confrontation between theologian and philosopher can even be called a "cooperation," though a strange one, for the two work in "opposite order and sequence" (which in turn is the cause of the confrontation) and for different ends and audiences.

The theological context of this enlarging conversation is Barth's sharper focus on the common history of God and humanity, narrated in the fourth volume of the *Church Dogmatics*. There is a striking analogy between Barth's consideration of worldly lights and secular parables and his later thoughts on the relation between theology and philosophy. The celebration of God's togetherness with humanity, of the fact that "the *deity* of the living God" finds "its meaning and its power only in the context of His history and of His dialogue with man,"[67] animates new horizontal patterns of relationship, even as it retains the vertical priority of God's grace. God speaks parables of his good will and action to and in the human. As such, Barth asks whether philosophy is one example of secular parables.

He makes two observations concerning this question. The first is that the theologian and philosopher should understand the sense of their cooperation as a confrontation with "the one, single, and whole Truth among all the differentiation of its components."[68] To be human means to be confronted with "the one whole Truth disclosing itself in its wholeness"; hence, to share with the philosopher in a "fellow-humanity" is to be his responsible "companion, comrade and colleague." The philosopher and the theologian pursue their respective tasks "on the basis of the one whole Truth as such," but yet importantly also on the basis of the presupposition that each may only circumnavigate this truth.[69]

Second, Barth claims that the extent to which the theologian and the philosopher succeed in speaking about "the one whole Truth" is proportionate to the extent to which they recognize their respective humanity, which disables both of the possibility of being in possession of the truth. Neither theologian nor philosopher has yet the capacity to lead truth into its discourse, "there to let it speak in behalf of his own subject matter and against that of the other."[70] Philosophy and theology should allow themselves to be grasped by a claim— or "let themselves both put forward a claim by means of [the Truth]"[71]—but they cannot presume to apprehend that claim itself by means of their own cunning. Barth's qualification: "They can both only be at its disposal, viz., to want to serve it."[72] Truth is superior to both.

Something like an "analogy of endeavors" intrudes between theologian and philosopher. The theologian attends to the "one whole Truth" as the living Creator, who through the Word established creation, reconciled it to himself, and redeems it toward full togetherness in life with God.[73] The theologian works in view of a double responsibility: to emphasize the priority of revelation in knowledge of the truth and the good news that God invites humanity to share in the truth. As Barth says, "[The theologian] focuses on the freedom of God for his human being."[74] The philosopher also has a twofold responsibility, though one different in scope from the theologian's. The philosopher is preoccupied with the binary oppositions of being and existence, spirit and its self-unfolding, logos and reason, *causa prima* and *causae secundae*, and idea and appearance.

Nevertheless, the analogy that presents itself must be scrutinized by the question whether the theologians and the philosophers dispose themselves toward the truth, or the respective truthfulness, of each other's investigation. Will philosophers be able to recognize their own limitations in view of God as living Creator and Word, and will theologians discern in the philosopher's conceptual pairs that which they understand as Creator and creation? As a theologian, Barth is skeptical of such an equanimity, for in his view, the ascending movement of philosophy must be considered a secondary movement, the primary being the "passing counter-movement" of the above toward the below. Consequently, the theologian holds that the philosopher's conceptual pairs are always asymetrical, with the first term having priority over the second (and thereby "logocentric" to the core!). The theologian sees the philosopher navigating the route from creation to Creator and then back again to terra firma. But unless theologians want to become cryptophilosophers, they shall resist charting the same course as the philosopher, and simply remain astonished that the philosopher "considers himself free and sees himself in a position to think and speak in view of both of the components of the one whole Truth so completely differently than the theologian himself."[75]

The seminal question, then, is how philosophical thought, which proceeds from creation to Creator and back to creation there to remain, shall be reconciled with theology, which takes the creating, living Word as its sole premise and presupposition? "How can the legitimacy of the one be said to be able to exist beside that of the other?"[76] This question is the rock upon which any cooperation of theologian and philosopher founders, for theology confesses that Jesus Christ alone is "the one whole Truth, through whom the path of his thought and speech has been cut off."[77] Not the Christ-idea, not symbol, vehicle, or cipher, but Jesus of Nazareth is true God and true human being who himself illuminates "the whole world and thus also the philosopher and the theologian!"[78] What perplexes and amazes the theologian most is that the philosopher, despite his or her situation *post Christum natum*, still wants "to seek, to find and to walk the path from human being to God . . . and to undertake among these or those indications and claims the construction of a hand of a clock moving from the right towards the left, which yet for him also has been antiquated in Jesus Christ."[79] Why *does* the philosopher continue seeking the truth on the basis of the created, when the Creator has revealed himself truthfully to humanity, and in so doing revealed to humanity the truth of creation? In Barth's view, the conversation between theologian and philosopher comes to a close on this note, even though they must remain within "earshot" of each other.

But if they must remain within earshot, will not the theologian occasionally hear a word that pricks his interest? If so, what sort of word might that be? What can the theologian learn while listening to (or at least eavesdropping on) the philosopher's varied disputations? For starters, the theologian admires the philosopher's enviable technical skills, conceptual creations, and innovations of idiom and idea—his "worldly wisdom." More importantly, the theologian welcomes the philosopher's appreciation of nature and culture as a healthy reminder that theology has spoken of worldliness too little in earnest. "The existence of the philosopher may be helpful to him, to awaken and to keep him on the alert in this respect."[80]

But that's about it. Theologians should not make it their business to develop a universally valid ontology, anthropology, or psychology. In fact, Barth's suggestion at the end of the essay is that the best response to the difference of theologian and philosopher is simply to let both be what they are in their difference. Theology is a speaking about God on the basis of God's self-witness in Jesus Christ; philosophy is thought thinking about itself and being on the basis of being. Perhaps it may happen that on occasion the philosopher's thinking has a place in the theologian's speaking; but there is no way to generalize from the particular case a uniform method of correspondence. The philosopher reminds the theologian that discernment of self, world, and ultimate is integral to any credible conception of the truth. Nonetheless, what the philosopher actually thinks about the self, world, and ultimate is in no way binding on the theologian. God has spoken decisively in Jesus Christ; this is the measure of all truth.

Benign Neglect

The event of revelation demonstrates that genuine thinking about God must be directed, guided, and ordered by "something superior to itself."[81] Obedience to the axiom of theology means affirming the first commandment as the sole criterion for judging the promise of any philosophical idea. In Barth's final analysis, theology should attend to its principal responsibility and do the academy the favor of not trying to pass itself off as philosophy dressed in sheep's clothing. However, the theologian who works in obedience to the first commandment must not presume that while other theologians have sold out to certain philosophical programs, one has oneself consistently spoken the unambiguous truth. Although Barth acknowledges the inevitability of using categories and concepts external to the word, there is no way to generalize from these occasions to a method which might regulate the practice of a philosophical theology. Theology's disinterest in other vocabularies arises from the character of God himself, for God cannot be derived from any reality other than himself. "[God is no] foreign word on the edge of existence, but existence itself, surging through the nothingness of all that is. . . . A living God, a God who is really God! . . . What a miracle this is: a God who is God and not the puny little idol we, in our weakness, have made of God."[82] This living God of the Bible cannot be identified with the concept of being, however venerated or exalted the concept may be. Neither can he be identified with the concept of history, for "[the] non-objectivity of the God of Revelation is not the non-objectivity of which idealism speaks."[83] But equally important, the faith of the living God cannot be pitted *against* philosophy, for faith resides (as Luther says) "outside, under, above, below, around, and beyond it."[84]

I suggest that Barth's attitude toward philosophy can be clarified by comparison with Richard Rorty's remark (in a quite different context) that the best way to get on with the business of saying something novel and interesting is to assume a "benign neglect" toward the whole weight of inherited and unsolved philosophical problems, contradictions, and interpretations.[85] Rorty explains, "The question is: suppose that one wants to escape from a philosophical vocabulary, to set it aside, to diagnose the problems posed in it as pseudo problems, how do you go about it?"[86] How can one escape from a slavish dependence on philosophy without inadvertently becoming a philosopher oneself? How does one overcome metaphysics without waxing metaphysical? To wit: "How can you maintain enough contact with the vocabulary in order to criticize it while getting far enough from it not to have to answer questions phrased in its terms?"[87]

Rorty's advice is a shrug of the shoulders. There is no way to scale the sheer immensity of the alpine philosophical tradition. One should just turn away from it and do something else. Adopting a "benign neglect" would amount to saying "that when you want to avoid discussing a controverted issue you should, in the manner of Wittgenstein, conscientiously refrain from answering questions formulated in the vocabulary in which that issue was stated."[88] One should not affect "a back-to-nature pose," for such a pose is "merely one more expression of the Platonic idea that the truth has always been within us."[89] One should not even follow Heidegger's path of searching for a vocabulary "which will 'place' and 'distance' the old controversy."[90] Rather, Rorty recommends that we would do better to admit that "the only cure for bad old controversies is temporary forgetfulness."[91] Benign neglect amounts to saying that we should try to create *causes* for dispensing with old controversies which are not *reasons* for forgetting them.[92]

Aside from the obvious disagreements between Rorty's and Barth's thought, I think Barth assumes just this posture. He does not develop arguments against the Bultmannians, the Schelerians, the Gundolfians, and "all the philosophers"; instead, he suggests that the surest way of getting beyond, behind, around, or over institutionalized and time-honored theological problems is to simply start speaking about God in a new way. If this catches on, so much the better; if it does not, there is no all-encompassing apologetic scheme that one can deploy against one's detractors. If by chance there is a convergence between the new way of speaking and a public need (or a new way of hearing), then the old paradigm fades from the scene. But this happens not because the criteria have finally been found which approximate the truth and which engender universal accessibility to this truth. It happens because the new world finds hearers—listeners—whose minds are inspired anew and whose hearts are enkindled toward faithfulness and charity. As Rorty says, "The moral is not that objective criteria for choice of vocabulary are to be replaced with subjective criteria, reason with will or feeling. It is rather that the notions of criteria and choice (including that of 'arbitrary' choice) are no longer in point when it comes to changes from one language game to another."[93]

Rorty unwittingly emancipates the theologian from the dreary task of prefixing talk about God with apologies, prolegomena, and polemics with other discourses. "The world does not speak," he says. Implicit in Barth's view is the concern that if we constantly try to attach theology to a philosophical addendum, might it not be fair to ask whether we really believe in God. That is, do we believe that God is *really there*, that beyond the networks of human vocabularies there is one who *encounters* us as really other, as unprecedentedly new and surprising—as the God revealed in Jesus Christ? Like Rorty, Barth challenges the assumption that philosophers have a privileged standpoint from which to evaluate time-honored issues like "truth," "essence," and "reality." He does not worry about whether he has "gotten beyond" philosophy, for, if one worries too much about whether one has gotten beyond metaphysics, then it will inevitably turn out that one has not. Barth's audacity as a thinker gives new life to Rorty's admonition: "It behooves philosophers who think that an issue has gone stale to find something fresh to do, and to leave it to the historians of the future to figure out whether or not they succeeded."[94] Similarly, Barth's theology is "self-nourished at its own source";[95] it cannot be called antirational (or rational for that matter) because it is not interested in, or dependent upon, appraisals of "antecedently-formulated criteria" for scientifically or philosophically rigorous discourse. Rorty's benign neglect illuminates the environment in which Barth works, sometimes iconoclastic toward philosophy, sometimes mildly approving, but always solely attuned to theology's own inner source.

3

Bonhoeffer's Christological Redescription of Philosophy

The Problem of System

In *Act and Being* Bonhoeffer provides what he calls a "typological sketch" of philosophers and philosophical theologians from both transcendental and ontological traditions as a means of evaluating their significance for theology. Among the representative figures of transcendental thought, Bonhoeffer discusses Hermann Cohen, Paul Natorp, Friedrich Brunstäd, and Reinhold Seeberg; from ontology, Edmund Husserl, Max Scheler, Martin Heidegger, and Erich Przywara. Readers looking for detailed theological analyses of these seminal thinkers will be disappointed. Bonhoeffer's purposes are twofold: first, to locate philosophical themes which can be applied to the theological project of reconciling concepts of act and being in a Christian reflection on God and revelation,[1] and, second, to show how philosophy can be taken into the service of explicating the secondary objectivity of revelation, that is, the worldliness of revelation.

At the conclusion of his typological sketch, Bonhoeffer asserts that even though revelation demonstrates the insufficiency of all self-enclosed systems of thought, ontological and transcendental theses are not to be rejected en masse without careful consideration. "In so far as both—the act as foundation of being, and being as foundation of act—evolve into the I-enclosed system (in that the I understands itself from itself, can place itself in truth), they offer no assistance in

understanding the idea of revelation."[2] However, within the circumference of revelation's new social space—"Christ existing as community"—certain contributions from "genuine" transcendentalism and
ontology are serviceable to theology.[3] The important qualification is
that in the course of theological redescription philosophical themes
will no doubt be construed in a "wholly new guise." Bonhoeffer contends that only thought "bound to the obedience of Christ 'is' *from*
the truth and can be placed into the truth."[4] Thus, when philosophy
is bound to Christ (in whatever form this may take), it is able to confess itself as "Christian philosophy," certain that "the place it wished
to usurp *is already* occupied by another—Christ."[5]

What does Bonhoeffer mean by the term "Christian philosophy"?
In *Sanctorum Communio* he argues that a Christian philosophy
should be developed in place "of the idealist philosophy of immanence."[6] The term is introduced in the context of discussing the four
historical schemes of social relation, the Aristotelian, the Stoical, the
Epicurean, and the idealist. In particular, Bonhoeffer is concerned with
the problem of idealism in thinking about the relations of God and
world, and self and other. He describes "christliche Philosophie" as
a kind of theological thinking which is grounded in the primacy of
revelation and shaped by receptivity to otherness, which inhibits a
conception of God and humankind subsumed into overarching totality. He says, "For a Christian philosophy, the human person exists
only in relation to the divine transcending it, in contradiction to it,
not as the overcoming of it."[7] Christian philosophy is then a manner
of thinking about God which is broken to divine otherness, humble
to the qualitative distinction between infinite and finite that under-
mines all claims to self-mastery.

In *Act and Being*, Bonhoeffer asks further how philosophical
notions can inform theology's reflection on the new being in Christ.
He agrees with Barth that revelation shatters the possibility of the I's
possession of itself outside of reference to God; faith is the existential expression of the fact that the self does not possess itself.[8] But
Bonhoeffer disagrees with Barth on the matter of the appropriateness
of employing certain philosophical themes in theological construction. Revelation yields its own epistemology, its own sociology and
social ontology. To the extent that theology remains faithful to the
distinctiveness of the new reality in Christ, philosophical themes are
to be treated with creative and disciplined respect. The work of Christian philosophy is able to unify the contributions of a pure transcendentalism and a pure ontology into an "ecclesial thought"

("kirchliches Denken").[9] As he states, "The relation of theology and philosophy requires a new clarification."[10]

When Bonhoeffer refers to the "problem of philosophy," which he does frequently in the early literature, he most often has in mind the distortions of a philosophical system. Although he attributes the modern origin of these aporias to Kant and Hegel, his notion *of Systemgedank*, or "systematic metaphysics," is most dramatically exemplified in terms of what Fichte means by the *Wissenschaftslehre*. Fichte's project is that of an extended demonstration of the systematic reflexivity that emerges in the science of logical thought. The original tautology of self-identity (I=I) is explicated in terms of the process of the unfolding of all principles of knowledge, which unfolds from and returns to the basic tautology as the perfect envelopment of the perfect system. Fichte persists in an effort to think rationally how the world came to be, to ask how it is possible to know anything at all. He says, "[My task] is intended to express that *Act*, which does not and cannot appear among the empirical states of our consciousness, but rather lies at the basis of all consciousness and alone makes it possible."[11] As such, the procedure of the science of logic is always the same. One starts with a single principle (identity, or the "I=I") and rigorously follows the dialectical method (difference, or the "I=not-I") until arriving back at the beginning through a synthesizing of the contradictions (limitation, or the "I and the not-I"). Thus, as a self-enclosed whole, Fichte's description of system approximates that idea brought into critical scrutiny by Bonhoeffer. The principal problem of philosophy, then, involves its totalizing claims.

However, Bonhoeffer not only criticizes the elegant closure of system illustrated by Fichtean logic; he also leaves open the possibility that negative or critical strategies contain totalizing proclivities. In this manner, there is an analogy between the distortions of philosophical system and what Jacques Derrida has counterposed to the meaning of "infrastructure." In such texts as *Writing and Difference*, *Dissemination*, and *Margins of Philosophy*,[12] Derrida has sought to illustrate the impossibility of reaching a single position based on one irreducible principle, inasmuch as there are irrevocable dualities even in purported unities. To be sure, a metaphysical system involves the search "for a centered structure," for a concept of meaning, "based on a fundamental ground . . . a play constituted on the basis of a fundamental immobility and a reassuring certitude, which is beyond the reach of play."[13] But system inevitably becomes *illusion*; thinking itself to be concrete unity, it disseminates into multiplicity—into pure heteroglossia. In the play of difference performed in textuality, the finite I is thrown into unending, inchoate revelry. Totalization is fractured. Since the system of knowledge is always beyond the grasp of the finite individual, every field of discourse is infinitely varied and discontinuous. In the event of writing, system is subverted.

Bonhoeffer agrees that the system is illusory. But his gloss on the Derridean critique would amount to the objection that the affirmation of infinite openness, even though occasioned by loss of meaning and radical finitude, betrays in its own idiosyncratic way a longing for overriding identity. In Derrida, what is at work under the pretenses of apocalyptic carnival is something like the narration of the absolute I, but an I wandering further into exile, colliding with other I's in a haze of diaphoristics, losing centeredness to a difference so complete as to be finally indistinguishable from totality. Bonhoeffer would see this as yet another variation on the theme of identity, even one calculated by insidious negativity.[14] Although Derrida claims that the decentering moment of inscription is not first and foremost an intellectual event but a political and social one,[15] his claim totters off into the esoteric when he fuses and confuses text and reality in much the same way that thought and being are unified in the systemizers he so brilliantly ridicules (see his cynical redescription of Nelson Mandela as grass-roots bricoleur).[16] From Bonhoeffer's vantage point, the workers at Manchester or the children in the urban ghettos would surely find Derrida's festival of play no less repressive in its shrewd monopolization of writing than the suffocating grandeur of Fichte's system. So sharp are Bonhoeffer's suspicions of system, so decisive is the preeminence of revelation, that not even the most rigorously critical philosophical scheme can speak truthfully about meaning and existence on its own terms.

Thus, philosophy as a mirror of finite reality does not grant any room to the event of revelation, which is why its concepts, categories, and models must be christologically redescribed. The project Bonhoeffer initiates in *Act and Being* involves a unification, that is, a sublation, of transcendental philosophy and ontology into a "kirchliches Denken." Therein certain philosophical themes gain clarity and illuminative power. Bonhoeffer explains in detail:

> Nevertheless, it may be that . . . we shall find in genuine transcendentalism and ontology (as distinct from idealism and phenomenology) certain contributions to the solution of the act-being problem *within* the concept of revelation, if only because they have exhaustively fathomed and argued the philosophical dilemma of act and being, or because we shall be able to adopt their polar standpoints of man as pure act "with

reference to," and thought "suspended" in being, in order to test against revelation, in the sharpest possible antithesis, the merits of explanation in terms of act or of being. If that is so, we may be sure that these theories will emerge from their encounter with the idea of revelation in a wholly new guise, but equally we shall know that the "with reference to" and the "suspension" are amenable to theological interpretation, hence, after all, of service in understanding the idea of revelation.[17]

Thus, Bonhoeffer's address to contemporary thought forms is not an accommodation to them but follows from his emphasis on the incarnational vigor of God's coming to the world in Jesus Christ. Bonhoeffer does not toss all conceptuality into an eschatological distance; his attentiveness to the concreteness of revelation compels him to arrange nontheological materials into a discourse of obedience and commitment shaped by the christological axiom—"Christ existing as community."

Before turning to the next division of the book, I wish to discuss a concern that must not be overlooked in the process of positioning Bonhoeffer within a larger intellectual framework, namely, how his theological use of philosophy differs from Paul Tillich's well-known and highly influential method of correlation. Most alternatives to Barth on this issue have tended to go the way of Tillich. But Bonhoeffer lays out a new synthesis that avoids a correlation method as commonly conceived.

Theology's Internal Correlation

In the essay "Philosophy and Theology" Paul Tillich introduces a typology of the relation of theology and philosophy. He begins by asking the question, "Does the term 'philosophical theology' itself have any objective content?" A negative answer is initially given in the form of a theological supranaturalism, which construes philosophical theology as the unlawful marriage of two contradictory ways of thinking. Here a confusion occurs between a first-order form (the ontologically immediate, or the order of religious symbols) and a second-order form (the interpretation of the first-order symbols, or theology). A theological supranaturalism disengages faith from the need for the second-order interpretive or critical task; therefore, it disavows the very propriety of the distinction between religious experience and theological reflection. In this approach the idea of a philosophical theology is regarded as "high treason against theology."[18]

Another negative response comes from a theological humanism or from philosophy itself, an objection shared by most philosophers of an Anglo-American bent. Like the supranatural form, theological humanism considers philosophical theology "an impure mixture of two incompatible methods of thought,"[19] but for different reasons. According to this objection, philosophy is a superior mode of thinking; too much intercourse with theology disturbs its serene rationality. The business of philosophical logic is to structure the investigation of religious concepts, and thereby resist confessional claims which are not consistent with its criteria.

Can philosophical theology be protected against the double assault of supranaturalism and theological humanism? Is there such an enterprise as philosophical theology? If so, what are its responsibilities? Tillich devotes most of the essay to these questions.

A theological construction is either "philosophical" (having some philosophical makeup) or it is "kerygmatic" (seeking to present the content of the Christian message "in an ordered and systematic way without reference to philosophy").[20] Of course, no two theological forms are positioned quite the same way along the spectrum of philosophical to kerygmatic. However, all forms gravitate toward one of the two poles—the philosophical or kerygmatic. (In the essay, Tillich mentions a third type, the "mystical," which is not discussed in any detail.) Let us look more closely at these two poles.

A philosophical theology explicates the content of the kerygma with close attention to philosophy. A kerygmatic theology explicates the content of the kerygma with attention to its internal terms without explicit reference to philosophy. Importantly, Tillich recognizes that no kerygmatic theologian is able to work in the absence of philosophy. Similarly, no philosophical theologian worth his money will ignore the content of the kerygma. "[The] theological ideal is the complete unity of both types, an ideal which is reached only by the greatest theologians and even by them only approximately."[21] Nevertheless, Tillich does not deny his own bias for the philosophical, and it is not clear from the essay that he is not promoting his own theology as the ideal itself.

To understand the ideal wherein theology and philosophy work together correlatively, we must first understand the respective tasks of the two disciplines. Philosophy is a type of inquiry concerned with the basic question of being itself, the *Seinsfrage*, "the question as to what being, simply being, means."[22] Philosophy is thought thinking about itself and being on the basis of being. As Tillich states in *Systematic Theology*, "Philosophy asks the question of reality as a whole; it asks the question of the structure of being."[23] As such, philosophy provides answers to the question of being in terms of "categories,

structural laws, and universal concepts"—it provides ontological formulations. Tillich holds that philosophy's answers are inevitably
ontological because ontology is the basic analysis of "those structures
of being which we encounter in every meeting with reality."[24] When
a definition of philosophy is cast in terms of the *Seinsfrage*, any separation between philosophy and theology becomes tenuous. Theology
needs philosophy for the reason that "any interpretation of the meaning and structure of being as being unavoidably has consequences for
the interpretation of God, man and the world in their interrelations."[25]

The similar, though not identical, purpose of theological thought
is to ask after being inasmuch as being elicits ultimate concern. He
says, "That which concerns us ultimately must belong to reality as a
whole; it must belong to being";[26] if it did not, we would not be able
to encounter it, and thus it would not concern us.[27] Theology seeks
expression of "the ultimate ground and power and norm and aim of
being . . . for the fulfilling and rejecting aim of *my* existence."[28] In
asking about ultimate concern, theology asks about God, for faith is
the state of being ultimately concerned.[29]

Therefore, a correlation exists between theology and philosophy.
A theological drive (ultimate concern) provides the "impulse to philosophy,"[30] and a philosophical question (the meaning of being) im-
plicates itself in all theological inquiry. In either discipline, Tillich
says, "the meaning of being manifests itself in the logos of being, that
is, in the rational word that grasps and embraces being and in which
being overcomes its hiddenness, its darkness, and becomes truth and
light."[31] Philosophy asks about "the way in which man can find the
revealing word, the logos of being."[32] Theology (of a Christian sort)
asks about the logos of being which appeared in the God-man Jesus
Christ. Thus, theology and philosophy both ask the question of being but from different perspectives. "Philosophy deals with the structure of being in itself; theology deals with the meaning of being for
us."[33]

The method of correlation, which moves from philosophical questioning to theological answering, is the motor of philosophical theology. The method operates by taking the concept and categories of
reason and proceeding to the existential problem implied in reason,
to which the answer is revelation;[34] by taking the concept and categories of being and proceeding to the existential problem implicit
in being, to which the answer is God; by taking the concept and categories of existence and proceeding to the existential problem implicit
in existence, to which the answer is Christ; and so on throughout the
catalog of relevant Christian doctrine. Symbolically expressed, God

answers humankind's questions.[35] As such, theology formulates the questions implicit in human existence, and it formulates the answers implicit in divine revelation "under the guidance of the questions implied in human existence."[36] This represents a circle from humankind's questions to theology's answers, which is repeatable, and which is, in fact, the very lifeblood of theology. The end of the possibility of correlation would signal the end of genuine Christian theology and the final silencing of the kerygma.

Does Bonhoeffer employ a correlation method, perhaps inadvertently, in his task of showing that theology answers the questions of philosophical thought? How are Bonhoeffer and Tillich situated with respect to each other's approach to philosophy and nontheological vocabularies? In fact, Bonhoeffer's christological approach differs from Tillich's method in several important ways. First, according to Bonhoeffer, theology always works in light of the presupposition of God's self-revelation in Jesus Christ. This event is not preconditioned by philosophical reasoning but is simply the basic fact. Despite the possibility that theology might at some point ask about "what concerns us inescapably, ultimately, unconditionally,"[37] theology is principally bound to the confession that God reconciled the world to himself in Jesus Christ, a confession that is neither anticipated nor contradicted by experience; this fact empowers its own questions. As Saint Paul writes, "If Christ has not been raised, our preaching is useless, and so is your faith" (I Cor. 15:14). Bonhoeffer would reject Tillich's conclusion that the answers implicit in the event of revelation are meaningful only "in so far as they are in correlation with questions concerning the whole of our existence."[38] For the questions concerning the whole of our existence are meaningful only in reference to the presupposition of God's self-revelation in Jesus Christ.

Second, to the extent that a correlation does exist between theology and philosophy, such correlation is possible only on the terms established by theology, that is, the correlation is internal to theology. Questions of philosophical anthropology become meaningful (not just theologically meaningful, but meaningful in themselves) only in the space of revelation. On the presuppositions established by theology, philosophy can be placed into truth. Thus, what can be positively stated of Bonhoeffer's relation to Tillich's theology it is that he christologically inverts the method of correlation. According to Bonhoeffer, theology begins with revelation and then proceeds to refigure philosophical concepts and categories of reason; it begins with God's self-witness and then proceeds to redescribe concepts and categories of being; it begins with the reality and presence of Christ and then proceeds to restructure philosophical concepts and categories of existence. In its refiguring philosophical themes theology shows that what philosophy labors to articulate about selfhood, world, and ultimacy is already contained in revelation's complex internality.

Thus, Bonhoeffer's approach cannot be called "correlation"; for even though "alien" vocabularies possess a relative significance, they cannot be said to lead to the truth that is unique to the saving God. Revelation yields its own epistemology, its own sociology and social ontology. Although the fact that the Word became flesh in Jesus Christ abolishes rigid dualisms between God and the world, and thereby abrogates bifurcations between theology and other discourses, it does so from the side of theology and not in correlation with other vocabularies.

In his 1931–1932 lectures on contemporary systematic theology at Berlin, Bonhoeffer argued that theology cannot be confused with either philosophy of religion or *Glaubenslehre*.[39] Philosophy of religion, he claims, must ground its own object; it must establish its own criteria and its own verification of truth. However, the object of theology is the Logos of God, which is self-grounding in God's own act.[40] This is truth's fundamental source, behind which it is not possible to go. Theology does not ground its own object but proceeds from the reality of God—the only reality that wholly grounds itself.

Is theology a positive science like biology? Only in a highly qualified sense, he explains in the lectures. The subject matter of other sciences can always be led back to a universal which lies behind it, and therein be grounded. But in theology the subject matter is "truth itself."[41] Theology's truth is not accessible through a phenomenological analysis of the structures of religious experience. As Bonhoeffer states, "Man becomes open to God only through God himself."[42] In the beginning stands the truth of God ("Gottesbeweis"), articulated by the Word of God which attests to itself. Theology's primary responsibility is to work out an "immanent criticism" ("immanente Kritik") in the context of revelation;[43] to become a mode of thinking internal to the terms established by the self-grounding truth of God. As a result, the relationship of theology and philosophy is given an altogether new clarification.[44]

To be sure, theology's immanent criticism is no simple matter. It certainly does not disengage the theologian of the need to employ philosophical sources in theology, just as faith does not offer the believer a shelter from the storms of our historical present. *Following after* the God who has revealed himself in Jesus Christ propels one into the very heart of worldliness, even as the longing for worldly wholeness and the inability to attain it necessitate the *extra nos* of God's promeity. Revelation creates a new space of human togetherness; in the service of celebrating this new reality, certain philosophical themes can bring to the theological task unexpectedly creative amplifications and illustrations of its own glad proclamation.

II

Life Together

4

Christ Between Totality and Otherness: Bonhoeffer's Earliest Theology

In 1927 Bonhoeffer qualified for the licentiate under Reinhold Seeberg at the University of Berlin with the dissertation *Sanctorum Communio: A Dogmatic Inquiry into the Sociology of the Church*. The book, as Bonhoeffer modestly describes it in the preface, is an attempt to position "social philosophy and sociology in the service of dogmatics."[1] The purpose is to understand the revelation of Jesus Christ in its constitutive sociality, without lapsing into a banal sociology or a bland ecclesiology.

According to Bonhoeffer, if fellowship with God also requires human community,[2] then all theological statements presuppose a social intention. "Community with God by definition establishes social community as well."[3] But this intention does not posit a correlation between sociality and revelation, that is, an interplay or equiprimordiality between the two. Rather, as he says, "the history of the Christian community proves to be defined by an inner history."[4] The new sociality of community is grounded in revelation. Thus, the creating Word *is* social and thereby precedes and establishes the integrity of human sociality; as in the words of Genesis, "Let us make humankind in our image" (1:26). Correspondingly, within the new social space of "Christ existing as community," Bonhoeffer seeks to describe the new patterns of ontic relation and, in this way, to further explicate the secondary objectivity of revelation.

Not surprisingly, his effort provoked much criticism. Socio-
logists pointed to the skewed way of reading contemporary sociological texts. The objective work of the social sciences cannot be achieved
in light of the specious presupposition of the Christian community.
Moreover, while liberal theologians were uncomfortable with the confessional nature of the study, many neoorthodox theologians puzzled
over the sociological and philosophical jargon. Yet after reading the
published text Barth himself called it nothing less than a "theological
miracle." What must have seemed impressive to him was the audacity of the twenty-one-year-old graduate student to integrate almost
every aspect of his theological training, as well as much of what was
currently fashionable in German and Swiss philosophy circles, into the
basic fact of God's self-witness in Jesus Christ. (Barth was also pleas-
antly surprised that the work came out of the "school of Seeberg").[5]

Of central importance to my interest in the dissertation is
Bonhoeffer's appropriation of one such philosophical trend, the philosophy of dialogue, as a means of bolstering his claim that revelation breaks
the hegemony of all totalizing systems of thought. In opposition to the
transcendental tradition, the influential dialogical philosophers argued
that the ethical encounter with the other subverts the pretensions of
any world-constituting subject. The self, in this sense, is not a substance
but a relation;[6] thus, the pretensions of self-sufficient subjectivity are
displaced by the priority of the dialogical "between."

I delineate two serious problems with the theological use of the
philosophy of dialogue. First, it remains within the hegemony of the
transcendental tradition in its rigorous inquiry into the conditions
of the possibility of personal encounter and in the final subjective
character of its claim. Second, the philosophy of dialogue is unable
to secure the continuity of human togetherness. Bonhoeffer wisely
abandons this vocabulary soon after completing the doctoral dissertation. Yet in the course of his experiment with dialogics, he touches
on several points critical to his developing christological reflection
on community. I will turn presently to these points.

However, I wish to emphasize at the outset that the focus of this
chapter is admittedly idiosyncratic, insofar as it takes a technical
interest in the first dissertation's rhetorical strategy. The logic of my
argument in the book as a whole will not be impaired should the
reader wish to proceed directly to Chapter 5.

Ethical Relation and the Place of the Other

"From the purely transcendental category of the universal," Bonhoeffer writes, "we can never reach the real existence of alien sub-

jects."[7] In the epistemological sphere, all knowledge of the other is a modification of self-relation and self-mediation. Only in the encounter with the other is there real social relation. Thus, the other remains constitutively different from the I and is not reducible to its ontologizing grasp. While the epistemological is characterized by ownership and control (and is the way of the same), the social is characterized by receptivity and reciprocity (and involves the encounter of the different).

Bonhoeffer argues that the integrity of the other, the other's irreducibility to the I—"to my thoughts and possessions"[8]—can only be realized in a social, ethical dynamic. When I am encountered by the dialogical other in ethical action, I am arrested in my own attempts to master the world; for in responding to the call of the Thou, I am taken out of myself and repositioned *in relation with the other*. I no longer control the other, nor does the other control me, but we both discover our individual and social identities in the place of our difference. In ethical encounter, we recognize that the source of our relation resides neither on the side of the subject nor on the side of the object but in the space of the relational between. In the act of being encountered by the other, I am shaken up and awakened from the dream of self-constitution. In ethical relations I discover that the other is "not the idealist's reasoning self or personified mind, but a particular living person."[9]

In the Hegelian phenomenology of subjectivity—against which Bonhoeffer's polemic is directed on this point—the identity of the self and other in subjectivity is expressed universally throughout the range of the alterity of objects, and this "despite the opposition of self to self."[10] Herein the difference is, in the end, not really different; "the I, as other, is not an 'other,'"[11] for the rich multiplicity of differences is reduced to the sameness of the single subject "I."[12] The vitality of conflict and the energy of diversity are subsumed into self-mediated homogeneity.

In Hegel's *Phenomenology of Spirit* the subject's others posit a provisional or penultimate limit to the I such that their differences are sublated in the movement of spirit. The universal undergoes diremption or separation into the provisional delimitation of the particular; thus, the particular is enabled to know itself as the universal in the individual. The movement from consciousness to self-consciousness takes form as the self recognizes in the other not a genuine strangeness but an estrangement of its own self. One discovers that the truth of absolute spirit *is* subjectivity—though not just individual subjectivity but universal self-consciousness. The living substance is that being which is truly subject—that which is truly realized and actual solely in the process of positing itself, or in mediating with its own self its transitions from one state or position to the opposite. "What seems to occur outside it," Hegel says, "is its own action."[13] Absolute spirit occasions the disappearance of both the opposition of knowledge and its truth and the opposition of substance with itself; otherness and identity are overcome in the realization of a final identity.

Although Bonhoeffer's principal conversation in *Sanctorum Communio* regarding the relation to the other is carried out with Hegel, the theme of the fracture between sociality and epistemology (which Bonhoeffer advances) is folded into the conversation of the entire transcendental tradition of the subject. This conversation refers to that narrative he calls the "metaphysical scheme."[14] The story told herein involves the various false starts and unfinished accounts of the mollification of the other's otherness in the activity of the self-reflective subject. According to Bonhoeffer, even Kant in his critical architectonic recites the way in which the opposition of subject and object is overcome in the sameness and interiority of intellectual intuition, for the relation of I and other is collapsed into the noetic locus of the subject and object schema (as opposed, for example, to a social or material locus).[15] In the well-known doctrine of the thing-in-itself, Kant holds that there is a component of experience which eludes cognition as the contrapuntal element of the known world. This doctrine is intended to militate against the two dogmas of absolute idealism and materialism. Since Kant construes time, space, and the categories as mental contributions to experience, and since these do not constitute the totality of the real, there must be something else, something other, that is unknown but real. Kant consigns the doctrine of things-in-themselves to the task of pleading that there is a reality sufficient to escape both the totalizing grasp of the I and the compression of the real to the empirical or material.

Bonhoeffer sharply criticizes what he sees as the contradictory claim implicit in Kant's critical epistemology: to the extent that the *ding-an-sich* is posed as barrier, Bonhoeffer says (in agreement with Hegel of the *Logic*), thinking has surpassed any limit. In conceiving the barrier of thought, thought has already gone beyond it; in order to conceive the limit one must already have gone beyond it.[16] He says in the christology lectures, "In so far as the logos limits itself it also establishes itself with power."[17] Bonhoeffer holds that one enters the social sphere only when a "barrier of principle appears at some point to my mind."[18] As long as mind is "dominant"[19] and asserts universality, and as long as the resolution of contradiction (even social contradictions) is achieved in thought, one has not entered the social sphere. The barrier must be established outside the perimeter of the individual I, since any barrier erected by the I is relativized from the start. Bonhoeffer uses this analysis as a way to bring home his point that totality is broken only in the encountering limit of the other in ethical relation.

The systemic fallacies of Kant and Hegel are constitutive of a single overarching claim, namely, that the resolution of the aporias of human relatedness is immanent in the unitary I, and thus the I is privileged with respect to knowledge and encounter of the other (and this even in the case of Kant, who holds forth the possibility, however suspiciously, of the other of thought in the thing-in-itself). If the I is conceived as the condition of the possibility of the other, then the I, as the all-constituting originary I, is also conceived as constituting the other, which is in turn itself all-constituting.[20] One thereby demeans the other inasmuch as one relegates the other's I to a derivative mode of subjectivity.[21]

I do not read Bonhoeffer to claim that the social and the epistemological are mutually exclusive categories. Rather, in *Sanctorum Communio* he is trying to think through the primary mode of human relatedness. With regard to the encounter of the other, there is a disjunction between the two spheres that cannot be bridged by the reflective subject but only encountered (and accepted) in social relation. As Bonhoeffer explains: "My I as a form of Thou can only be experienced by the other I; my I as a form of I can only be experienced by myself. Thus in the experience of a Thou the I-form of the other is never immediately given. . . . So the Thou-form is to be defined as the other who places me before a moral decision. With this I-Thou relationship as the basic Christian relation we have left the epistemological subject-object relationship behind."[22]

This relation can be subject to reflection, but reflection has no role in shaping its source. The relation to the other has simply nothing to do with a monopolizing ego.

Alterity and Community

Accordingly, Bonhoeffer's earliest theological response to the transcendental tradition is his attempt to conceptualize what he calls a "non-synthetic" description of I and other, a conception in which the difference of I and other remains in every case uncompromised. In a nonsynthetic relation, the other remains different, even in the space of revelation, and this difference emerges time and again out of the performance of the dialogical encounter.

Nonetheless, a conflict emerges here in *Sanctorum Communio*'s stated intentions. If social relations are "ever falling apart," and if they are shaped by the act-oriented claims of the other, it would seem to be the case that community, and also subjectivity itself, splinters into particularized acts of encounter. Yet Bonhoeffer must try to show that individuals embedded in "an infinite abundance of possibilities of expression and understanding" are able to come together in community. At least, this is the crucible of his attempt to demonstrate the continuity of community in Christ. If a connection cannot be made between the *difference* of I and other and the *unity* of their life together, then we must concede that Bonhoeffer fails to carry through on his promise that "Christ existing as community" offers a compelling conception of the self with others that avoids many of the pitfalls of the transcendental tradition.

This raises the question whether Bonhoeffer's use of the philosophy of dialogue militates against the possibility of genuine community and defeats his main purpose. Does he overdefine his concept of person to the extent that, though constitutionally separate from the other, it is also atomistic or monadological? Certainly, he recognizes the problem when he asks, "Does the proposition that the Thou is not necessarily an I, not conflict with the concept of community based on persons? Is not the person in the last resort completely isolated?"[23] If the relation of I and other cannot be reduced to the identity of I and other, but is animated by the ethical demand of the Thou, then the pivotal question must be addressed of how I and other can be thought together in community.

Bonhoeffer answers the question in shotgun fashion. He offers a number of resolutions, some of which are incompatible with others. These answers can be divided into two sorts: first, those which are simply suggestions but are given under the pretext of argument; second, those which can be combined to shape a single christological response but which presuppose a social ontology lacking philosophical coherence and theological adequacy.

I will simply provide a summary of the two suggestions given in the first type. First, Bonhoeffer recommends that the link between the dialogical relation and community be made through the conception of God as the Thou who wills the human Thou and imbues it with God's image.[24] According to this proposal, the absolute will of the divine Thou frames the concrete Thou of human sociality.[25] The divine claim confronts the person in every encounter with human otherness such that every encounter of the human Thou is a reflection of, and is based on, the divine Thou. The problem with this suggestion is that if the way to the other person is in fact the way to the divine Thou (a way of recognition or rejection, he emphasizes), and the encounter of the other person is based on my encounter with God, then community as the source of all relationality is fragmented by the formalism or decisionism of the divine acts. Community grounded in the dialectical assertions of the divine Thou becomes itself as discontinuous as the radically eschatological presence of God in time and history. This notion backslides to the equivocal terms of Barth's crisis theology and does not advance the discussion beyond the impasse of otherness and totality.

The second suggestion involves the event of communicative action through language. Speech unites in itself the intentions of objective meaning, subjective reference, and empirical aspects (acoustics and graphics) in which persons overcome isolation by entering into networks of communication. Language is the material which "the formative spirit," given in social intention, makes objectively and subjectively fruitful.[26] Language connects the socially coherent relations of community through the coordination of speaker, word, and hearer in shared linguistic patterns. Bonhoeffer says, "With language a system of social and spiritual interconnections is set within human experience; in other words 'objective spirit' has become effective in history."[27] However, this promising suggestion is not expanded in any significant way in the argument; he simply raises the possibility and then drops it.

Bonhoeffer's sustained response in the dissertation to the quandary of the *separateness* of persons and their life together in *inseparable* community is christological in character. He names Christ as the source of life together. As such, his response involves two steps: he identifies (by explicating the nature of) the source, and he names the source Christ. I will now examine this response in greater detail.

In *Sanctorum Communio*, Bonhoeffer pursues a description of the real and social presence of Christ in the church—not in potentiality but in reality. The doctrine of the Holy Spirit, often construed as a derivative notion in Bonhoeffer's theology, must take into account the fact that the Spirit does not make the church actual.[28] The church is "completely established in Christ as a reality which is necessarily made actual."[29] The Holy Spirit dwelling in the church is actualized solely by revelation in Christ; therefore the Spirit does not reside independently of the church. "As Christ and the new humanity now necessarily belong together, so the Holy Spirit too is to be seen as

effectual only within this humanity."[30] Bonhoeffer rejects the Troelt-
schian view of the church as oriented exclusively on the Word, which
holds that where the Word is to be found, there the church is, even
in the total absence of hearers.[31] Rather, according to Bonhoeffer,
where the church is, there the Spirit dwells in the reality of Christ.
He writes, "The Holy Spirit is solely in the church and the church is
solely in the Spirit."[32] Pneumatology is based strictly on christology:
"[The] Holy Spirit has no other content than the fact of Christ."[33]

In trying to reconcile the structural separateness of persons and
their inseparable life in community, Bonhoeffer thinks of God in his
revealed love in Christ as the divine Thou who becomes the divine I
in the reality of the church. If God is conceived not as the formalistic
Thou of the divine claim but as the Thou becoming I as community,
then community itself can be conceived as the christological I which
is the source of the self and other. He states, "Then it will become
clear that the Christian person achieves his true nature when God
does not confront him as Thou, but 'enters into' him as I."[34] Revelation as community surpasses any reduction to idealist-transcendental epistemologies and their various architectures. Constructions of
the nonobjectivity or otherness of God, as well as constructions of
the objectivity or immanence of God, are herein expressed by the
thought of Christ as the divine subject appearing in and as the difference of the I and other.

"Christ existing as community" is then taken to be the source of
both the *difference* of the unique person and the *continuity* of their
basic relations in the church. "In Christ this tension between being
isolated and being bound to others is really abolished"[35]—but not for
the reason that Christ is the instantiation of difference but because
Christ is the origin both of the difference of persons and of their life
together. This point Bonhoeffer asserts with great force. "The thread
between God and humankind which the first Adam severed is joined
anew by God, by his revealing his love in Christ."[36] The isolation of
the monadic I—the *cor curvum in se*—is broken such that the person is restored to the source of its genuine meaning in community.
In Christ, God no longer confronts humankind with the claim of the
divine Thou—in "demands and summons"—but God, as Bonhoeffer
says, "gives himself as an I, opening his heart."[37] The person living
in the fellowship of the I-Thou "no longer sees the other members of
the community essentially as a claim, but as a gift, as a revelation of
his love, that is, of God's love, and of his heart, that is, of God's heart,
so that the Thou is to the I no longer law but gospel, and hence an
object of love."[38] Importantly, Christ as the source of the social rela-

tion energizes the vicarious fulfillment of the other's claim, which means that I am able not only to be free for the other, but to be free from the bondage of the I, and thereby am able to give myself to the other. Without any vanishing of the barrier of I and other, there arises the reality of a *gemeinsames Leben*. Bonhoeffer says, "[Community] is based upon the separateness of persons. Hence communion is never 'being at one,' nor is it a final 'being One' in the sense of a mystical fusion. . . . Communion based on love is based upon each person's complete surrender for the neighbor."[39] Structural togetherness and separateness originate in the being of Christ as community, reshaping the will in love and sacrifice for the neighbor.

This insightful explication of community as the divine I becoming concrete in Christ is Bonhoeffer's most important point in *Sanctorum Communio*—at least with respect to matters at hand. However, more constructive use of this insight cannot be made because of his appropriation of the philosophy of dialogue to account for community's inner-relational content. Community based on dialogue, difference, and the occurrence of the between forfeits the continuity insinuated in the rich conception of God's I becoming concrete in Christ—a conception that requires thicker ontological and christological expression. I will approach this dilemma initially by a brief evaluation of another theologian who ponders the dialogical relation.

When Martin Buber explores the situation of the meeting (*Begegnung*), he is eager to show that the source of the I and Thou is neither external to nor internal to the relation but "between" it. "Spirit is not in the I but between I and You."[40] Buber holds that the relation of I and other originates in a source that precedes the meeting. As he writes in *I and Thou*, "In the beginning is the relation."[41] This sphere of the "between" is the originary category of human reality, and, as such, it provides a way of thinking an ontology of the inner human reality. For Buber, real conversation is not an affair of one participant or the other, nor resident in some impartial world that embraces both, but, as he says, "in the most precise sense between both, in a dimension, so to speak, that is only accessible to them both."[42] The dialogical meeting then can never be formed by the actions or works of the participants, but happens "out of will and grace in one." Buber says, "The 'Thou-effecting-I' accordingly describes the 'grace' that confronts me in the experience of the meeting, and 'I-effecting-Thou' the same grace as it manifests itself to the other. 'I-effecting-Thou and Thou-effecting-I' then means: in its self-occurrence, the meeting happens at the same time to I and Thou."[43] The Thou encounters me, eliciting from me a direct relationship.[44] Thus, the individual is neither the starting point nor the end point of the human world. "What counts is not these products of analysis and reflection," Buber says, "but the genuine original unity, the lived relationship."[45]

Certainly Buber and Bonhoeffer are different in significantly particular ways. Nonetheless, in my view, Bonhoeffer uses the situation of the meeting in *Sanctorum Communio* to illuminate the inner-relational content of "Christ existing as community." The person, he argues, consists in a "continual coming into being" which proceeds out of the christological between. The answer to the question concerning the connection between individual I's and others and their being in community is given in this context. Christ is the divine subjective ground of the I and other; Christ as *between* is the source of community.

In this light, I disagree with Ernst Feil's claim that *Sanctorum Communio* is bereft of a strong christological imagination.[46] Feil argues that Bonhoeffer does not speak of Jesus Christ in his attempt to develop a concept of ethical transcendence, personal difference, and community, and he criticizes Bonhoeffer for failing to christologically interpret the ethical other. He states, "It seems that Bonhoeffer [in *Sanctorum Communio*] made things more difficult for himself by developing a concept of person in which the neighbor becomes a 'thou' through God or the Holy Spirit, and the true boundary is established by the 'thou' of God or the neighbor, instead of developing it on the basis of Jesus Christ, the mediator."[47] But the text of the dissertation contradicts Feil's conjecture. Bonhoeffer writes, "The man whose life is lived in love is Christ in respect of his neighbor."[48] Great pains are taken to show that Luther's notion of "being transformed into one another through love" is a penetrating description of the christological character of community. Bonhoeffer says, "Each man can and will become Christ for his fellow man."[49] What it means for Christ to exist as community is that the I is opened up to be with and for the other.[50] Thus, Bonhoeffer does not disregard christology in *Sanctorum Communio*, rather—and here is the real shortcoming—the christological terms he uses are in large part informed by the language of dialogue. The dialogical terms of the dissertation do not obscure a christological focus; they pattern the very social-ontological texture of christology. In *Sanctorum Communio*, dialogue is the grammar of christology.

Nevertheless, for two reasons this grammar fails to meaningfully explicate the conception of community that Bonhoeffer seeks in his earliest theology. The first involves the question of philosophical coherence; the second the issue of theological adequacy.

First, the appropriation of a philosophy of dialogue to counter-act the systematic-subjective legacy of the transcendental tradition rests upon shaky premises. Although the priority of dialogue might ostensibly dispense with transcendental philosophy, it carries out this rejection only on the foundations (be they ruined or collapsing) of transcendental philosophy. Dialogics is itself an inquiry into the condition of the possibility of the self's being a self; it does not—and cannot—dispense with the originality of the self in the equiprimordial occurrence of the between. Moreover, dialogical thought does not escape the speculative curiosity of the transcendental tradition, that is, if "philosophizing means risking failure by venturing upon the unthought."[51] Indeed from this perspective dialogics appears to be *more* philosophical than transcendental thought, which attains less problematic results precisely because its approach is less audacious from the start. Therefore, as a rejection of the philosophy of the universal subject and a turning toward the factical human I, the philosophy of dialogue belongs entirely to the same movement of thought as transcendental inquiry. We cannot simply exchange dialogicalism for transcendentalism and claim that we have gotten beyond the synthetic grasp of the Kantian subject.

A better way of looking at the matter is to recognize that the two claims of transcendental and dialogical philosophy contain truths which, in fact, are compatible (particularly, as I will show, when theologically reconfigured). Dialogical thinking can demonstrate the hubris of transcendental thought's claim to demonstrate the subjective constitution of the other by attending to the interplay of the other's difference and its intractability to subjective reductions. But transcendental philosophy can emphasize the impossibility of imagining the relation to the other in terms of immediacy, since all experience is self-mediated at some level. It would be nonsensical to hold that the self's mediations are never its own.

The core of the misunderstanding, as Michael Theunissen argues in his penetrating study of social ontology,[52] is that the two options make mutually different claims which are *not* in fact contradictory. The transcendental project of social ontology tells us important things about the inescapable subjectivity of the dialogical partners, which cannot be entirely swept into the between. Similarly, dialogics provides a dramatic description of the teleology, or the futural character, of the relation. Genuine selfhood may then be conceived as a movement from subjective origins to dialogical communion; the former involves means and the latter ends. Theunissen suggests that the philosophy of dialogue drop the claim of the between as the source which is always prior to the I and other. Rather than the equiprimordiality of the "between," Theunissen recommends the notion of "the dialogical self-becoming of the individual I," a notion he thinks has the power to facilitate a mediation between transcendental philosophy and the philosophy of dialogue, but from the side of dialogue.[53] He says, "[This model] would put us in a position to settle the conflict between the claims to originality by allowing us to grant to transcendental philosophy the originality of the beginning and to the philosophy of dialogue the originality of the goal, of the completed end."[54] The beginning of the social relation would reside in the I proper, while the end would be the I's reconfiguration in the meeting with the other. In this way one could hold that the recentering of the I is initiated *in the I's* movement *to the other*, though not as a recontainment of the other in subjectivity, but as a pulling of the subject out of itself into social relation. Something must take place in subjectivity that inaugurates the reshaping of self in community.

Theunissen cannot say, as a philosopher, what this something is. But a theological narrative such as Bonhoeffer incipiently develops in *Sanctorum Communio* and strengthens in subsequent writings provides an eloquent account of the conversion of the solitary I to agapeic togetherness. In this manner, I suggest that we see Bonhoeffer as sketching the following social-ontological description: the new I in Christ does not recontain the world in identity, rather in being pulled out of itself in communion with the other, the new I remains, as an extended self, always with the other. Thus, the human being who, as transcendental archimedean point of the world, initially posits its I against the other, does not turn back into his I through an assimilation of the other.[55] Through the grounding of the self upon Christ existing as community, the person discovers that Christ is the basis of the capacity for self-being and being with others.

In *Sanctorum Communio* Bonhoeffer has yet to explore the ontological significance of Christ as the *intermediation* of self and other (even though this is precisely the direction he turns in his next book, *Act and Being*). In part, I think the dialogical categories of *Sanctorum Communio* restrict him from conceiving this dialectic as one that sustains both I and other in continuous fellowship—as a movement like the dialogical self-becoming of the individual I. Bonhoeffer's alliance with the philosophy of dialogue in *Sanctorum Communio* protects the difference of I and other, but at the expense of failing to appreciate the continuity of their life together.

The second reason dialogue fails to explicate the sociality of Christ involves the issue of theological adequacy. If the place of the person's encounter with the absolute is taken by his encounter with the Thou of his neighbor, and if the I's claim to be absolute is transferred willy-nilly to the encounter by the other in the between, then what occurs is not the overcoming of the absolute claim per se to master the world but the inversion of the absolute claim from the I to the encountering other. (This is a conclusion which Buber rejects, but which Emmanuel Levinas, for example, recognizes to be the inevitable next step beyond Buber.)[56] According to Bonhoeffer, the result of such inversion is an "ethicized version" of the gospel, and even more problematic, a loss of the priority of revelation in knowledge of the other. In dialogue truth remains immanent in the reciprocity of encounter; thus, even dialogue, which rejects transcendental philosophy in the name of critical reflection, remains encased in systematic fixtures. To be sure, dialogue comes close to Christian theology when it shows that humankind can only be shown the way to reality from the outside. However, Bonhoeffer insists that the person's first intimation of this "from outside" is not supplied by his contact with his neighbor's claim but "is supplied by his encounter with *something* that at the same time enables him to understand the 'from outside' in a meaningful sense—revelation accepted in faith."[57] Dialogics' will to refrain from the transcendental system becomes a new and more subtle attempt "to trap reality," albeit in an ostensibly unsystematic way. As Bonhoeffer says, "Even a critical philosophy is powerless to place the philosopher in truth, because its criticism issues from itself, and the seeming reality is still subservient to the (in this case undemanding) claims of the *cor curvum in se*."[58]

Even more, the language of encounter is unable to grasp the continuity of life together. Any continuity between dialogical occurrences would signal some mediation, and therefore destroy the "integrity and simplicity" of the event.[59] From decision, or from a sequence of decisions, continuity is not forthcoming. However, community cannot be sustained on the basis of encountering acts, for the relation of I and other is present not only in its act but in its perduring being. Revelation textured by dialogue scatters the concreteness of Christ into disparate points of decision and etherealizes the concreteness of being-in Christ. As Emmanuel Levinas states in a different context, "Each encounter must be considered as a unique event, a momentary present which cannot be connected to other temporal instants in order to form a history or biography. . . . The relation is a fulguration of moments without continuity, not a coherent connection of parts nor a final possession."[60]

Rather than thinking the place of Christ as the dialogical between,

Bonhoeffer attempts in subsequent works to conceive Christ as the very being of community—the inner content of which is the conversion of individual I's into agapeic togetherness, the external meaning of which is the concrete, worldly gathering. The self positioned in community does not return back into the I-ness of the I as a transcendentally accessible point of reference, but it dwells with the other in love within the indwelling of "Christ existing as community." In these later works, community is not based on a dialogical Christ but on the richer conception of a Christ who as the center of all the real comes to the person as his or her ownmost center and thereby creates a new social ontology. Whether Bonhoeffer turns out to be a Hegelian by default is a question that must not be ignored.

5

Christ as the Mediation
of the Other

Karl Barth once said that we must always think three times before contradicting Hegel's system, "because we might find that everything we are tempted to say in contradiction to it has already been said within it."[1] Hegel wanted his thought to mirror the full movement of life, and to Barth (avid moviegoer no less than Mozart aficionado) this movement proceeds like the film of the cinematograph, though one so extraordinary that it depicts "the rhythm of life itself," running exhaustively through the fullness of history, capturing the "exact recollection" of the observed plenitude of being.[2] Barth would find incredible Richard Rorty's comment that the *Phenomenology of Spirit* is not so much "an argumentative procedure or a way of unifying subject and object, but simply a literary skill—skill at producing surprising gestalt switches by making smooth, rapid transitions from one terminology to another."[3] When Hegel concludes the magisterial section on absolute knowledge with the statement that here "Spirit has wound up the process of its embodiment,"[4] he is not, as Rorty cavalierly suggests, recommending a new and improved vocabulary[5] but is celebrating the complete infusion of truth into the dialectic of knowing. As Barth says, "Truth is necessary to [Hegel] and necessary to him in its unity, in its actuality, in the divine rigor inherent in it."[6]

Indeed, for Barth it is precisely this extraordinary confidence that is most problematic—the way Spirit trots through history with predictability and necessity, and reason's grand claims to truth. God and humankind can never confront one another in a relation that is genuinely encounter; "a word, a new word revelatory in the strict sense, cannot pass between them; it cannot be uttered and cannot be heeded."[7] All truth is discovered in the "ceaseless completion of the circle, all error is contained in stopping and staying at one of the moments of the concept, which are necessary as stages, but are thought of not as points to be stopped at but as points to be passed through."[8] As the place of the divine mind incarnate, human thinking embodies the fullness of divine reason, and in its consummation as absolute knowledge, thought overcomes the conceptual division between finite and infinite. Barth's obvious sympathies with Hegel are always qualified by this architecture of knowing.[9]

Dietrich Bonhoeffer, who we have seen was one of Barth's earliest followers, as well as one of his earliest and most perceptive critics, also took on the unenviable task of proposing a critique of Hegel. But in his reflection on the axiom "Christ existing as community," Bonhoeffer directs his criticisms not primarily toward Hegel's softening of the *otherness* of God and the novelty of revelation (as does Barth) but precisely toward Hegel's thinking about the *presence* of God in the world.[10] As early as *Sanctorum Communio* (1927), Bonhoeffer claimed that Hegel's philosophy of religion misrepresents much of what is fundamental to a Christian reflection on God and the new social ontology of the church. In subsequent writings, Bonhoeffer sharpens this critique and argues that though Hegel shows a keen appreciation of Christ as reconciler of God and the world, he fails to see how utterly critical it is to acknowledge Jesus Christ as the sole mediation of truth and experience. Thus, while Barth dissents from Hegel on the issue of the *alterity* of the Word of God, Bonhoeffer's dispute is based on the question of the *concrete* place of God's incarnate Word. As such, his concern is to explicate the secondary objectivity of revelation in view of the challenges presented by Hegel's demanding reflections on divine reconciliation.

This chapter is divided into four parts. In the first part I discuss the meaning of community in Hegel's philosophy of religion by providing a summary of his view of the relation between the divine being and human experience. In the second I examine the way Bonhoeffer's description of community is influenced by Hegel and in this context give special consideration to the themes of reconciliation, divine promeity, and absolute knowledge. In the third part I turn to Bonhoeffer's *Ethics* in order to consider his attempt to explicate the concreteness of community in relation to (what I call) its extrinsic and intrinsic reference. The place of Christ as community is not abandoned in Bonhoeffer's later writings—yielding to various general patterns of social relation—but becomes instead the paradigm for interpreting genuine worldliness, expressing of Christ in a *relational* form what the world expresses in a *creational* form. Although this is not an entirely neat analogy, it does help to clarify the important point that Bonhoeffer does not give up the christological axiom "Christ existing as community" in his later theology. Rather, he explicates it in terms which address both the worldly, external meaning and the internal or social ontological character of life with others. In these later writings, Bonhoeffer continues to work in view of Hegel's challenge, though less overtly than in the early texts, inasmuch as he positions his conversation about worldliness and being-for-others in the Hegelian problematic of identity and universal subjectivity.[11] Most of his later conversations with Hegel are subtextual. Finally, I conclude the chapter with the proposal that for Bonhoeffer human subjectivity consummated in servanthood represents the realization of revealed religion. Thus, the christological transformation of the person in agapeic togetherness—an idea narrated in various forms throughout all of his writings—demonstrates the sharpest difference between theologian and philosopher.

Whether, in the end, Bonhoeffer's own description of reconciliation and life with God succeeds in illustrating a different theological conception than Hegel's is a complicated question. Bonhoeffer hearkens to Hegel's grand celebration of the reconciliation of God and the world and is clearly influenced by Hegel on this theme. It is also true that both are trying to articulate the heart of the gospel in a fresh and meaningful way, and thus are both involved in a common task of theological *nachdenken*.[12] I submit that we think of Bonhoeffer after the doctoral dissertation as trying not so hard to contradict Hegel as to correct him theologically from the inside—internally—specifically to argue that conceptions of the relation between God and world and between self and other as *self-mediated* must be redescribed by a conception of human sociality as *Christ-mediated*. Bonhoeffer's appropriation of Hegelian themes is always one of creative and critical redescription in light of his christological axiom.

Hegel on Spirit in Community

According to Hegel, the content of the Christian faith is presented in the life of the single individual Jesus of Nazareth. As the God-man, Jesus was not only concretely real as a living historical person, but through the torment of his death he becomes present in community. The life of Jesus is an essential moment in the life of Spirit's self-discovery, for unless Spirit assumes objectivity and appears to finite humanity as a single individual in embodied form, we can say of God only that he exists in static symbol or eschatological distance, but not in the fullness of the divine presence. Yet the sensuous moment of the God-man must be sublated, raised up, and preserved, to a "real signification" such that the single individual gives way to its eternally true essence. Only then can the abstractness of the metaphysical deity, one of whose principal masks was substance, be transformed into real, simple, and universal self-consciousness. Thus, even as Hegel emphasizes the necessity of Spirit's incarnation as a historical event, he further emphasizes the necessity of moving beyond the historical vesture so that the truth disclosed in that event might be grasped in its universal significance.[13]

Hegel sees a correlation between the religious narrative of the God-man and the dialectic of sense certainty, recited in the first chapter of the *Phenomenology of Spirit*. In this anatomy of self-consciousness, Hegel follows the way in which a concept of the general (the *allgemein*) emerges from immediate sense impressions. The "this" of sense certainty signifies in linguistic form a demonstrative pronoun that, from the standpoint of the observer, is said to refer to definite particulars. As such, sense certainty is the immediate awareness of the world, an awareness boasting the empirical confidence that "one has immediately achieved knowledge of the truth of things as they really are."[14] However, Hegel shows that in this immediacy language plays a trick on the individual, for while presuming that the *particular* "this" is a discrete entity, grammatical necessity betrays the *general* referential significance of the pronoun. The "this" can be applied to *anything*; "universality is the real truth of sense certainty."[15] Accordingly, sense-certainty in its essential nature demonstrates the universal to be the truth of its object.[16] As Hegel says, "When I say: 'a single thing,' I am really saying what it is from a wholly universal point of view, for everything is a single thing; and likewise 'this thing' is anything you like."[17] What was originally imagined to be a particular sensation turns out instead to be part of an interconnected whole. The "this" becomes a total reference of objects, "a collection of universal properties."[18]

In sense certainty it becomes clear that experience of the particular is not immediate, but always mediated by a universal. Charles Taylor says, "If being aware of something is being able to say something about it, then it involves grasping the objects before us through aspects they have in common or could have in common with other things, rather than in their own particularity."[19] The "this" or "now" of sense certainty cannot be affixed to the brute sense object, but as a universal it applies to other contents as well. Sense certainty confirms the fact that all relations to the other are intermediate, never in truth immediate. Thus, taken in itself sense certainty offers no account of the coherence and depth of experience, because it apprehends the world as a constellation of autonomous, independent objects, existing in-and-for-themselves and external to the self. In the consciousness of sense certainty, truth is estranged from the self— "the truth of consciousness is something other than consciousness itself."[20] For consciousness to graduate to self-consciousness it is necessary that the self know in the other not an objectified strangeness but its own self.[21] Hegel says, "It is in self-consciousness, in the Notion of spirit, that consciousness first finds its turning-point, where it leaves behind it the colourful show of the sensuous here-and-now and the nightlike void of the supersensible beyond, and steps out into the spiritual daylight of the present."[22]

Similarly, in the religious self-consciousness, the image of the God-man Jesus remains historically buried in autonomous particularity and does not ascend to its proper universality when our thinking about the cross fails to reckon with the seriousness of the death of God. What is the meaning of this event of the cross? Hegel says, "The death of the picture-thought contains, therefore, at the same time the death of the *abstraction of the divine Being* which is not posited as Self. That death is the painful feeling of the Unhappy Consciousness that *God Himself is dead.* This hard saying is the expression of innermost simple self-knowledge, the return of consciousness into the depths of the night in which 'I'='I,' a night which no longer distinguishes or knows anything outside of it."[23] The man who is beheld sensuously and immediately as the historical Jesus of Nazareth reemerges through the dark night of divine self-negation as the universal reconciler of God and the world. The "harsh utterance" of the death of God expresses the movement of knowledge which, through "the loss of the Substance and of its objective existence over against consciousness," allows "the return of consciousness into the depth of darkness where Ego is nothing but bare identity with Ego."[24] This return enables "the pure subjectivity of Substance, the pure certainty of itself" to appear and substance to become subject.[25]

Thus, according to Hegel, Spirit animates the event of the God-man to become infinitely more than a historical moment, indeed to become "the axis on which world history turns."[26] Spirit is the dynamic process by which the implicit unity of the divine and human natures is actualized and assumes concrete existence. In overcoming the separation of God and world, Spirit moves into, through, and beyond contradiction, not as a static reconciliation occurring once and for all in the bluntness of a past history but in restless activity and freedom. The divine being, says Hegel in the *Phenomenology*, is "reconciled with its existence through an event,—the event of God's emptying Himself of His divine Being through His factual Incarnation and His Death."[27] For this reason, the death of God must be regarded as the tremendous moment in which *even death itself* ceases to mean the nonexistence of *this* particular individual; for the dead God is resurrected "into the universality of the Spirit, which lives in its own communion, dies there daily, and daily rises again."[28] Thus, the knowledge that lives in the "yea, yea" of divine reconciliation does away with the separation between the self and that which it observes and to which it relates.

In *Lectures on the Philosophy of Religion* Hegel contends that the religious mode through which this reconciliation is concretely experienced is the spiritual community. "[In the community]," he writes, "Spirit is the infinite return into itself, infinite subjectivity, not represented but actual divinity, the *presence* of God."[29] The significance of this point is twofold. First, community illustrates that the moment of the God-man, or the otherness of the Son, gives way to a higher truth, and is thus not a permanent and absolute moment;[30] and second, that even within this concrete mode of reconciliation, separation is not fully overcome. In religious community the divine Idea is still held forth to consciousness as an otherness that stands beyond subjectivity—outside the self—even though the verbal proclamation of the event of reconciliation is heard and often acknowledged. Like the event of the God-man, community constitutes a moment (necessary and true but *a moment*) in Spirit's ascent to absolute thought. Hegel says, "The 'now' of communion dissolves in its representation, partly into a beyond, an otherworldly heaven, partly into the past, and partly into the future."[31] As a result, the spiritual community remains estranged from the full recognition of the truthfulness of Spirit's self-unfolding insofar as it deflects the content of self-consciousness in a certain imagery, in the form of a pictorial or historical idea or even in conceptual representation such as doctrine.[32] But Spirit requires more than "confused images";[33] it demands a "fulfilled present," nothing less than that the content of truth should itself be experienced.[34]

According to Hegel, the religious self-consciousness remains unaware that the reconciliation of subject and object is not external to itself in various representations but immanent in its own self-consciousness. Of course, in the community there is the awareness that God's reconciliation of the world to himself is a reconciliation *for* humanity; the celebration of this event is the veritable heart of the church's worship and compassion. However, the celebration of this event, sublime as it may be and altogether true in its heart, still sunders into two the full reconciliation of Spirit in the world. Although the religious community cannot help but comport itself toward a future in the eschaton or nostalgically attempt to recover a lost past in a primitive or biblical community, it does this at the expense of casting away from itself the "church triumphal" and forfeiting its possibilities of realizing the fullness of the divine presence in the pure subjectivity of thought. In the community, the conceptual truth of the idea of God continues to be suppressed in a thinking shaped by difference and alienation; Spirit has not become self-conscious subject. As Hegel says, "This religious communion, therefore, is not yet fulfilled in this its self-consciousness. Its content, in general, is put before it in the form of a pictorial idea; so that this disruption still attaches even to the actual spiritual character of the communion . . . just as the element of pure thought itself was also hampered with that opposition."[35] Thus, thought must yet ascend to the point where the difference contained in the description of reconciliation as the event of the God-man Jesus (an image external to the self) is shown to be an event internal to consciousness itself. Until this happens, religious thinking—representational thinking—obscures the full possibilities of human reason and the community remains a halfway house for Spirit on the way to its subjective maturity. The book cannot end.

In the nick of time the philosopher arrives on the scene and gets to work on the final chapter. His writing is therapeutic; the last infirmity of thought is healed in the process, discord is harmonized, religion and reason reconciled. Why is this so? Philosophy inaugurates the reconciliation of God with himself and nature so as to undo the seemingly irreconcilable division between logos and nature. Both logos and nature, as well as the opposition of the preceding moments and all possible oppositions, are recognized to be "the works of the self which poses itself, and insofar as it poses itself in a determinateness, opposes itself to itself."[36] In philosophy, the same divine being is present which is depicted figuratively in religion, but now the form of this presence is philosophy's own infinite self-consciousness. Spirit wraps up the process of its embodiment, theo-logic becomes "ontologic,"[37] for Hegel has shown that all duality is annulled in the ascendence of pure knowing. Only now can the content of truth take refuge in the concept, demonstrating with final clarity that the "witness of spirit is thought."[38]

"Christ Existing as Community"

In the terms of Hegel's religious thought, Bonhoeffer's axiom "Christ existing as community" signifies a reality that is true in content (God is *for* the world) but incomplete in form (God remains *other than* the world in his prevenient grace). God in the concreteness of Jesus Christ enacts a dialectical intensification such that God's being who he is in inner-trinitarian community is accompanied by God's being with humanity in the resilient light of redemption. This is the Barthian texture of Bonhoeffer's thought which is never explicated in full, precisely because it is always presupposed in Bonhoeffer's perduring emphasis on the promeity of God toward humanity. As being-himself, being-for humanity, and being with others God establishes a community grounded in his *miraculous free decision to save*. Thus, in Bonhoeffer's view the incompleteness (from Hegel's perspective) is precisely what preserves the integrity of the gospel.

As we have seen, in *Sanctorum Communio* Bonhoeffer argues that the difference of God and world must be thought *alongside their unity*, that unity should not absorb difference, and thus that the difference of God and humanity can never be sublated in descriptions of their reconciliation. Reconciliation in the sense the gospel proclaims is efficacious solely on the basis of God's prevenient difference. Bonhoeffer criticizes "the idealist goal of totality"[39] by keeping in dialectical tension the relation of self and other. He says, "The idealist concept must be overcome by a concept which preserves the concrete individual concept of the person as ultimate [*endgültig*] and willed by God."[40] That concept is the "non-synthetic" description of I and Thou, a relation grounded in the constitutive alterity of grace. In fact, the nonsynthetic description of God's self-relation to the world grounds the relationship of the I and the other, for "the divine Thou creates the human Thou" and "the other man is Thou only in so far as God makes him this."[41] God's Thou reveals itself originally in the nonsynthetic event of revelation, and dependently in the encounter of the ethical other. Experience of the Thou in the limit of the moral demand sustains a "dialectics of otherness,"[42] not simply because ethical encounter elicits the indigenous strangeness of the Thou, but much more for the reason that "the other presents us with the same problem of cognition as does God himself."[43] In this context, Bonhoeffer maintains that the dialogical description of I and other avoids the totalizing impulse of idealism and concords favorably with christological redescription.

But what is the texture of Hegel's so-called totality? Is the difference of God and world annulled in Hegel's religious philosophy, as Bonhoeffer seems to think? What about the difference of I and other? These questions involve a complex set of responses, nuanced interpretations, and clarification, about which Bonhoeffer remains frustratingly silent in the doctoral dissertation. His criticisms there are submitted almost entirely without reference to specific texts, certainly without adequate explanation of his frequent generalizations of not only Hegel but the whole of German idealism.

Does Bonhoeffer maintain this harsh view of Hegel throughout his later writings? Does his reading of Hegel mature after *Sanctorum Communio*? I wish to begin to put Bonhoeffer's criticisms of Hegel in perspective in order to discern what is most important, perceptive, and promising for philosophical theological reflection (as opposed to his criticisms that are conventional and stock). Suffice it to say, the argument is superficial that charges Hegel with the full-scale demolition of difference in his phenomenology of Spirit. Hegel realizes that every synthesis always preserves a place for separation as well as identity.[44] William Desmond rightly explains, "The [Hegelian] relation asserts that the self as a unity in itself is also able to encompass some degree of difference. It does not exclude difference and complexity from itself; nor does it define external difference as an absolute exclusion between irreconcilable opposites."[45] Separation is indispensable for attaining rational autonomy. Hegel attacked mercilessly the murky romantic desire for self-abandonment in communion with nature. In his view, separation and difference are necessary for the unifying executions of reason. Indeed, his description of the overcoming of otherness is not a description of obliteration; as Merold Westphal says, "it rather presupposes a continuing otherness of the object, though not a brute otherness."[46] The goal of the self is rather to be "at home in its otherness as such."[47]

Thus, Hegel's solution to the question of how to bring to unity the demands of freedom and the desire for expressive identity cannot be reduced to a victory of one side over the other, that is, by simply absorbing separation into unity. There is an inner complexity at work in the unity of Spirit that sustains difference, a complexity empowered by contradiction. "The motor of these dialectics is contradiction," Charles Taylor says, "and the contradiction consists in this, that finite beings just in virtue of existing externally in space and time make a claim to independence, while the very basis of their existence is that they express a spirit which cannot brook this independence."[48] In Hegel's philosophical system, contradiction or conflict is not incompatible with the reconciliation of subject and object, for in a critical sense, the whole "lives on contradiction."[49] His metaphor from the preface to the *Phenomenology* dramatizes this sense quite vividly, that the "bacchanalian whirl" of the whole is not monotonous conformity or docile assimilation to a cosmic fusion, but the struggle of opposition and contradiction in which "no member is not drunken."[50]

What Taylor overlooks in Hegel's description (but Desmond sees with remarkable clarity) is the fact that though difference and contradiction are not obliterated by an all-consuming monism, neither is difference mediated by the *different* or *the other itself*: the other is *self-mediated*. While Hegel understands being as more complex than simple unmediated unity, he is still inclined to reduce all mediations to self-mediation. Desmond says, "The dialectical approach faces the problem of avoiding a final reduction of the other ways of being mindful to the self-mediation of philosophy's own thought."[51] Its mediation of "dispersing difference" runs the risk of reducing all relations to others "to something that must be dialectically subordinated to the putative primacy of self-mediation."[52] Difference is contained, or recontained, within the sameness of the self. As Hegel writes in the *Phenemenology*, "Only this self-*restoring* sameness, or this reflection in otherness within itself—not an *original* or *immediate* unity as such—is the True."[53]

Does Bonhoeffer's interpretation of Hegel after the doctoral dissertation come to acknowledge a greater subtlety and intricacy of description? I think so for the following reasons. After completing *Sanctorum Communio*, Bonhoeffer spent considerable time carefully reading Hegel's primary texts, and to good effect.[54] His 1933 Hegel seminar in Berlin demonstrates an unexpected sympathy for the breadth of Hegel's theological significance. The Hungarian student Ferenc Lehel, whose notes were the basis for the published edition of the Hegel seminar, recalls his surprise that Bonhoeffer discussed Hegel with obvious admiration and approval.[55] Unlike most other contemporary anti-idealist theologians, Bonhoeffer recognized an undeniable value in Hegel. Lehel says, "Bonhoeffer handled Hegel eclectically to the extent that he examined and emphasized that which to the theologian appeared useful."[56] The transcripts of the Berlin seminar, while offering no new insights into Hegel's thought, give us a clear sense of

Bonhoeffer's openness to and interest in the theological dimensions of *The Phenomenology of Spirit* and *Lectures on the Philosophy of Religion*. This is but one indication of the fact that after the dissertation, Bonhoeffer's approach toward Hegel matures strikingly. His writings become more attentive to the richness and polyvalence of Hegel's thought. He is less concerned with overcoming Hegel than in thinking along with the philosopher on the meaning of God's presence in the complex drama of divine worldliness. Bonhoeffer will no longer argue the case that Hegel proffers a crude totality that stamps out all particularity and difference, but he will, for example, try to think of the totality proper to the biblical witness of God's redemptive story, and in this way revise Hegel's description from the inside out, that is, theologically.

As I see it, there are three points at which Hegel's influence in Bonhoeffer's theology needs to be addressed in a circumspect and sober-minded way. I will turn now to these issues.

Community and Reconciliation

Both thinkers understand spiritual community to be the place where humanity is aware of its reconciliation with God, a reconciliation that, as Hegel says, "exists for Man."[57] This reconciliation of God and the world achieved by Jesus Christ and preserved by the Spirit in community *is* a present reality, through which the oneness of "all finite life is fulfilled" without negating the particularity of individuality.[58] Bonhoeffer appreciates the ornate spiritual texture of Hegel's description, particularly his emphasis that the unity of the infinite and finite demonstrated in community is not a mere interconnection of natural objects—"in no way a sensuous, worldly connection of things"[59]—but a spiritual unity, real for the whole life of the individual. As Hegel writes, "The Christian religion is the religion of reconciliation."[60]

Moreover, in community God shows that not even the finite human is alien to him, but "that this otherness, this self-distinguishing, finitude as it is expressed, is a moment in God himself, although, to be sure, it is a disappearing moment."[61] Hegel's idea of reconciliation includes the stark presentation of the God who takes into himself the negativity and sorrow of the world, and the narration of this moment in light of the suffering Jesus. He wishes to rewrite "the poetry of Protestant grief"—to redress the historical uneasiness with the idea that God might dwell amid the quotidian finitude of the earthly—by showing how the finite is the pathway of Spirit to itself.

He says, "The life of the Spirit is not the life that shrinks from death and keeps itself untouched by devastation, but rather the life that endures it and maintains itself in it."[62] In the words of one of his aphorisms from Jena, "God sacrifices himself, gives himself up to destruction. God himself is dead; the highest despair of complete forsakeness by God."[63] God gives himself to destruction in order to reconcile the finite and infinite, and to demonstrate that the anguish of creation is part of God's own history: "[The] pure concept or infinity as the abyss of nothingness in which all being is engulfed, must signify the infinite grief [of the finite] purely as a moment of the supreme Idea."[64] Hegel's imagery is strikingly Pauline: Christ did not consider equality with God something to be demanded but took the form of a servant and humbled himself even unto the death on the cross, to that which indeed was most alien to him, so that now he bears the mark of mortality in himself (Phil. 2:6–11). In Jesus Christ, God turns himself totally to the finite. In the life of the God-man, God enters history and becomes a reality which is subject to perishing.[65]

In becoming a reality which is subject to perishing, God manifests himself in the world, is taken into custody and murdered, in order that he may take into himself the "pinnacle of negation," "finitude in its highest extreme."[66] Although Golgaltha's harsh message that "God himself is dead" is "a monstrous, fearful picture, which brings before the imagination the deepest abyss of cleavage,"[67] it is at the same time the expression of the highest love. "The death of Christ is the vision of this love itself—not [love merely] for or on behalf of others, but precisely divinity in this universal identity with other-being, death."[68] Thus, in the "totality of the history of redemption," that is, in the process of the going forth of the divine idea into the uttermost abyss, even unto death, God's highest love generates the negation of negation within itself and achieves the "absolute reconciliation."[69] "The end is [presented] as a resolution into glory, the festive assumption of humanity in the divine idea."[70] The dialectical tension between God and world and between God and human negativity is resolved in the course of Spirit's self-realization.

Nevertheless, the second half of the well-known Philippians hymn, that God exalted the Son (not humanity) to the highest place, "that at the name of Jesus every knee should bow, in heaven and on earth and under the earth" (2:10), is conspicuously understated in Hegel's description. I think this problem is corrected by Bonhoeffer. In texts after the doctoral dissertation, he shows an increased confidence in the christocentric mediation and refiguration of all reality and is able thereby to take considerable freedom in playing with

Hegelian images of divine reconciliation. Let me explain by summarizing several of these expositions.

In *Act and Being*, Bonhoeffer's new emphasis is signaled by his bold claim that all ontological definitions are connected with God's self-witness in Jesus Christ. Christ refashions the ontological structure of being itself such that all reality has Christ as its vital center. As community, Christ precedes both I and other as their source and mediation, engendering a new ontology of relation based on the coming of God into worldly experience.[71]

The 1933 Christology lectures (*Christ the Center*) provide a more direct statement of Christ as mediator of reality. In rephrasing the central question of christology from "what is he?" to "who are you?", Bonhoeffer argues that Christ is the Word of God who is both at the boundary of the real (in the act of creating the world) and at center of the real (as the new being). He portrays the centrality of Christ in a threefold way. First, Christ is the center of *human existence*, that is, the center of the self, the source of I and other, and the reconciliation of humanity and God. Second, Christ is the center of *human history*; therefore, the story of history is tied up with the event which takes place in the depth and hiddenness of Jesus Christ. Bonhoeffer says, "The meaning of history is found in the humiliated Christ."[72] Third, Christ is the center *between God and nature*, for he is the new creature, the redemption of the fallen and the liberation of enslaved nature. As mediator between God and sinful humanity, Christ draws all things into the redemptive center of the new world of God.

In *Creation and Fall* (1933) Bonhoeffer reflects on the self-recognition of God in creation. He poses several critical questions that arise from the conversation with Hegel. Does God see himself in his created work, and thus recognize himself in his other? If so, what are the conditions for the divine self-discovery? How shall God find himself in his work?[73] These are crucial questions, for the God of the Bible is a God who wills to see himself in his creation and to take delight in the goodness of his covenant with the world. According to Bonhoeffer, this can happen only if the created work upon which God looks is free in its otherness. But how can the created other be free? Is it not bound to God through the necessity of God's creative will? According to Bonhoeffer, God creates his image on earth in creating a humanity which is free for community. Humanity created in freedom is the only image of the free creation that "fully proclaims the honour of its Creator."[74] Humankind is free by the event of God's creating word; and because humankind is free God recognizes himself in the world.

Significantly, in *Creation and Fall* Bonhoeffer stresses that freedom is not a possession over which the person has control but "something he has for others."[75] God's being is a being-in-relation; God is
one who is always on the way toward the other in communion. Consequently, the person enters most fully in the sacramental dance of
creation when he or she turns (and is turned) outward toward others
in agapeic love. Bonhoeffer says, "Only in relationship with the other
am I free."[76] The message of the gospel is that God has decided to
bind us to himself in freedom, that is, to embrace us and thus allow
us to be who we are as humans in loving relationship to God; God
has not chosen to contain his freedom for himself, but to pour his
freedom outward to humanity. Christ mediates God's overabounding
love such that those of us who live "in the middle" between God and
God, between resurrection and resurrection, live in freedom only
through Christ.[77] For only through Christ is God's freedom able to
dwell among us in body, word, and truth; only through Christ can I
in my creatureliness belong fully to God and to this world; only
through Christ as creator does God see himself in humanity. Therefore, while Bonhoeffer can conceive of reconciliation in the quasi-
Hegelian language of divine self-recognition, he subverts the preeminence of speculative, subjective knowledge by the insistence that the
source of the affinity of God and humankind resides in the unconditional sacrifice of Christ the mediator. The essence of divine knowing is the love, compassion, and solidarity demonstrated by this sacrifice.

In *Life Together* (1939) Bonhoeffer with eloquent simplicity further describes the Christian's relation to others as mediated and
opened up through the person of Jesus Christ alone. Without Christ
humanity would know neither God nor the neighbor, for the way to
the other is always constricted by the ego. However, Christ opens up
the way to the other by pulling the self out of itself into life with others
and by drawing the person into faithful togetherness. Bonhoeffer
writes, "Now Christians can live with one another in peace; they can
love and serve one another; they can become one. But they can continue to do so only by way of Jesus Christ. Only in Jesus Christ are
we one, only through him are we bound together. To eternity he remains the one Mediator."[78] In liberating the person for life with others, Jesus Christ discloses far more than the simple dialogical meeting of I and other; rather, he actively refigures the self in faith such
that openness to and life for the other become the new ontological
description of being-in Christ. As such, the mediation of Jesus Christ
empowers a relating to the other (what Bonhoeffer here calls "spiri-

tual love") that allows the other to remain in its difference, even within our common history in life with God. What "human love" cannot attain in manipulating the other into the sameness of the self (even in heroic or charitable acts), spiritual love enkindled by the transforming love of Christ does, namely, the grace to release the other from the I's grasp and to give the other over to its integrity and to its otherness. Bonhoeffer says, "Because Christ stands between me and others, I dare not desire direct fellowship with them. . . . This means that I must release the other person from every attempt of mine to regulate, coerce, and dominate him with my love. . . . Because Christ has long since acted decisively for my brother, before I could begin to act, I must leave him his freedom to be Christ's; I must meet him only as the person that he already is in Christ's eyes."[79] This giving others over to their own integrity is not a further sign of my cunning and mastery to dominate but an expression of my humility; for only in Christ do I even know who the other is. However, of equal importance is the observation that giving others over to their otherness is not driven by resignation or quietism; rather, my being with and for others requires that I respect their terms and contingencies (that is, their freedom to reject me or turn away from me), and that my giving others over to an integral difference is a simultaneous reaching out to them in love and solidarity.

Moreover, only in Christ am I aware that the other is not simply the one standing with me in family, cult, ideology or creed, but also the victims, the weak, and "the seemingly useless people." Christ as mediator stretches our moral imagination to the point at which our own capacity to discern who the other is is broken, and replaced by the discernment that in Christ all have been reconciled to God (Gal. 3:26–29). As George Hunsinger writes, "The history of Jesus is viewed as included in that of every human being."[80] No one is excluded from the efficacy of the salvific work of Jesus Christ, for through his action an "ontological connection" is forged between humanity and God, which is grounded not in ourselves but in Christ's action alone. Bonhoeffer writes in *Ethics*: "In Jesus Christ, the original source of humankind is given back to it"[81] ("Der Ursprung ist ihm wieder-geschenkt").

These texts make clear that in Bonhoeffer's theology all genuine relations to the other are mediated by Christ. Although it is quite appropriate to question the dialectical self-mediation of the other, to antagonize the preeminence of the subject in the knowledge of self, world and God, a genuinely christological alternative must remain discontent with even the commendable "metaxological" or dialogical celebration of the middle as open to mediation not only from the self but also from the other.[82] For Jesus Christ shows humanity not what it can be if it attunes itself to a certain way of being, but what it can never be except through the miraculous gift of the new being of God in life together. Bonhoeffer writes, "The ground of God's love towards humanity does not lie in humankind but solely in God Himself. And again, the reason why we can live as real humanity and can love the real person at our side is to be found solely in the incarnation of God, in the unfathomable love of God for humankind."[83]

Community as the Overturning of the Metaphysical God

A second Hegelian theme which Bonhoeffer takes to heart is that the community bears witness to the dissimilarity between the God of revelation (Christ as reconciler of God and the world) and the God of the metaphysical or onto-theological tradition (that reified bundle of complex properties known as Unmoved Mover, First Cause, Being itself, and the like). What makes a conception of God abstract and illegitimate for Hegel? Precisely when that conception holds that God is a "mere object" standing over against consciousness.[84] As such, Bonhoeffer's "Christ existing as community" shows that God's being is not frozen in transcendence and ineffable otherness but is living, historically animating Spirit. Nonetheless, while Hegel's idea of spiritual community is propelled by the restless play of its conceptual incompleteness toward philosophical transparency (and to the final sublation of a communal representation), in Bonhoeffer's view, God draws near to us and is with us in human togetherness, there to remain as Christ's real presence. While Hegel's understanding of the death and resurrection of Christ has its pedagogical end in the universal self-consciousness of the community, for Bonhoeffer the divine abstractness is transfigured into the veritable heart of community. God enters into the concrete structure of finitude and assumes the form of human community. A God who "is there" in some primordial a priori givenness is not the God of Jesus Christ, who "is" always in personal relation and whose being is personal.[85] What God gives of himself in Jesus Christ cannot be surpassed, for although revelation is not exhaustive of God's trinitarian mystery, it does witness to him truthfully and consistently such that what it says of God is final and decisive. To be sure, for both Bonhoeffer and Hegel the event of the Incarnation witnesses to the good news that the infinite and the finite are inseparably connected.[86] But when Hegel takes this one step further—"Humanity . . . bears within itself the *divine idea*, not bearing it within itself like something from somewhere else but as its own substantial nature[87]—Bonhoeffer refuses to concede the move, which he thinks incommodes a theology grounded in the priority of God's own self-grounding.

Precisely at this point the suspicion arises that Hegel's attempt to overcome the difference between God and humanity is intended not primarily to emphasize God's gracious promeity but to elevate humanity to God. Eberhard Jüngel thinks this tendency to deify humanity remains the most critical theological problem in Hegel. Hegel's God reaches out to humanity out of a fierce longing for his other, and in this meeting humanity becomes itself divine.[88] According to Jüngel, there are two possibilities contained in Hegel's thought for explicating this double movement. On the one hand, it may be that in the process of coming to himself in his other God *uses* humankind; that is, in the course of his self-development God elevates humanity to himself for the purpose of coming to himself. On the other hand, it may be that in the process of arriving at the depths of its spirit humankind uses God, so that instead of crying out to God "from the deeps" (*de profundis*), humanity raises itself up to its true height "out of the deeps" (*e profundis*).[89] However, in either case, the end result is that one of the two parties exploits and degrades the other. It is insignificant in this respect whether humankind is the one who uses God or vice versa, since the concrete distinction between God and humankind is threatened in both possibilities.[90] Jüngel's contrast is reminiscent of Bonhoeffer's concern, that it is crucial to recognize God in the crucified one, who because he is both divine and human prevents humankind from becoming God and, in this manner, frees humankind to be itself and nothing other than itself.

The recognition that God remains God in the crucified one is enforced by Bonhoeffer's commitment to Luther's *finitum capax infiniti*, the twofold thought that God's reaching out of himself in Jesus Christ as community coinheres with God's reaching out to his other in himself in the mystery of his Triune sociality. The finite contains the infinite without loss of the propriety of their distinction, precisely because Jesus Christ comes out of the inpenetrable mystery of God into the resplendent multiplicity of the world to bring the world home to God without collapsing the difference between the two. In the homecoming is redemption—not the identification of God and world but the recovery of the divinity of God and the humanity of the person. We might think then of Bonhoeffer's reading of Hegel at this point as a celebration of the God who becomes present in experience; however, in Bonhoeffer's case, God is not one who becomes identical to experience. The place of God is Jesus Christ existing as community, and in this way God joins the world to himself in a common history; but this commonality does not indicate an identity between God and the world. It is Christ who mediates the togetherness of I and other and who thereby accomplishes their intermediation, not the self which seeks the assimilation of its others into the final univocal sameness of self-mediation.

Importantly, because of this description Bonhoeffer is able to accord to community a concreteness and a relative autonomy that seem mollified in Hegel's system. By illustrating that God is one whose being in himself is a being for his other (while not being the other), the concreteness of revelation expresses of God that he is for the world without being the world. God is neither totally other than nor identical to the world but is together with the world because God remains God and humanity remains human. To insist with Hegel that the community is not yet fulfilled in its self-consciousness, that it must—and can—throw off its figurative impediments and become the perfect speculative mode of consciousness is to entertain an unrealistic hope. It is to miss the truth of Kierkegaard's statement that "spiritually speaking, everything is possible, but in the world of the finite there is much which is not possible."[91] It is to obfuscate the epistemological and social message of sin, that community as a gathering of fallen men and women is embraced in unity by the forgiving and reconciling presence of Jesus Christ. For however much Bonhoeffer emphasizes the gracious and real presence of Christ in community, he recognizes that it remains a broken totality. The togetherness of I and other in Christ is a space secured by Christ alone; the natural tendencies of the person (which do not cease to assert themselves) seek to monopolize all commerce with others. "Being transformed into the other through love," in Luther's expression, occurs as a miracle, as something not our own achievement.[92] Bonhoeffer thinks Hegel delineates the indefatigable movement of self-knowing spirit in terms which ride roughshod over the brokenness of human life. But the transformation of human sociality in faith happens quite apart from the person's natural inclinations to dominate and control.

In this manner, we cannot regard the event of revelation as an *interplay* or a *reciprocity* between God and humankind, between grace and nature.[93] If we want to call the event of revelation a self-enclosed totality, we can only do so from the perspective of God's prevenient action. As Karl Barth writes in *Church Dogmatics* I/2, "Not only the objective but also the subjective element in revelation, not only its actuality but also its potentiality, is the being and action of the self-revealing God alone."[94]

Christ as Absolute Knowledge

The third Hegelian influence in Bonhoeffer I wish to explore is the idea of absolute knowledge, that pure reflexive thought in which content and form are unified, in which the thinking of theological thought becomes the thinking of thinking itself, which is in turn the thinking of all things in their conceptual fullness.

In *Act and Being*, Bonhoeffer's most demanding academic work, christology is put in the conversation of the transcendental tradition in order to show that revelation as community surpasses any analytical reduction to idealist-transcendental epistemologies and their various architectures as well as to existential-phenomenological possibilities of existence. He holds that neither Kantian nor Hegelian systems are adequate to encompass the christological description of community. Constructions of the nonobjectivity or otherness of God (the Kantian tradition), as well as constructions of the objectivity or immanence of God (the Hegelian tradition), are redescribed by the idea of Jesus Christ existing as community.

In the gospel narrative, Jesus Christ shows that God is the one who comes to his other in redemptive togetherness. In coming to his other, Jesus Christ shows originally who he is as God and thus who God *is*; in coming to his other, Jesus Christ simultaneously shows what humanity is as humanity and thus what humanity *is*. The distinguishing feature of divine majesty is, as Eberhard Jüngel says in agreement with Bonhoeffer, "a ceaseless movement into the *depths.*" God in Jesus Christ enacts a dialectical intensification such that God's being *who he is* is always accompanied by God's being *with humanity* in grace and redemption. As a ceaseless movement into the depths, divine majesty shows itself as ceaseless movement toward humanity; movement into the depths is "the *human* movement of divine majesty." Thus, the conception of God's being in himself is inseparable from the conception of God's coming into the depths of the world in life with humanity.

How does Bonhoeffer attempt to explain this complex notion, apart from appropriating yet another primary philosophical model? He begins at the place Hegel ends, with the problem of divine knowing. He asks, what is the texture of God's own knowing such that God is other than experience and yet concrete subject in experience? The surpassing of otherness and totality in Christ is possible only if revelation is the event for which God is active subject; only if God is subject of the knowing of revelation and is thereby understood as the divine I who at once *stands against* and *embraces* the human subject in the prevenience of his knowing. Bonhoeffer writes in *Act and Being*, "God is in revelation only in the act of understanding himself."[95] The *subject* of the act of the divine knowing is God Himself revealed in Jesus Christ; the *originary location* of this revelation is the story of Jesus of Nazareth narrated in the biblical texts; the *perduring place* wherein Jesus is present and the story celebrated in proclamation, forgiveness, and fellowship is the gathering of the faithful. Our knowledge of God is then bound up with whether God has known us in Christ.[96] As such, the thought of divine identity runs aground because it overlooks the personal-structural character of community. Similarly, the thought of divine difference is inadequate because it misses the truth of the basic theological axiom that what it means for God to be *bei sich selbst* is that he is always also *bei uns*. God knows humankind because Christ stands vicariously in its place, thus God's knowing humankind is God's knowing it in Christ. And for Bonhoeffer, God's knowing humankind in Christ is inseparable from God's knowing it in community.

In advancing the idea that "God is in revelation only in the act of understanding himself"—a phrase sounding brashly Hegelian— Bonhoeffer insists that he diverges from the philosopher at two crucial points. First, the *freedom* of God is not brought into question. With respect to the being of God, the community is not a prerequisite for God's own understanding of himself. God is the actively knowing subject whose knowing binds itself in life together. God's free being for us is, as a relational expression, the repetition of the free self-relation of God in his being as Father, Son, and Holy Spirit. Second, as mediated by Jesus Christ, God's self-understanding embraces humanity without abolishing the difference between God and the world. God's self-understanding always comes to the human I from a source outside itself—prior to its own self-understanding. Yet Bonhoeffer does not position the transsubjective divine self-understanding in the dialectical transcendence of the Word. This is not what he means in this context by trans-subjective. Rather, the place—the "where"—of the act of divine self-knowing is life with others. Bonhoeffer says, "[God's] binding in the community is the freedom of God."[97] Hence, God can never be discovered in my consciousness for a reflection on this act;[98] if Christ exists as community, then Christ must be found apart from my individual act.[99] God as divine subject revealed in Jesus Christ is not confined to the immanent movement of absolute knowing or to radical transcendence, for God's self-understanding is shared with human being through the *act* of faith and within the *being* of revelation—in the togetherness of God and humanity enacted in Jesus Christ.[100]

Community, World, and Obedience

The question that needs to be addressed at this juncture is how Bonhoeffer understands, in a concrete way, human community as the act of God's self-understanding mediated by Jesus Christ. If God exists as community in the act of understanding himself, then we must ask how this self-understanding is imbricated in human knowledge. Put differently, in what mode is divine self-understanding present in the texture of human experience?

Bonhoeffer provides a complex answer to these questions in his later ethics, particularly in the texts "God's Love and the World" and "Christ, Reality and the Good." His approach is twofold: to understand life together in terms of both an *extrinsic* reference to the world and an *intrinsic* reference to the reconfigured self in Christ.

The Worldliness of Community

In its extrinsic reference, the *sanctorum communio* illustrates the place *within the world* in which the lordship of Christ *over all the world* is demonstrated. Although one of Bonhoeffer's primary concerns in the later writings is an exploration of the worldly shape of God's redemptive act in Jesus Christ, it cannot be said that he abandons his principal axiom, "Christ existing as community." Human togetherness becomes instead the paradigm for considering the christomorphic recapitulation of the world as a whole. He says, "If God in Jesus Christ claims space in the world . . . then in this narrow space He comprises together the whole reality of the world at once and reveals the ultimate basis of this reality. And so, too, the Church of Jesus Christ is the place, in other words the space in the world, at which the reign of Jesus Christ over the whole world is evidenced and proclaimed."[101] The community, like the person in its particularity, cannot be regarded as an isolated or self-enclosed reality; for "from the outset it is something which reaches out far beyond itself"[102] and is the place "where testimony is given to the foundation of all reality in Jesus Christ."[103] The community, then, is not a privileged gathering which denies the world its integrity or opposes the world as its militant opposite. As the place of reconciliation, the Christ who exists as community redemptively draws all things to himself and in doing so shows that the world is the world and God is God. (In *Life Together* Bonhoeffer goes so far as to say that our being with others in Christ is the basis of the certainty of the living God and the assurance of faith. He says, "Our brother has been given me that even here and now I may be made certain through him of the reality of God in His judgment and His grace."[104] The brother or sister breaks the "circle of self-deception" such that the certitude of God's presence in the world is attested in the very presence of the other.)

In this *extrinsic* response, Bonhoeffer's conversation with Hegel is focused largely on the meaning of the Incarnation. Like Hegel, Bonhoeffer places great weight on God's becoming human as the decisive event in history—as the axis on which world history turns. But Bonhoeffer is unyielding in his commitment to the historical concreteness of Jesus, not just to his historically redemptive benefits— the former a matter on which Hegel seems indifferent. Hegel's references to the Incarnation are ahistorical in tenor; one could say that he looks in and through rather than at history, so that although God manifests himself in history and history is transformed, the "ever-changing historical vesture has no ultimate and lasting import."[105] Hegel is not able to employ Johannine language to speak of God's sending the Son into the world as the revelation of what is new and altogether unanticipated precisely for the reason that the self-narrating life of Spirit is the description of a process which is immanent within, and whose potential resides within, history.[106] Although for Hegel the extreme form of the estrangement of God and world occurs in the dark night of the cross when otherness or negation is recognized to be a moment of the divine nature, what is actually attained here is a spiritual truth or a conceptual discovery, a knowing of the divine which exploits the concrete historically particular event for the sake of Spirit's universal self-discovery. The signification attached to death is that in death "the human element is stripped away and the divine glory comes into view once more—death is a stripping away of the human, the negative."[107] Thus, for Hegel a sustained or mutually interpreting dialectic of divine humility and divine exaltation interpreted by and through Jesus Christ is ruled out from the start.

Moreover, while certainly agreeing that the "spiritual element" of the Incarnation is an integral part of the persona Christi, Bonhoeffer insists that the embodiment of Christ in the flesh punctuates this event with a significance that must not be overlooked. In "Christ, Reality and the Good" he connects the embodiment of God in creaturely form with the cosmic efficacy of redemption. "In the body of

Jesus Christ, God is united with humanity, the whole of humanity is accepted by God, and the world is reconciled with God."[108] That Jesus suffered in spirit and body means, for Bonhoeffer, that the Incarnation is an event which transforms the total structures of the world; the spiritual and the creational are part of the detailed integration of this transformation. Since estrangement affects the being of the person as a unity of thinking, feeling, and acting, the form of redemption must embrace this unity in a complete embodiment. The body is to be enjoyed and celebrated because Jesus Christ assumed bodily form; and because Jesus Christ assumed bodily form, the body is central to every aspect of life together. Bonhoeffer explains: "Man was created a body, the Son of God appeared on earth in the body, he was raised in the body, in the sacrament the believer receives the Lord Christ in the body, and the resurrection of the dead will bring about the perfected fellowship of God's spiritual-physical creatures. The believer therefore lauds the Creator, the Redeemer, God, Father, Son and Holy Spirit, for the bodily presence of a brother."[109] The Incarnation of the Word in suffering flesh makes it hereafter impossible to speak of the world as estranged by God or the body as unaffected by the scope of redemption.

Nonetheless, what distinguishes Bonhoeffer's description from Hegel's is not so much the emphasis on divine embodiment but his sweeping, uncompromising christocentricism. God as the "ultimate reality" is no other than the one who "shows forth, manifests and reveals Himself, that is to say, God in Jesus Christ."[110] In Jesus Christ the reality of God entered the reality of the world, as a result of which the reality of God and the reality of the world are explicated by the name Jesus Christ. "All concepts of reality which do not take account of Him are abstractions."[111] Beyond this name there is no appeal, neither to self-reflexive subjectivity nor to some mystical insight. Thus, Bonhoeffer claims that the thinking of God in two spheres is overcome only in Christ, who as true God and true human reconciles God and world in himself. He says, "There are not two realities, but only one reality, and that is the reality of God, which has become manifest in Christ in the reality of the world. . . . The reality of Christ comprises the reality of the world within itself."[112]

Yet Bonhoeffer seems to push too far his emphasis on Christ as the center of the real. For example, he says that because of Christ's propitiation of estranged humanity before the Father, the world "has no reality of its own, independently of the revelation of God in Christ."[113] Further, "[The] whole reality of the world is already drawn into Christ and bound together in Him, and the movement of history consists solely in divergence and convergence in relation to this center."[114] The world, the natural, the profane, and the sacred are now all taken up into God (he does not here use *aufgehoben* but *hineingenommen*). Does he not push the theme of recapitulation in Christ to such a point that the difference between Christ and world is jeopardized (despite his criticisms of Hegel on precisely this point)?

I take Bonhoeffer to be saying in *Ethics* that the Christian message of reconciliation cannot help but speak of the redemptive work of Christ in language that (at least initially) sounds monistic. For there are no longer two spheres, the human and divine, standing in opposition to each other, but only "the one sphere of the realization of Christ, in which the reality of God and the reality of the world are united."[115]

As I see it, the influence in Bonhoeffer's critique of thinking of God in two spheres is not directly Hegel or even Luther (compare the theme of God's condescension and passion and the *finitum capax infiniti*) but Saint Paul and the second-century theologian Irenaeus. Saint Paul's high christological language in Colossians is a clear antecedent to this tendency of appearing to endorse a divine monism: "For God was pleased to have all his fullness dwell in him, and through him to reconcile to himself all things, whether things on earth or things in heaven" (1:20). Similar language is found in Ephesians: "And he made known to us the mystery of his will according to his good pleasure, which he purposed in Christ, to be put into effect when the times will have reached their fulfillment—to bring all things in heaven and on earth together under one head, even Christ" (1:9–10). Specific to Irenaeus is the notion of "recapitulation" or "anacephalaeosis," in which the whole of creation is conceived to be re-constituted, "gathered together, included and comprised" in Christ. When Irenaeus uses the term *recapitulation* he intends to denote that the entire scope of creation is gathered up into the Incarnation of God; consequently, creation as such must be understood as a preparation for reuniting the fellowhip of God with humanity.[116] Irenaeus writes in *Against Heresies*:

> In every respect, too, Christ is man, the formation of God; and thus He took up man into Himself, the invisible becoming visible, the incomprehensible being made comprehensible, the impassible becoming capable of suffering, and the Word being made man, thus summing up all things in Himself; so that as in super-celestial, spiritual and invisible things, the Word of God is supreme, so also in things visible and corporeal He might possess the supremacy, and, taking to Himself the preeminence, as well as constituting Himself Head of the Church, He might draw all things to Himself at the proper time.[117]

In this way, in the present economy, Christ must not only be confessed as the goal of creation and the new Adam but as the one who atones for the sins of humanity; and as the firstborn from the dead, his absolute comprehension of every stage of history has redeemed, reconstructed and "re-constituted" that creation which until the Incarnation had been subjected to corruption and was receding into non-being.[118] Christ represents in word and truth the second Adam, and as in the Lucan genealogy, Christ recapitulates in himself "all the dispersed peoples dating back to Adam, all tongues and the whole race of mankind, along with Adam himself."[119] In becoming incarnate, Christ "recapitulated in Himself the long sequence of mankind," so that now in the new covenant Christ, who atones for the disobedience of Adam, can be celebrated as the beginning of a redeemed humanity.[120] Bonhoeffer's interest in this theme further evidences his desire to think the great expanse of the christological transfiguration of the world, and to employ ontological concepts when appropriate. One hears echoes of this theme in his letter "Advent IV" when he writes, "Nothing is lost, everything is taken up in Christ, although it is transformed, made transparent, clear and free from all selfish desire. Christ restores all this as God originally intended it to be."[121] This "magnificient conception," which Bonhoeffer recalls as "full of comfort," gives voice in an extraordinarily clear way to the mysterious heart of grace, that it is not we who shall take creation back to its original glory, and thus it is not we who shape and reshape the real in the image of ourselves, but it is Christ who shall "give it back to us."[122] Therefore, the "ecstatic longing" of Paul Gerhardt's hymns or the Augustinian *O bone Jesu* in Heinrich Schütz's motet bears witness to the "'bringing again' of all earthly desire" as the new creation of the Holy Spirit.[123]

However, in acknowledging the monistic tenor of much of his language, Bonhoeffer does not fail to recognize the possible dangers of pushing the "one reality" image too far. In the ethics texts, as in numerous other works, he guards his view from an extreme kenotic position by arguing that the togetherness of Christ with the world always preserves the prevenience of God's grace and thus the difference of God and the world. He says, "The unity of the reality of God and of the world, which has been accomplished in Christ, is repeated, or more exactly, is realized ever afresh in human life. And yet what is Christian is not identical with what is of the world. The natural is not identical with the supernatural or the revelational with the rational. But between the two there is in each case a unity which derives solely from faith in this ultimate reality."[124] It is the "shared reality" of God and humanity that Bonhoeffer emphasizes, not the necessary identity of the two. Similarly, this shared reality, mediated by Christ alone, militates against all conceptions of totality as self-mediated, as he affirms nowhere more elegantly than in the theme of the recapitulation of the world in Jesus Christ.

Obedience as the Inner Logic of Community

In considering the *intrinsic* approach to the concrete meaning of community in his ethics, Bonhoeffer wants to cast light on the inner logic of "Christ existing as community." As such, he returns to the problem of divine knowing, though now to the way it articulates itself in human experience. He writes, "Whoever knows God in His revelation in Jesus Christ, whoever knows the crucified and risen God, he knows all things that are in heaven, on earth and beneath the earth. He knows God as the ending of all disunion, all judgement and all condemnation, as the One who loves and as the One who lives."[125] The point at hand is crucial because it elicits a confrontation with Hegel's affirmation of the conceptual locus of revelation. Bonhoeffer seems to give a high (and admittedly singular) christological gloss on the idea of universal self-consciousness. What does he mean by his reference to a knowledge that knows all things in Jesus Christ?

The context of the citation is Bonhoeffer's intriguing discussion of the knowledge of the Pharisee in "The Love of God and the Decay of the World," the one whose thinking of God is "dead and barren" and pervasively egotistical. He contrasts the "new knowledge" given in revelation to the "legalistic nihilism" of the Pharisee.[126] "The knowledge of the Pharisee," he writes, "is the negation of all true action, but the knowledge of Jesus and of His own consists solely in action."[127] This is a significant statement. One hears echoes of the distinction in *Act and Being* between the *actus directus* and the *actus reflectus*; the former employed in order to describe the direct intentionality of the person to Christ, a relationship based not on speculative or theological knowledge but on steadfast obedience. He says, "The clinging to Christ does not need to be conscious of itself for it is fully taken up into the execution of the act itself."[128] The *actus directus* interrupts all introspection because the I taken out of itself in the call of Jesus Christ ceases to be *self-reflective*, becoming instead *deflective* of the saving God. Based on the objectivity of the call in Word and sacrament, *fides directa* is exemplified in the power of the call to pull the I out of its self-encapsulation and into the extrinsicality of life together.

Bonhoeffer continues to develop the theme of the *actus directus* in *The Cost of Discipleship*. Reading the Marcan account of Levi's decision to follow Christ (Mark 2:14), he notes that the only claim the text makes about discipleship is: follow Christ.[129] That is all. An "abstract Christology," a christology which is oriented in a system of doctrine or a general religious knowledge, is placed in contrast to a discipleship bound to Christ. Knowledge of Christ does not just incite a certain course of behavior or an admirable example of the life best lived. Knowing Christ *is* following Christ—it *is* obedience. Bonhoeffer says, "And what does the text inform us about the content of discipleship? It is nothing else than bondage to Jesus Christ alone, completely breaking through every program, every ideal, every set of laws. No other significance is possible, since Jesus is the only significance."[130] Of course, the historical context of this exegesis, written from the seminary of the Confessing Church at Finkenwalde in 1936 and 1937, emphasizes the utter subversiveness of such radical simplicity (and hence its extraordinary complexity!). Even here Bonhoeffer is seeking for a way to express the glad fellowship of humanity's life with God that is not affixed to the self-mediations of the dialectical system.

Bonhoeffer's emphasis on the immediacy of the call of Jesus Christ should not be misunderstood as a compromise of the priority of Christ as mediator. There is no unbroken way between God and humanity, but a fracture (*ein Bruch*) which Christ always fills.[131] The immediacy Bonhoeffer conceives involves the radical renunciation of false gods and the simple turning to Jesus Christ as the salvation of humanity and the way to the other. This is no mystical fusion—no overcoming of the difference of God and self. As Andre Dumas writes, "The role of faith is thus not to erect delaying and hesitant preconditions but to simplify the ambiguity of circumstances so that they can highlight the unambiguous nature of obedience."[132] Christ is the mediator who empowers the simple following after which cuts away all other finite claims to truth. The directness of the obedient response to the call "arises from the fact that Christ 'is the One beyond any Other.'"[133]

Thus, in "The Love of God and the Decay of the World," Bonhoeffer invokes the *actus directus* in his discussion of the meaning of the "new knowledge" in Christ. "The knowledge of Jesus is entirely transformed into action, without any reflection upon a person's self."[134] There is no essential conflict between knowledge and practice in this regard, for the knowledge of Christ *is* the call of liberation, the call which "negates the old knowledge of the apostasy and which imparts the new knowledge of Jesus, that knowledge which is entirely contained in the doing of the will of God."[135] Expressed differently in Saint Paul's words, "The Kingdom of God is not a matter of talk but of power" (I Cor. 4:20).

One can then say that the new I in Christ does not venture forth in a gesture of trying to re-contain the world as identity (in universality), but it is called out in simple obedience, *not* to return as a recovered I but to remain, extended in life with others, always more than the I. This transformation illustrates the inner content of community or its intrinsic reference.

Subjectivity as Servanthood

Do we then say that, for Hegel, reconciliation is finally consummated in philosophical thought, and for Bonhoeffer, appropriated in obedience to Christ? I think this is the right direction, but we cannot overlook the subtlety of the distinction between reflection and action. It might be wise to heed Eberhard Jüngel's advice that the more similar two things are the more carefully they must be distinguished.[136]

In the *Phenomenology of Spirit* and the *Lectures on the Philosophy of Religion*, Hegel designates the instantiation of the reconciliation of God and world as the noetic mastery of philosophical thinking. However, throughout his writings Bonhoeffer understands the experience of reconciliation as a life with others shaped by agapeic love, sacrificial responsibility, and delight in our natural being.[137] For both Hegel and Bonhoeffer the earth and all its fullness is the Lord's. But Bonhoeffer's vision does not lead the self back into subjectivity, however consummated in its universality this subjectivity might be. Bonhoeffer's vision leads the person as subject—even more now as servant—back into the world that has been reconciled to God. As Jörg Rades wrote in his unfinished manuscript on Bonhoeffer and Hegel, "Action is where we find freedom. What sets us free is the stepping out of ourselves . . . to grasp reality which is only in Christ."[138] I have tried to follow Bonhoeffer's reading of Hegel toward this end.

It would seem, then, that Bonhoeffer does distinguish his christological description of community from Hegel's understanding. Certainly when Hegel states that the very possibility of reconciliation depends on the recognition of the "implicit unity" of the divine and human natures, the differences between Bonhoeffer's priority of the graciousness and freedom of God and Hegel's view of the necessary self-development of Spirit appear to be decisive. There is no implicit unity between God and community, or God and world, although there is fellowship through the redemptive work of Christ. Christ is present among us as the concretion of being-for-others in life together. But this being-for is not propelled by ethical action as such but by the deep transformation of the self in faith. Again in Saint Paul's words, "Therefore, if anyone is in Christ, he is a *new creation*; the old has gone, the new has come" (II Cor. 5:17). As Bonhoeffer says, "Christ existing as community . . . turns man's eyes away from self and gives him his direction to Christ the Crucified and Risen, who is the defeat of temptation to death."[139] The experience of reconciliation is not a project of speculative reason but a life of responsibility, commitment, and risk.[140] Bonhoeffer activates Hegel's dialectic toward compassionate engagement and self-forgetfulness at the point where, for Hegel, it becomes the complete recovery of subjectivity through universal self-knowledge.

In life together we are not only confronted with the *promise* of our redemption, but much more we enter into "*the Christmas-world*"—the "Weihnachtswelt."[141] It is not the subject, love, or even life itself which provides the paradigm of the real, but Christ alone.

6

On Heidegger and Life with Others

Dietrich Bonhoeffer and Martin Heidegger led remarkably different lives. On 27 May 1933 Heidegger became rector of the University of Freiburg, eager to encourage pedagogical reforms consistent with the ideals of National Socialism. Less than a month earlier, at the end of April, Bonhoeffer had issued his first public defense of the Jews and condemnation of the Ayran Clause in his address "The Church and the Jewish Question," followed in August by the "Bethel Confession."

Yet there was a time during the previous decade in which their lives intersected in an altogether different way. When Heidegger's *Being and Time* appeared in the early part of 1927, Bonhoeffer was completing work on his doctoral dissertation, *Sanctorum Communio*, under the direction of Reinhold Seeberg at the University of Berlin. Bonhoeffer's cousin Hans-Christoph von Hase, the same cousin who earlier introduced him to Barth's theology, spoke enthusiastically to him of Heidegger, possibly as early as 1924.[1] Bonhoeffer may have read *Being and Time* (or previously published sections of the book) while he wrote the dissertation, though there is no evidence of this in the text. But in 1929, just months after Bonhoeffer assumed the position of "Volontärassistent" in the Berlin theological faculty, Professor Wilhelm Lütgert referred to him in a conversation with von Hase as a Heideggerian and a neo-Thomist, notwithstanding the cousin's protests.[2] During Bonhoeffer's postdoctoral work as a Sloan Fellow at Union Theological Seminary in New York City (1930–1931), John

Baillie relied on him for "detailed information" about Heidegger and other contemporary Continental thinkers such as Bultmann, Gogarten, and Barth.[3]

Importantly, the influence of Heidegger's *Being and Time* is unmistakably present in *Act and Being*, which Bonhoeffer wrote in the summer and winter of 1929. Eberhard Bethge has noted that there are more references to Heidegger in this book than to any other thinker except Martin Luther.[4] Although Lütgert exaggerates Bonhoeffer's relation to Heidegger's philosophy (as well as his relation to neo-Thomism), there are important connections between their thought that have not been explored.[5] Namely, in an attempt to shape reflection in a way that is not determined by the totality of the self-reflective subject but emerges from a source prior to and external to the individual, Bonhoeffer finds certain themes in Heidegger's fundamental ontology congenial to his theological purposes. Bonhoeffer subjects these themes to christological redescription, and thus does not appropriate existential analysis *tout court*. Nonetheless, Heidegger's notions of potentiality-for-being, authenticity, and being-with others push Bonhoeffer in his thinking about human selfhood and sociality to recognize specific social-ontological distinctions and concepts critical to his developing christology.

In this chapter I wish to bring theological clarity to Bonhoeffer's reading of Heidegger. But, more important, I will show the implications of Bonhoeffer's critique for his sustained reflection on the secondary objectivity of revelation, in this case with close attention to the christological texture of community. My purpose in this task is to delineate the central issues at stake in their differences and also to suggest that Bonhoeffer's best insights have powerful contemporary significance.

Self and World in Being and Time

According to Heidegger, one of the pervasive consequences of the Western metaphysical tradition for contemporary theological and philosophical thought is that the question of essence is answered by explaining what something is—by attending to the quiddity of a thing. As such, the standard way of explaining the meaning of a thing is to show and then to define the object. One cannot define what has not shown itself or what has not been shown as the object to be defined. For example, in defining a tree, one points to the particular woody object to say that this thing here is a tree, and then one proceeds to define the very tree-ness appropriate to the observed thing. Three elements are fundamental to the process of definition: (1) the demonstrative term—"This is a tree."; (2) a name given to the object—"A tree is . . ."; and (3) a definition proper—"A tree is a permanently woody plant, and so forth." Thinking about the essence of a thing means coming to terms with a description of the nature of the thing. Aristotle's classic illustration of the point is that when considering the nature of human beings, we do not define them as featherless bipeds but as those who possess the *Logos*, as those who have the capacity to talk.

Heidegger's most dramatic break with the metaphysical tradition in his existential phenomenology of human being is his bold rejection of this descriptive procedure. The philosopher should not say *what* human being is, but only that it is *there*. Human existence always constricts its significations to the first person singular. In contrast to the generic classification of human being as rational animal, according to Heidegger, all I can say about what I am is that *I am here*. Thus, Heidegger employs the term *Dasein*, or being-there— that is, being that is there—to signify the individual human being. Dasein is one who has its essence in its own existence; thus, the individualizing or discriminating factor is not the materiality of a thing but its location in a certain historicized network of relations. Moreover, the fact that human being is there as a specific location presupposes a network of concern in which human being is always a there of "being." This network is the world. As a result, questions that might have traditionally been asked of the world as nature or as *res extensa* (Descartes's notion of the world as an extended thing) such as, "How do we come to know it?" or "Through what mode can (or ought) we most truthfully experience it?" are for Heidegger derivative of the concrete, worldly character of Dasein, for whom the *da* is always *in der Welt*. Being-in-the-world should not then invoke a spatial metaphor of being-in like the worm in the tequila bottle,[6] for being-in-the-world is a unity constitutive of Dasein itself. Being in the world and not of the world means to have worldliness as part of one's own being. Heidegger intends his notion of world to reach beyond the subject-object or mind-body distinction, as well as beyond certain modes of *being-in-relation* (including the theological mode), by showing the way in which *relation* per se and the subject and object of particular relations is derived from the basic unity of Dasein's being-in-the-world.

Heidegger never achieved the goals he set for himself; he grew disenchanted by the inescapable *da* which seems to obscure Being's unguarded presence. He discovered that even though it is possible to get at the being that is there in Dasein, it is never possible to strip away the "there" and to arrive at a pure understanding of *Sein* itself. Heidegger's later writings on the meaning of poetical discourse are meditations on whether it is possible for being itself to speak in the "purest poetry of the essence of poetry" and for the poetical words of Dasein to bespeak the meaning of *Sein*. Philosophy itself becomes an exercise of meditation on the primordial, formative words of the tradition—a listening, an attunement, a waiting.

Yet although there is material in the later Heidegger amenable to theological construction,[7] it is the focus on the analysis of human existence, as developed in *Being and Time*, that, as Jeff Prudhomme says, "helped redirect theological reflection from a metaphysical dogmatism and to the issues of lived existence."[8] In a stunning exercise of phenomenological reflection, Heidegger investigates the ekstatic structure of that peculiar one Dasein which *stands out* into time by means of a certain comportment toward location and place. If *Sein* is always located in a network of relations peculiar to the *da*, then it must be the case that an analysis of this location will illuminate the meaning of being. Temporality for Heidegger does not mean the simple coming and going of time as *chronology (kronos)*; rather, it indicates *the horizon of all understanding of the being of Dasein* as a being extended over and into time, over and into a past, a present, and a future. Temporality is particular to the being of Dasein itself.[9] Heidegger says, "In our thesis that temporality is primordially finite, we are not disputing that 'time goes on'; we are simply holding fast to the phenomenal character of primordial temporality—a character which shows itself in what is projected in Dasein's primordial existential projecting."[10] In this way, *Being and Time* constitutes an analysis of time "explicated primordially as the horizon for the understanding of Being" (190:234). Chronological time is then derivative of the existential analytic of Dasein's own temporality.

Three aspects constitute the unitary structure of Dasein's being-in-the-world. First, being-in-the-world involves the notion of being-in as an *existenzial*. More clearly stated, Heidegger contrasts the first-order existential (*existenzial*) examination of the *ontological* structure of human being with the second-order exisentiell (*existenziell*) investigation of the *ontic* structure of human existence. Dasein's being-in-the-world is not to be understood as something "present-at-hand" (*Vorhandensein*), as though the world existed for Dasein as an objectification to be manipulated for certain means; nor is it to be conceived as being-present or alongside-of, *Mitvorhandensein*, or as spatially "in." By calling these states "existentiell," Heidegger means that these relations are contingent on certain ontic conditions of Dasein—and thereby construe human being as some sort of object or thing. On the other hand, Being-in as an existential takes its designation from *innan* ("to reside"), *habitare* ("to dwell"), and most significantly, the simple *ich bin*, which in connection to the preposition *bei* means "I reside" or "I dwell alongside." Heidegger shows that the infinitive *sein* or the first person *ich bin* entails more than being in the particular sense of persisting through space and time according to a certain, temporal form; indeed, *sein* means "to reside alongside" or "to be always in a dwelling." Being-in, then, is "the formal existential expression for the Being of Dasein, which has Being-in-the-world as its essential state" (54:80).

Second, the existential mode of concern secures Dasein's place among a grid of practical tasks and projects as the mode in which Dasein is most immediately aware of the world. Heidegger says, "Taking up relationships towards the world is possible only because Dasein, as Being-in-the-world, is as it is. This state of Being does not arise just because some other entity is present-at-hand outside of Dasein and meets up with it. Such an entity can 'meet up with' Dasein only in so far as it can, of its own accord, show itself within a world" (57:84). The point at which Dasein "meets up with" an entity of concern (*Besorgen*) occasions a manifestation or disclosure of the world; herein the phenomenon of the world is grasped as the end point of concern. Knowing the world ("noein") and discussing it ("Logos") are ancillary to the more fundamental description of the world disclosing itself in concern. Otto Pöggeler says, "Dasein becomes transparent to itself as Being-in-the-world, as the 'circumspection of concern,' as the 'considerateness of care-for-others,' and as the 'sight of Being as such for the sake of which Dasein in each case is as it is.'"[11] Conceived otherwise than as a constellation of practical concerns, the world is taken as an object of theoretical study—a natural or physical datum—and its primary existential character is concealed.

The third aspect of the unitary structure of Dasein's being-in-the-world engages the question of the self for, as we saw in *Being and Time*, the *da* of *Sein* is always the point of departure in the investigation of Dasein. To pursue the description of the concept of world one must raise the question of how the world at first shows itself. Heidegger turns in this context to the use of tools. In the concept of the tool (*Zeug*) Heidegger wishes to restore the existential power of the term he thinks was eviscerated of its connotative force when the

Greek word *pragmata* came to mean merely those things close-at-hand. As *zuhanden* (ready-to-hand), a tool manifests a practical-existential significance (*Bedeutsamkeit*); this is quite a different matter than the concept of tool as *vorhanden* (present-at-hand), the denotation of a mere conspicuous object. For in the everyday appropriation of tools, Dasein finds itself in this network of connections that is the world. A hammer is used to build a table; a table is built to serve a useful purpose for human beings. Insofar as one achieves in this way a world which can be made subject to reflection—to this end a world that can be thematized—the equipmental thing must become at once *Vorhandensein* and *Zuhandensein*. The tool must overcome its inconspicuousness and yet remain potentially a tool—a tool must break down. Then as Heidegger says, "The modes of conspicuousness, obtrusiveness, and obstinacy all have the function of bringing to the fore the characteristic of presence-at-hand in what is ready-to-hand" (74:104). This singular mode represents a way in which the world can be thematized, but not, of course, as one might "throw a 'signification' over some naked thing which is present-at-hand" (150:190). Rather, a broken tool provides a clear example of how the interpretive task always proceeds for Dasein. The thing in question, the broken, obtrusive tool, is grasped as already involved in our understanding of the world, so that the purpose of the interpretation of the tool itself is to illuminate the understanding that was previously there in the use of the tools.

The world is therefore built within Dasein's understanding *as a referential totality*, because the equipmental thing never discloses itself as unconnected to other things but always as discovered alongside and with something else. Because tools present themselves as a total network of useful references, their end purpose coincides with self-understanding. When the reliability of tools gives way to uselessness—when the tool breaks—Dasein understands what it had already preunderstood in the mode of reliability, it understands that *it is where it is*, indeed that Dasein *is* a historicized location of concerns and cares. The hermeneutical circle originates in the very self-understanding of Dasein; as a result, all specific, ontic, or local strategies of interpretation presuppose the primordial ground of existential self-understanding.

There is, of course, more that could be said here in summary of the principal themes in *Being and Time*, especially about the matter of the self's relations with others. However, I will discuss this and related matters later in the chapter. I now turn to Bonhoeffer's direct response to Heidegger's analysis of human being.

Bonhoeffer and Heidegger Against the Self-Reflective Subject

Interpreters of Bonhoeffer have almost uniformly assumed that his assessment of Heidegger, given the immense political and religious differences between the two thinkers, is entirely pessimistic. Ernst Feil, in an otherwise insightful study of Bonhoeffer's theology of the world, summarizes the conventional wisdom: "[Heidegger's] concept of existence, derived from the human and not from revelation, was, for Bonhoeffer, theologically unusable."[12] In my view, Feil's comment too quickly glosses over Bonhoeffer's own use of various aspects of Heidegger's existential analysis, including (at least in *Act and Being*) terms and expressions derived from the Heideggerian idiolectic. That Bonhoeffer does finally reject the fundamental ontology on theological grounds should not obscure his admiration for *Being and Time*'s attempt to "destrue" or destructure the history of ontology. Heidegger's desire to reawaken the question of Being in his analysis of concrete existence, as well as his project of reaching or questioning back to a place anterior to the split of act and being, captured Bonhoeffer's imagination in a decisive way.

In particular, there are four themes in *Being and Time* that Bonhoeffer critically appropriates for his own theological purposes. First, Bonhoeffer follows Heidegger in his effort to debunk the hegemony of the self-reflective subject; he is impressed with the claim that human subjectivity is not the creative center of human being's existence. One of Bonhoeffer's primary theological aims was to show that self-reflection is itself always preceded (and thus, broken of its pretensions to primacy) through a prior being-known by God; it is never the case that the concrete person is in complete possession of himself. He writes, "Whoever countenances the idea that he need only arrive at himself to be in God is doomed to hideous disillusion in experiencing the utter introversion, the treadmill confinement to the self, of the very loneliest solitude, with its tormenting desolation and sterility."[13] Rather, the person is always placed in a contingent here and now "as one who has to find his whereabouts by asking, thinking and doing, one who has to relate to himself the position pre-given to him and at the same time define himself 'in reference to' it."[14] The "imposition" of already being with reference to a network of concerns is quite a different matter than the presumption to master or constitute the world by means of a world-constitutive subject.

While Heidegger's mentor Edmund Husserl pondered the texture of "pure transcendental consciousness," Heidegger takes as the basic subject of the phenomenological inquiry "Dasein," or "there-being," the one who concretely raises the question of being that is its own; not timeless essentialities and values, as one finds (for example) in Husserl and Max Scheler, but temporal Dasein caught up in a concrete network of concerns. The aristocracy of the self-reflective subject and the privileges accorded its cognitive domain are contested in Heidegger's attempt to deconstruct the whole architecture of the philosophy of subjectivity. Heidegger aspires to retell the story of Western philosophy so as to make clear that the *cogito ergo sum* is not possible unless there already "*is* something such as understanding of being."[15] (For this reason Descartes, whose *cogito ergo sum* isolates only the *cogitare* of the *ego*, fails to reckon with the plenitude of the *sum*.) Thought itself must be understood as constitutive of Dasein's network of concerns. As Bonhoeffer himself explains, "Thus even thought does not produce its world for itself, but finds itself, as Dasein, in a world."[16] Dasein (the one who is always already in the world) is not the creator of its own facticity nor of the facticity of the world; rather, Dasein is the recipient of the world.[17]

Second, Bonhoeffer thinks Heidegger's analysis of being-in-the-world points a way toward a viable interrelation of being and thought in which mind no longer has priority over being nor is being relegated to a modification of mind. Although being understands itself in Dasein, Dasein is human being's understanding in historicity, in the given temporal context of unique decisions.[18] Neither pure consciousness in the Husserlian sense nor the supraformal a priori in Scheler's sense remains the dominant term. Bonhoeffer says with approval, "Heidegger has succeeded in forcing act and being into partnership in the concept of Dasein—that is to say, the actual decidings of Dasein coincide with its given decidedness."[19]

Nonetheless, Bonhoeffer thinks Heidegger contradicts his own attempt to overturn the preeminence of the world-constituting subject in his claim that Dasein in temporality already possesses understanding of being and is consequently "open" to itself.[20] Bonhoeffer says, "The genuinely ontological development of the suspension of thought in being is permeated by the systematic theme of man's having, qua Dasein, an understanding of being at his disposal."[21] Bonhoeffer's sympathies with Heidegger are checked by the implication that no room is left for the novelty of revelation. In contesting the domination of act over being, Heidegger winds up inverting the relation such that being absorbs act. I will amplify Bonhoeffer's point in the following section.

Third, fundamental to Heidegger's investigation of the *Seinsfrage* is his distinction between any particular being (*Seiende*) and being itself (*Sein*). Heidegger thinks that careful reflection on this distinction can facilitate the overcoming of the onto-theological mistake of identifying highest being and God. The nature of this historical problem—a problem that has led all too often to the mistaken identification of God and being as such—is that being is construed in objective terms with the result that the difference between being (*Sein*) and beings (*Seiende*) is obscured. Inasmuch as the Western metaphysical tradition has forgotten the difference between the question about being as such and the question about any particular being, it has also forgotten being itself. Metaphysics describes the nature and hierarchy of beings while overlooking the fundamental question about Being itself—about the "is."[22] To ameliorate this fateful neglect, Heidegger thematizes the theological difference between God and beings in light of the basic ontological difference between God and being.[23]

What interests Bonhoeffer in this task is Heidegger's refusal to answer the question of being by reference to another (yet more exotic and compelling) being (*Seiend*). Instead he begins with the *difference* between being and beings. Being itself is not understood by means of the observation of particular beings but in attending to the way being shows itself.[24] This approach plays a significant role in shaping Bonhoeffer's claim that the revealing act of God in Jesus Christ demonstrates the basic difference between human and divine being. The self-witness of God in the revelation of Jesus Christ is the reality within which the difference between human and divine is articulated, within which God shows himself to be God and humanity is given the freedom to be humanity. Bonhoeffer's theological description coheres nicely with Heidegger's phenomenological methodology to the extent that being (or Bonhoeffer's God revealed in Jesus Christ) is not considered to be derived from an investigation of entities or beings, or from a general description of being, but articulates itself in the way it shows itself to be.

Fourth, Bonhoeffer is influenced by Heidegger's claim that the understanding of being is possible through the disciplined exercise of "authentic questioning."[25] As we have seen, Heidegger does not question after *a* being but after being that is there in Dasein, for Dasein is that one which is distinguished by the capacity of asking the question of its own being (the *Sinn von Sein*). Correspondingly, in the christology lectures of 1933, Bonhoeffer considers the classifying schemes of the ontic sciences inappropriate forms for understanding encounter with Christ. He rejects the purely ontic questions of "How?" or "What?" He writes, "When the Counter-logos appears in history, no longer as an idea, but as 'Word' become flesh, there is no longer any possibility of assimilating him into the existing order of the human logos."[26] As noted earlier, the only genuine question remains, "Who are you?" The "who" directs a personal address to the one who already confronts the person in decision. One hears echoes of Heidegger's authentic questioning in Bonhoeffer's proposal:

> The question, "Who?", expresses the strangeness and the otherness of the one encountered and at the same time it is shown to be the question concerning the very existence of the questioner. He is asking about . . . the boundaries of his own existence. . . . With the answer that his logos has reached its boundary he faces the boundary of his own existence. So the question of transcendence is the question of existence, and the question of existence is the question of transcendence. In theological terms: it is only from God that man knows who he is.[27]

That there is almost a reversal in Bonhoeffer's question of "Who are you?"—you Jesus Christ, the one who encounters me in the saving event of revelation—of Heidegger's *Seinsfrage* does not negate the shared assumption that the authentic question is not primarily an address to particular beings in their ontic character (entities) but is the decisive way of turning to the original source of human being (of being attuned to the voice of the call).

These important and overlooked ontological and methodological affinities undoubtedly influence the shape of Bonhoeffer's philosophical theology. But these affinities must be put in the context of Bonhoeffer's critical reading of Heidegger on the issues of potentiality, personal continuity, and being-with others.

The Problem of Potentiality in Theology

With respect to the issue of selfhood, Bonhoeffer raises two objections against the existential analytic of Dasein. He criticizes Heidegger's claim that Dasein contains—immanent to its own structure—the potentiality for authentic being-in-the-world and his description of the continuity of human being.

In *Being and Time* Heidegger describes Dasein's potentiality for authentic existence as an ontological feature of human being inasmuch as it is integrally related to both temporality and ecstasis. As the temporal form of ecstasis or projectedness, temporality signifies the way human being is *always already* projected in time toward the future, always ahead of itself in a bending toward the not-yet. Temporality, says Heidegger, is "essentially ecstatical" (331:380). Prior to the classification of human being in biological or genetic terms, Dasein should be conceived as a potentiality that projects itself into temporality; indeed, this is its primoridal constitution. Even the activity of understanding itself, in its basic existential rendering, involves nothing less than the "projecting towards a potentiality-for-Being for the sake of which any Dasein exists" (336:385). As Heidegger says, "Dasein is not something present-at-hand which possesses its competence for something by way of an extra; it is primarily Being-possible" (143:183). Dasein *is* "that which it *can be*," for as Pöggeler says, Dasein is "primarily a Being-possible."[28] When resolutely determined to confront its future as its own finite possession, human being is able to save itself from fallenness—from losing its way in the pedestrian trivialities of the common—and to do so precisely for the purpose of being more authentically there in the "Situation" at hand (328:376).

Therefore, it is the temporal direction of the future that makes ontologically possible that entity Dasein which exists "understandingly in its potentiality-for-Being" (336:385). "Projection is basically futural" (336:385), and *as* projection, Dasein is always comported toward the future in a concrete way. Either I fall inauthentically into the dronelike blandness of "the they" (*das Man*) and thereby insist on relating myself to the future in terms of a "making present" and of a "backing away," or I turn resolutely toward death for the purpose of becoming authentic to my most basic possibility—my absolute end. In acknowledging and accepting the death that is unconditionally mine, I am enabled to return to my ownmost potentiality-for-Being. I become authentic.

Heidegger effectively correlates the ecstatic nature of time and the exsistent standing-forth of Dasein as a way of answering the question of how it is possible for the self to be both within itself and ahead of itself in the world. Because Dasein stands out into time as potentiality, it is able to achieve unity in "the totality of the structure of care" (328:376). Temporal ecstasis makes it possible for Dasein "to be able to take over resolutely that entity which it already is" (339:388); being-there qua human being is a self-projecting potentiality-for-Being. More importantly, human being's potentiality toward the unity of understanding emphasizes the extent to which truth belongs to Dasein in its existence. Heidegger says, "There-being is 'in the truth.'"[29] As the disclosedness of Dasein's being what it is, truth is not a cognitive property but a primordial feature of human being. Truth and being are equiprimordial to human being.

Bonhoeffer takes exception to this description of Dasein's potentiality for authentic being—for dwelling in the truth. According to Heidegger, the comprehension of the being of beings is possible as part of the structure of human being's finite understanding. According to Bonhoeffer, the capacity to attain self-authentication by means of the resources of finite existence denies the invidious circuity of the *cor curvum in se*, the verities of moral and spiritual fallibility whose recalcitrance and pervasiveness Bonhoeffer (writing in the 1930s) has no intention to ignore. He protests the Heideggerian self-sufficient finitude on the grounds that the existential analytic of finite self-understanding is itself an inadequate foundation on which to think of human identity in its most concrete expression.

In his inaugural lecture at Berlin, "Man in Contemporary Philosophy and Theology" (1930), Bonhoeffer provides a more nuanced account of this criticism. He argues here that Heidegger actually abandons the ostensible phenomenological limitations of the investigation in his discussion of potentiality-for-being. When responding to the call of conscience, Dasein is able to snatch itself away from fallenness in the world by taking its guilt and the nullity of life into itself in order to become resolutely directed toward the most intractable of all powers, death.[30] Dasein's summons to resoluteness or authenticity is invoked not by any reality outside human being but by the immanent call of conscience. Conscience invokes a kind of nagging recollection of the home place from which one has strayed. The truth of human being as self-contained projection or projectedness is elicited by the individualized acknowledgment of its end—that is, in turning toward the end as the turning toward authentic being. As the "most indeterminate, the final and the most authentic potentiality of Therebeing,"[31] death is Dasein's extreme possibility. Death, writes Heidegger, is "die Möglichkeit als die der Unmöglichkeit der Existenz überhaupt" (262:307).

Bonhoeffer recognizes that up to this point Heidegger has remained consistent with his stated intentions of carrying through a rigorous investigation of finite human being. Yet when he narrates the account of Dasein bringing itself face-to-face with the possibility of being itself in an "impassioned freedom towards death," thereby achieving facticity, self-certainty, and release from the "they," he overleaps the constraints of human finitude. Bonhoeffer says, "[Human being] does not come to the end, but to the fulfillment, the totality of Dasein."[32] In seizing its authentic possibilities for being, Dasein is made master of the world and soars above itself "to tragic solitude."[33] In grasping its existence entirely in this world, Dasein is finally able to overpower the world.[34] In this manner, falling into the world becomes a vehicle for spirit discovering itself.[35] Bonhoeffer concludes, "Certainly Heidegger fully understands the man questioning himself to be the basic problem, but in the end, the question becomes the answer, man in fact has knowledge of himself, the question has no ultimate seriousness."[36] Once again a conception of human being ("solipsistically posited Dasein"), though guised in a new and arresting terminology, asserts the supremacy of transcendental subjectivity.[37]

What does Bonhoeffer make of Dasein's final presumption to dominate the world? Clearly, he does not see this as philosophy's triumph but as yet another symptom of the self turned inward. "The I really remains in itself and that is not its credit, but its guilt."[38] To be sure, theology's own thinking of the person is governed by its reference to limitedness (*die Schranke*); but limitation, in Bonhoeffer's view, can only be established by God. Any limit internal to experience is subverted by the possibility of going beyond it. (This is the reflexive irony the idealist philosophers detected in Kant's doctrine of the thing-in-itself; conceiving the limit is already a step beyond it.) But as Bonhoeffer argues, in the divine confrontation with the living God of Jesus Christ, the person is "taken out of himself" and turned outward before God so that now in this recentering of self, "the question [of being] becomes serious because it no longer itself includes its answer, but instead the answer is given completely freely and completely afresh to the person by God."[39] Only in the act of God's self-witness in Jesus Christ is human being faced with the truth of being.

Thus, Bonhoeffer holds that the category of potentiality can have no place in a theology of revelation, for revelation is based on the decisive event of Jesus Christ, fully actualized in time and history. In the inaugural lecture, he summarizes his point.

First, potentiality presumes the supremacy of self-mediation as the final arbiter of truth. Second, potentiality "rationalizes" reality, defining it in the fashion of a logical entity. Rationalization of the real carries with it the implicit claim that the location of the unity of self-understanding is the I. In Bonhoeffer's view this claim leads to the idea that thinking of God and thinking about thinking are one in the same activity. Thus, the relation between self and God is construed as fluid and interchangeable such that the interplay and interpenetration of human and divine overrides the decisive limitation enacted by revelation. Third, *potentiality* as a theological category obscures the *reality* that the person either stands in or outside revelation. More to the point, as a self-generated reality, there is nothing in the event of revelation that warrants its qualification as a possible state of affairs. God has spoken of himself truthfully in Jesus Christ; this event narrates the decisive *identity* of God that must in all cases precede and regulate descriptions of the *presence* of God.[40] Fourth, a theology shaped by potentiality is vulnerable to lapses into semi-Pelagianism. If sin and faith reside within humankind's potentialities, then, according to Bonhoeffer, "the complete incomprehensibility, inexcusability, infinity of the fall is rationalized into an explicable realization of immanent possibilities."[41] According to Bonhoeffer, sin is not an ontic or "existentiell" quality of which fallenness, guilt, and the like are ontological or "existential" interpretations, for sin is fundamentally—pervasively—ontological. Sin is the *primordial condition* within which any genuine theology must be situated. Finally, the concept of potentiality compromises the provisionality of a limit between human and divine. If being in truth is part of the person's potentiality-for-Being, then revelation's prevenience appears compromised. Yet Bonhoeffer—not wanting to capitulate to metaphysical dualisms—uses caution in his argument for the necessity of limitation by adding a threefold clarification to his point. (1) The limit between God and world is not the "formal limit" of structural difference as between two entities. Rather, the theological limit is personal in nature; difference is shaped by the moral disposition of respect and love. (2) The content of the limit with regard to the relation of God and humankind is defined by the concepts of sin and holiness— by an anthropological and a theological axiom. Anthropologically, human reason is fallen and cannot properly understand God apart from God's prevenient self-articulation. Theologically, humanity cannot know God apart from an original being known by God for, as in Luther's simple apology, only God is God.[42] Theological and anthropological realities coalesce in the shaping of the barrier between God and humankind. (3) Theology's glad message is the crossing of this limit *by God* through the forgiveness of sins in redemption and reconciliation and the nurturing of people by the Holy Spirit in sanctification. The concept of the limit in theology is delineated only by the dynamic reality of God.[43]

If the theologian must reject the category of potentiality for a thinking about God, world, and self, a positive consideration must be put in its place: humankind does not understand itself in self-reflection but only in the act of reference to God.[44] Only in the *actus directus* of faith toward Christ is there real self-understanding, for the object of faith (Jesus Christ) empowers the self to be drawn out of its insularity into sacrificial and agapeic relation with others. Hans-Richard Reuter says, "Individualistic striving for dominance of the self-empowered subjectivity is broken in 'obedience' and 'following.'"[45] The I becomes the child, the child becomes the disciple, and the disciple follows after in togetherness with others.[46]

The Continuity of Community

In *Act and Being* Bonhoeffer raises the question of personal continuity as a critical theological issue. There is an important theological background to this question that I will briefly describe.

As I explained in Chapter 1, Bonhoeffer's early criticisms of Barth are focused primarily on the problem of continuity implicit in the actualistic description of revelation. Barth demonstrated repeatedly the dialectical pattern of presenting the futility of the theological task (for only God can speak a truthful word about God) alongside the urgency of taking the risk to speak about God (despite God's unspeakability). This paradox is not resolved in Barth's early thought but weaves itself into the very fabric of theological discourse. Bonhoeffer finds no coherent way in Barth's dialectical theology to conceive the continuity of the new I in Christ. As Barth says, "[By] faith we are what we are not."[47] Bonhoeffer wants instead to understand the connection between the act and being of God so as to ensure the continuities of (1) God in himself, (2) God in relation to the world, (3) human community, and (4) individual subjectivity in itself.

Similarly, Bonhoeffer insists that Heidegger's being-toward-death cannot secure personal continuity since the return to authenticity (*Sein-zum-Tode*) from the condition of being-in guilt (*Schuldigsein*) is contingent on Dasein's own resoluteness and potentiality-for-being. Potentiality scatters the historical and personal concreteness of the self, and concomitantly the totality of revelation, into an impressionism of decisions, resolutions, and repetitions. Bonhoeffer remarks, "The problem here is how Dasein *qua* decision can be envisaged in continuity. This might appear simple if Dasein could be thought to decide over and over again for the 'possibility most its own.'"[48] But in fact there is a continual straying of Dasein from the authenticating mark of the total end. Authentic being is realized only as an "intermittence" of inauthentic being. There is an entrenchment of Dasein into the redundancies and circularities of the everyday, which impedes the continuity of human being's authentic existence.

Like Barth, Bonhoeffer holds that continuity is gained only through a movement extrinsic to the person. A continuity which does not impinge on existence is not the continuity of Christian revelation; it is not continuous *being* but fleeting, passing-by *entity*. However, unlike the dialectical Barth and in anticipation of the Barth of the *Church Dogmatics*, Bonhoeffer holds that theology must establish of revelation that God "is" in it, and of the person that he "is" before he acts and acts only out of that "being."[49] Revelation must be understood such that its being and existence underlie, precede, and embrace the being and existence of the I—such that the being of God underlies, precedes, and embraces the human being in the act of revealing himself in Jesus Christ. Bonhoeffer says, "This is where a *genuine* ontology comes into its own, inasmuch as it defines the 'being in . . .' in such a way that cognition, finding itself in the world of entity, suspends itself when confronted by the being of the entity and does not force it under its control."[50] What is meant, then, by the unity of the historical I in faith is unity in life together (both preceding and embracing personal identity, both transcending and preserving personal identity), in the historical community which is confessed in word and sacrament. Bonhoeffer explains as follows: "Because the humanity wherein I stand, which I myself also am, prays for me, forgives sins (in preaching and sacrament) independently of me, being always the whole humanity wherever I am, just because I am its member, my everydayness is overcome within the communion: only there am I embraced both as individual and as humanity, in existentiality and continuity."[51]

Thus, the being of God in revelation is not being-in-potentiality ("Sein als Seinskönnen") but being in Christ as the concreteness of community. The difference of God and world is preserved through the good news that God in his freedom shows himself to be with the world without either forsaking his divinity or annulling the world's worldliness. God is recognized to be a God who because he is for himself in trinitarian community is also for the world in human community. As Jüngel puts it, "From all eternity, God *is in and of himself* in such a way that he is *for* man. As the Eternal he is for perishable man, whose perishability has its ground in this Pro-Being of God, a ground which prevents the process of perishing from ending in nothingness."[52] In Bonhoeffer's axiom "Christus als Gemeinde existierend," God differentiates himself from himself, without ceasing to be the one living God in this self-differentiation.[53] God abdicates total difference from the world for the sake of being for us, with us, and among us in life together.

Being-in Christ

In my view, Bonhoeffer's most important criticism of Heidegger is implicit in the difference between Heidegger's conception of being-with others and Bonhoeffer's being-in Christ. My discussion of this criticism involves explicating its far-ranging implications for theological thinking about the meaning of selfhood, otherness, and community.

From the outset Bonhoeffer dismisses the identification of being-in Christ with doctrine, institution, or psychic experience. All three are inadequate because they have the effect of reducing the divine being to an entity in the world. Since in principle the being of any entity is objective for proof (*Aufweis*) or for intuitive perception (*für das Schauen*), the crucial issue for Bonhoeffer is to conceive God in contradistinctive priority to any entity.[54] This amounts to thinking how revelation is prior to and yet present in life together. Bonhoeffer claims that the axiom "Christ existing as community" allows one to proceed beyond the impasse of imagining revelation in terms of either strict nonobjective conceptions of God (God as the "not" of any entitative designation) or strict objective conceptions of God (God as some entity); for as community God enjoys "a mode of being which embraces both entity and non-entity, while at the same time 'suspending' within itself man's intention of it."[55] As Bonhoeffer puts the point theologically, revelation as the concrete reality prior to any ontology of relationality must (1) challenge and constrain the self, (2) be independent of its being known, and (3) confront the self in such a way that the person's own relations to and knowledge of others are based on and suspended in a being-already related to and known. Conceived as entity, revelation would be malleable to human knowledge; it would be a deposit over which the person or the collection of persons could have recourse at will. But conceived as community, revelation satisfies these criteria in a number of different ways.

Bonhoeffer's way of keeping either of the two philosophical terms *difference* and *identity*—otherness or totality—from becoming exclusive descriptions of God and world is the christological conviction: God is the divine subject self-witnessed in the presence of Christ as community. As such, God shows himself to be a God whose aseity is interpreted by his promeity. God relinquishes total aseity for the sake of the world, but in relinquishing aseity for the sake of the world God demonstrates the aseity proper to his being: his being is always a being-for.

One way of illustrating this point, a way that also avoids the mistake of conceiving divine relinquishment as divine self-negation, is to think of God's turning out from trinitarian community toward humanity as the overflowing of God—as God's overabounding of himself in love. That is, God's never-exhausted giving of mercy and grace cannot be counted a possession in which he indulges himself; rather, it is an overabundance; "a going with himself beyond himself."[56] Inasmuch as God's going with himself out of himself expresses the very essence of God, this creative activity also determines the essence of humanity. As Saint Augustine said, because God is love, *we are*.[57] Or stated in a revision of Western trinitarian thought, *Christ* is the *vinculum amoris*; as the mediator of genuine, agapeic love, Christ is the ecstasy of the Godhead. The love of the Father, the Son, and the Holy Spirit is great enough to embrace the whole world.[58] However, God's promeity ought not to be understood as an effect emanating from him, nor as an accident, but as the essence, the being of the personal God himself."[59] God's being there is always a being-there for the world. Therefore, to think of the world as the overflowing of God's love, and thereby to *begin* with God alone, to see all the world as a movement between God and God, means to begin with the "infinitely abundant God" whose abundance should be understood not as ownership or possession but as overflowing. John J. O'Donnell's assessment of this trinitarian perspective applies directly to Bonhoeffer's purpose: "God is neither supreme object over against humanity nor the supreme Thou depending on the human I for fulfillment. God is in his own life interpersonal communion, and because God in his own being is love, God can be love for us, a love which is free and gratuitous. The love which God *is* overflows into creation and time."[60] God's overabounding love in Jesus Christ is then the source from which human overabounding in togetherness freely springs. God redefines or reenacts the meaning of God *a se*, so that a-seity *is* always in reference to an other.[61] In this manner, those who are in Christ are freed to live for and with the other.

I take all of this also to be part of Bonhoeffer's corrective of Heidegger. In Christ, the I is drawn out of itself "into the social sphere of persons,"[62] though not as a self-losing into sheer equivocal difference but as a self-finding in life together. In responding faithfully to the call of Christ, the self is reshaped as a self for others. Bonhoeffer says, "Where the I has truly come to the end, truly reaches out of itself, where its grasp is more than a final 'seeking of the self in the self,' there Christ is at work."[63] Without Christ my neighbor is no more than the possibility of my own self-assertion.[64]

However, since Bonhoeffer does not provide a sustained critique of Heidegger at the level of a theological social ontology of intersubjectivity, I would like to venture what I think is Bonhoeffer's legacy for this critical task.

If the fundamental *theological* question Bonhoeffer addresses to Heidegger is "What are the implications of the existential analytic of Dasein for an understanding of revelation?" the fundamental *anthropological* question he raises is "What are the implications of the existential analytic for an understanding of human togetherness?" Heidegger claims to get beyond the isolated subject of the transcendental tradition in his description of Dasein's constitutive being-with others. In projecting itself, Dasein projects a world which is always with the others (*Mitwelt*). He says, "Being-in is Being-with Others" (118:155). Others are encountered from out of the world in which human being essentially dwells, in its "with-world" of Dasein such that the worldliness of Dasein connects the other to the I. "This Dasein-with of the Others is disclosed within-the-world for a Dasein, and so too for those who are Daseins with us, only because *Dasein in itself is essentially Being-with*" (120:156). Heidegger claims that Being-with and Dasein-with are structures of human being that are equiprimordial with Being-in-the-World (114:149). Our being in the world is always a being with others. Thus, the original interrelation of being-with and being-in-the-world confirms that the being-there-with of the other is co-present in Dasein, and thereby always already understood in the elemental world projection.[65]

But problems immediately arise with Heidegger's description. Despite whatever intentions he might have to depict togetherness as aboriginal to Dasein, his description has the consequent effect of consolidating the other with the I. Although Heidegger argues that Dasein-with is a characteristic of Dasein's other through the being-with of Dasein's being-in-the-world, nonetheless, the world is always a referential totality *for the sake of the I that is Dasein.*[66] Thus, being-with-one-another is represented by *my relation* to the other and not by the relation of the other to me.[67] Although it is true that human being does not encounter the other through knowing but in *caring for* ("Fürsorge") and *taking care of* ("Besorgen"), the other is still recontained in the I such that the conception of the self-finding or self-discovery of the I in the other can never be attained. Alien being-there, to the extent that it is mediated by world, is worked down to the point that is in itself empty, for the other "receives its determinateness only out of 'with-like' ("mithaften") traces in the 'world,'"[68] In short, Being-with and Dasein-with constitute "structures of Dasein" (114:149): the experience of the other remains thoroughly self-mediated.

The connection Heidegger makes between being-with others and the "they" ("das Man") only exacerbates the problem. One's own Dasein, like the Dasein-with of others, is encountered originally in terms of the *with-world*, with which and in which we are environmentally concerned, that world of our everyday intercourse with people (125:163). In this everyday world, others are encountered "as what they are" (126:163); the "who" of these others is the "they." For example, in using public transportation, information services, and similar conveniences of modern technology, every other becomes indistinguishable from the next. We take pleasure and enjoyment in terms dictated by what "they" consider pleasurable and enjoyable.[69] The "they self" approximates the "self of everyday Dasein," or in more familiar words, the inauthentic self. Worst of all, inauthentic existence distorts the elemental voice of Being and suppresses the question of being in the numbing multiplicity of the everyday's demands and requirements. "Overnight, everything that is primordial gets glossed over as something that has long been well known. Everything gained by a struggle becomes just something to be manipulated. Every secret loses its force. The care of averageness reveals in turn an essential tendency of Dasein which we call the 'leveling down' of all possibilities of Being" (127:165). The social self is tantamount to the inauthentic self.

Why is this the case? Inauthentic Dasein does not understand itself from its own potentiality but from the world of public concern. Inauthentic Dasein is the one that is "completely fascinated by the 'world' and by the Dasein-with of Others in the they" (176:220). In Theunissen's reading of Heidegger, fallenness in the world is nothing less than fascination with others.[70] Consequently, since inauthenticity awaits Dasein's entrance into the "they," Dasein ascends to authentic being not only by freeing itself *from* the domination of others but by turning away from others—by turning to its authentic end in the process of radical individualization.[71] To be sure, individualization for Heidegger is reputed to make authentic being-with possible, for Dasein individualized down to its ownmost possibility remains authentic being that is in the world and thus still with the other. But there persists the nagging question of how individual and community (or individualization and communalization) can even be concretely brought together in Heidegger's ontology. Has his analysis, as Bonhoeffer suspected, fallen into the univocal sameness of self-constitution and turned out to be simply (and yet) another narrative of the I's mastery over self, world, and God?

Heidegger very often equates inauthentic everydayness with

being with others. The real potentialities of Dasein are not realized through the quotidian banalities and artistries (let us not forget) of the everyday, which are reportedly governed by indifference and shallowness.[72] For the "who" of the everyday is everybody and nobody.[73] Inauthenticity shapes the general character of being-with-one-another, for authentic being occurs only as an "intermittence" of inauthentic being—"its authenticity lies in such an indirectness because, in another sense, it enjoys no authentic, that is, direct, being-with-one-another."[74] Thus, the intermittence of authenticity occurs only in the process of individualization, in that most extreme of solitary comportments, being-toward-death. Heidegger says, "In the anticipatory revealing of this potentiality-for-Being, Dasein discloses itself to itself as regards its uttermost possibility" (262:307). What it means to be authentic is this winnowing down of the self that dwells alongside and with others to its innermost individuality. Death throws Dasein back from togetherness to its sequestered singleness. Inasmuch as death is my ownmost possibility, it is also the enactment of pure nonrelationality. Heidegger explains as follows: "The non-relational character of death, as understood in anticipation, individualizes Dasein down to itself. This individualizing is a way in which the 'there' is disclosed for existence. It makes manifest that all Being-alongside the things with which we concern ourselves, and all Being-with others, will fail us when our ownmost potentiality-for-Being is the issue. Dasein can be *authentically itself* only if it makes this possible for itself of its own accord" (263:308). Dasein is then only authentic if it projects itself upon its ultimate possibility-for-being, rather than upon the possibilities of other selves. Even if authentic Dasein can exist formally as a being-with others, the latter never works its way into my ownmost being.[75]

To be sure, Heidegger does think that Dasein's ultimate possibility-for-being enables it precisely to have "some understanding of the potentiality-for-Being of Others" (264:309). Being-toward-death breaks the shackles of Dasein's domination of the other by giving the other over to its ownmost possibility, in freeing the other to be itself. Dasein's resoluteness toward death makes it possible for others to be freed in their being-toward-death from attempts to control them. But despite Heidegger's belief that freeing the other to itself is a positive consequence of Dasein's being-toward-death, the result of such freeing is the disconnection of any genuine bond between I and other. Habermas is correct to say that the idea that subjects are coterminously "individuated and socialized . . . cannot be accommodated in Heidegger's view.[76] For Dasein as in each case my own "constitutes being-with in the same way that the transcendental ego constitutes the inter-subjectivity of the world shared by myself and others."[77] Since Dasein lives in and through the other in inauthenticity, anticipatory resoluteness, that is, authenticity, brings about the dispossession of the other. Others can only be freed *for themselves* to the extent to which they are freed *from me*.[78] Further, others can only be freed *for themselves* to the extent to which they are freed *from me* and freed from me for the sake of the I that is Dasein.

Let me make one more point before concluding. In discussing authentic being-with, Heidegger attends to the difference between (what he calls) Dasein's "leaping-in" for the other and its "leaping ahead" of him. The former—a leaping-in—involves a domination of the other through a kind of violent divestiture of the other's own concerns. "This kind of solicitude takes over for the other that with which he is to concern himself" (122:158). The latter—a leaping ahead—is a way of relating to the other that does not dispossess the other of its own concerns but gives them back to him "authentically as such for the first time" (122:159). In both cases, however, being-with comes about through "indirectness" and "negativity." The originary I has no constitutive partner. For either I can make the other person's concerns my own and thus dominate him or her or I can free the other from me.[79] In both cases again, the result is the aboriginal aloneness of the self.[80] Theunissen's bleak assessment follows: "The unrelatedness of death casts its shadow upon every communication and, in the voice of conscience, gives the listening Dasein to understand that, in the final analysis, it is alone."[81]

Bonhoeffer's purpose in *Act and Being* is to celebrate the turning of the self outward in community. The one who is in Christ is released from the absolute solitariness of death. Directed toward the crucified and risen Christ, our own deaths have this twofold intention of suffering and gladness. It is important to recognize that Bonhoeffer is not advancing a kind of cheap atonement that would abrogate the integrity and concreteness of human agony; we are not immune from suffering and pain. As he says in the christology lectures, "We have the Exalted One only as the Crucified, the Sinless One only as the one laden with guilt, the Risen One only as the Humiliated One."[82] All human suffering and weakness are a sharing in God's own suffering and in God's weakness in the world. Our suffering is, in a real way, a participation in the sufferings of God, for God is a God who suffers, who knows powerlessness and humility. Yet the powerlessness of God coinheres in God's power, suffering coinheres in wholeness, death in resurrection. In this coinherence Christ assumes life (power) and perishability (powerlessness) for the sake of life (power which knows powerlessness).[83]

Christ existing as community provides the space wherein I move from the powerlessness and agony of *my* individual death to the gladness of *our* dying in Christ—and hence our being given new life. In Christ death no longer confronts me as my ownmost individualizing prospect. For even as I am now more than the "I am here," namely, "I am in Christ together with others," my death is a dying into this mysterious togetherness. The sense here is not the facile notion that when I die, a part of the community goes with me—as Bonhoeffer says of Luther's idea of death, "He is not trying to express the platitudinous and doubtful wisdom that a sorrow shared is a sorrow halved"[84]—but rather that my death is a dying into community, and, as a result, not even my death breaks the continuity of being-in Christ. Bonhoeffer says, "Sin and death, therefore reach into the communion of Christ, but this they do in such a way that the communion now bears with me my sin and my death, while I likewise no longer see sin and death in the communion—in Christ himself—but only forgiveness and life."[85] Death is thus no longer "my central condemnation." Its individualizing solitariness is displaced by the active subject of Christ existing as community.

Bonhoeffer then gives voice to the magnificient theme of *Act and Being*: "The freedom of God has bound itself into the personal communion, and precisely that demonstrates itself as God's freedom—that God should bind Himself to humanity."[86] Binding is not a metaphor that indicates identity or monistic domination, but communion with others. Therefore, in genuine community I am not freed from the other, nor do I give the other over to its alien autonomy, but I am free for and with the other. "Christ as the one for others" is not merely an exemplary ethical standard but an expression of, and a way of talking in concrete terms about, the ontological transformation of people in Christ. Bonhoeffer says, "Christ is Christ, not just for himself, but in relation to me. His being Christ is his being for me, *pro me*. The core of the person himself is the *pro me*."[87] God's overabundant love is the cosmic and personal source of Christ's overabounding of the person in community.

Resistance

What is finally most troublesome about Heidegger's attempts to understand the meaning of Being by attending to the way Being discloses itself (either through Dasein or later through the elemental words of Being) is that talk about Being becomes "propositionally contentless speech."[88] "Being," or even its authentic mode of being-toward-death, lacks coherent ethical content and too easily disposes one toward resignation to fate. Of course, fate itself means nothing more than the shaping of specific historical-political powers in concrete situations. Hence, the practical-political side of authentic Dasein consists, as Habermas obliquely says, in "the perlocutionary effect of a diffuse readiness to obey in relation to an auratic but indeterminate authority."[89] There is a loss of the objective framework of human society and "an idealistic compression" of historical consciousness into the domain of self-experience.[90]

When Bonhoeffer says in *Life Together* that "one is a brother to another person only through Jesus Christ," he is emphasizing that self-relation and relation with others must be mediated in a theologically and ethically meaningful way; they cannot be adequately explained in terms of an empty resoluteness. Empty resoluteness lends itself readily to giddy jingoism. But Christ existing as community militates against the presumption of any institution or world leader to boast divine certification. In confessing Christ, we are saying Christ, not Hitler, not America, not anything or anyone else. Even so, Christ means even more than the negation of all idols. As life together, Christ repositions the person in a being in and out of agapeic togetherness. As life together, Christ activates the living consciousness of the other as neighbor and enables the self to have found once again an origin that was obscured when the I indulged itself in "that 'solitude' out of which it constitutes the world as its own."[91] For Christ is present in the world as the overflowing love of God, turning us away from self-will and self-determination, outward to life for the sake of others.

III

The Self for Others

7

The Overabundant I

On 30 May 1944, Bonhoeffer, in Tegel prison more than a year, wrote to his friend Eberhard Bethge:

> I'm sitting alone upstairs. Everything is quiet in this building; a few birds are singing outside, and I can even hear the cuckoo in the distance. I find these long, warm summer evenings, which I'm living through here for the second time, rather trying. I long to be outside, and if I were not "reasonable," I might do something foolish. I wonder whether we have become too reasonable. When you've deliberately suppressed every desire for so long, it may have one of two bad results: either it burns you up inside, or it all gets so bottled up that one day there is a terrific explosion. It is, of course, conceivable that one may become completely selfless, and I know better than anyone else that that hasn't happened to me. Perhaps you will say that one oughtn't to suppress one's desires, and I expect you would be right. But look, this evening for example I couldn't dare to give really full rein to my imagination and picture myself and Maria at your house, sitting in the garden by the water and talking together into the night etc. etc. That is simply self-torture, and gives one physical pain. So I take refuge in thinking, in writing letters, in delighting in your good fortune, and curb my desires as a measure of self-protection. However paradoxical it may sound, it would be more selfless if I didn't need to be so afraid of my desires, and could give them free rein—but that is very difficult.[1]

Bonhoeffer longs to be outside, to be free of the unbearable tedium of confinement and seclusion. His thoughts digress. "Separation from people, from work, from the past, from the future, from marriage, from God. . . . Smoke in the emptiness of time. . . . The significance of illusion. . . . Suicide not because of consciousness of guilt but because I am already dead."[2] Prison—the metaphor of intolerable self-enclosure—has now become real, ironically vicious and mocking. "Dissatisfaction, tension, impatience, longing, boredom, sick—profoundly alone, indifference."[3]

In *Act and Being*, written a decade and a half earlier in 1929, Bonhoeffer described the world-constitutive claims of autonomous reason as a cry that only "dissembles the mute loneliness of isolation," sounding "without echo into the world governed and construed by the self," keeping the self a "prisoner to itself."[4] Human identity conceived as self-idenfication approximates the anthropological postulate of humanity ruled by the will to self.[5] In this situation, which Bonhoeffer calls being in Adam, the person "reaches the confines of his solitude."[6] Thinking itself to be knowledgeable of the truth, the self-sufficient subject turns ever inward: all relations to others are reduced to relations of the self as an *inconcussum fundamentum veritatis*, an incorrigible foundation of truth.[7] There is convolution of a most insidious kind in this adamic self. How does one get outside? How does one break free?

In another letter from Tegel, this time to his parents the morning after a long night of air raids and sirens, Bonhoeffer's thoughts about himself turn in a different direction. "It's remarkable how we think at such time about the people that we should not like to live without, and almost or entirely forget about ourselves. It is only then we feel how closely our own lives are bound up with other people's, and in fact how the center of our own lives is outside ourselves, and how little we are separate entities."[8] In an eloquent and tragic way, Bonhoeffer's prison inscriptions illuminate the glad deliverance of life together. "Our relation to God is a new life in 'existence for others,' through participation in the being of Jesus."[9] Bonhoeffer envisions a motion of the self toward the other and of the other toward the self that recreates both in agapeic fellowship. Indeed, Christ calling the person to follow after is the way into this extrinsicality, for in the calling, the "twisted and intricate knottiness" (Augustine) of self-encapsulation is disentangled and redirected toward "the Crucified and Risen One."[10] Christ's calling is God's saving act and humanity's salvation, an invitation, as in Rilke's poem, "to step out of my heart and go walking beneath the enormous sky."[11] The ever-spiraling circuities of monadological solitude are interrupted in the alternating movement of summons and obedience.

In this chapter I will conclude Bonhoeffer's explication of the secondary objectivity of revelation by focusing on the particular question of selfhood. How is the self reshaped in the life of following after Jesus Christ? I provide a more systematic account of the refigured self than developed in the preceding chapters. I wish to show that the continuity of revelation is not particular only to (1) God in himself (*a se*), (2) God in relation to the world (*ad extra*), and (3) human community, or the continuity of the self and its others, but also to (4) selfhood, or human subjectivity in itself. I proceed as follows. First, I discuss Bonhoeffer's conception of christological relation in the context of the person in fellowship with others. Second, I engage this conception with Robert Scharlemann's postmodern description of the ecstatic I of "acoluthetic reason" (or "reason that follows"). I offer a response to Scharlemann from the perspective of the logic of following implicit in Bonhoeffer's theology. From this vantage point, I discuss the theological and ethical problems in Scharlemann's argument and explain why Bonhoeffer's approach renders inadequate his depiction of the "ecstatic I" as the primary mode of christological experience. Finally, I conclude by offering a constructive proposal for developing a conception of selfhood informed by Bonhoeffer's theology—one which might be called trinitarian self-becoming.

Christological Relation

As early as 1928, while working as an assistant minister to the German-speaking congregation in Barcelona, Bonhoeffer was intrigued by the ecstatic quality of life in Christ. In these early manuscripts, the dynamic of faith was understood in reference to faith's character as a disposition of freedom. For example, in the essay "What Is a Christian Ethic?" Bonhoeffer stood in solidarity with his unlikely cobelligerent Friedrich Nietzsche against the notion of Christianity as ethical religion. Without knowing it, Bonhoeffer says, Nietzsche introduces in the concept of the *Übermensch* many aspects of the freedom of being-in Christ. "Time-honored morals . . . can never for the Christian become the standard of action."[12] Ethics contrives eternal norms, deracinating them from time and circumstance; it signifies the hubris of the desire to live above the complexity of concrete situations.[13] Contrarily, the Nietzschean sense of the I in faith, as the young Bonhoeffer envisages it, involves the tellurian pulse of freedom in Christ. In faith, the person does not ascend into a realm of atemporal ethical norms or become paradoxically related to time and history. "[The] one who would leave the earth, who would depart from the present anxieties, forsakes the power which holds him."[14] Rather, faith liberates the person precisely to "remain earthbound," for "a glimpse of eternity is revealed only through the depths of our earth."[15] This is the Christian's song of earth.

There are resonances in the Barcelona text that Bonhoeffer would soon silence. Theologically, he grew to distrust his Kierkegaardian and existentialist description of the self-God encounter, exemplified by a claim such as: "Only through the call of God does this 'I' become isolated from all others, drawn into responsibility by God, knowing itself to confront eternity alone."[16] Yet there are also momentous historical factors that propel his increasing uneasiness with many of the images of his Barcelona lecture. When Bonhoeffer returned to Berlin in February 1929, he entered a Germany in which enormous political changes were under way. He quickly became more clear-headed, less mawkish, about the matter of the self's transmorality of freedom, and for good reason. During the autumn of the same year, the "Stahlhelm," the nationalists, and the Nazis (the last weak in numbers but highly vociferous) collectively organized a national petition for the drafting of a law against the enslavement of the German people by the Young Plan (a program of reparations denounced by the Nazis as the cowardice of defeatist politicians accepting the Treaty of Versailles).[17] Racist sentiment was emerging; blood, soil, and earth jargon found favor among even the nation's most tenacious thinkers. Consequently, jingoistic passages such as occur in the Barcelona addresses never cross Bonhoeffer's lips again, for, as Bethge says, "he now saw them transformed into nationalistic slogans and bound up with anti-Semitic propaganda."[18]

Nevertheless, the texts of the Spanish interlude call attention to a theme which takes on an almost compulsive role in the works to follow: the new self does not try to contain others in self-mediating identity, but in Christ the person is reconfigured in the freedom of life with others. As Bonhoeffer says, "When Jesus places men immediately under God, new and afresh at each moment, he restores to mankind the immense gift which it had lost, freedom."[19] In becoming the new center of the real, Jesus Christ is the new center of human being, in both its unique particularity and its corporate expressiveness. This double emphasis cannot be compromised for the important reason that from the start Bonhoeffer refuses to decimate the inner integrity of the person in his explication of the christological axiom "Christ existing as community." Although some passages in the literature seem to intimate self-negation, nonetheless, one of his most important and consistent anthropological claims is that being in Christ in no way occasions the diffusion of the individual into a communal monism.[20] Rather, between individual and community a reciprocity coheres which is enriched through a dialectical fertilization of self and other. As a result, Bonhoeffer can show that even though there is an unavoidable teleological structure in the relation of individual and community, inasmuch as life with others capacitates the person's genuine humanity, the integrity of the particular individual remains indispensable. I *am* incomplete when I am alone, but when I live together with others in community, the I that I am does not disseminate into plurality (nor does it consume the plurality of others); rather, it remains what it is even while being more than it is in Christ's overabounding love.

Therefore, according to Bonhoeffer, the claim of the other that fractures the infrastructural totality of the system and intrudes into the presumed continuities of self-identity qua self-mediation does not incite the disappearance of the self. The loss of the centered self (the self whose identity with others is secured in self-centering) does not warrant frenetic announcements of the disappeared self. While the other is constitutively different from the I and is not reducible to the grasp of the subject, neither is the subject in turn absorbed by the other.[21] Decentering as nihilation, dissemination, and the like might energize strategies useful to wage war against the idols, but it can never inspire the coherence which fashions community. In the striking language of the Epistle to the Hebrews: "We are not of those who shrink back to destruction, but of those who have faith in the preserving of the soul" (10:39). Life together establishes and restores our genuine humanity as individual persons, even as our individuality attains authenticity only in life with others.

In losing ourselves we find ourselves; and in finding ourselves we lose ourselves. There is a kind of swinging from the losing to the finding and back again, and this is the new song and the new life of God in Jesus Christ; this is the dynamic that protests against the static, and the continuity that defeats disintegration. Likewise, in the new space of revelation, there can be movement away from the center of Christ, and then back from the periphery to the center; the center always holds sure.

I think it is helpful to understand the seemingly paradoxical conception of self-losing and self-finding in terms of a social ontology which makes a distinction between the *genesis* and the *goal* of the self. In this manner, from the perspective of a christological model we can redescribe the transcendental interpretation of intersubjectivity—that view that considers the self the center of all relations to others. I turn again to Michael Theunissen's work in social ontology for conceptual help in this task of redescription. Theunissen offers the intriguing suggestion that we consider the source of the self as the "dialogical self-becoming of the individual I."[22] This is neither a concession to the philosophy of dialogue nor to transcendental intersubjectivity but a means of moving beyond these exhausted options to a conception which resolves their respective contradictions. How is this the case? According to Theunissen, the contradiction, often construed as constitutional between the philosophy of dialogue and transcendental intersubjectivity, runs to the effect that the latter affirms as the absolute original (in short, self-mediating subjectivity as the condition of the possibility of relation with others) what the former affirms as futural (relation with the other as the condition of the possibility of self-relation), and that the discourse of the other ascribes primacy to the veritable reality (meeting the other, or the between of I and other) to which the transcendental tradition endows only a secondary significance.[23] What is required in order to overcome the contradiction is that an intersection between the two be located on which to proceed even in view of their mutual shortcomings. Theunissen holds that conceiving selfhood in terms of the dialogical self-becoming of the individual I puts us in a position to reckon with the conflict between these respective claims to originality by granting to transcendental philosophy the originality of genesis and to the philosophy of dialogue the originality of the goal or completed end.[24] He says, "The beginning would be my individual I, the goal the self that proceeds from the meeting."[25] Self-mediation is essential at the level of the genesis of the self, but it must be reshaped in the complex dynamic of community. Therefore, in thinking through the dialogical self-becoming of the individual I we sacrifice neither the integrity of subjectivity (its desires and dreams, its intractable and psychic need of care and attention) nor the necessity of life together. However, as Theunissen admits, it is not clear how to imagine the source of this self. *Something* must reconfigure selfhood, and the identities of the I, in order for the self to be what it is intended to be in togetherness with others. What this "something" is Theunissen cannot say.

The promise of Bonhoeffer's christological explication of the self for others is precisely its capacity to illustrate in an exquisitely nuanced way a conception of life together that originates in the identity of the subject and yet requires the movement of and to the outside to achieve its completed end. As I take it, Bonhoeffer's description of the movement of the subject as genesis (or original site of the departure to the other) to self-becoming in life with others is driven by the self's reconstitution in the christological relation—Christ as the source of the I becoming itself in the other, Christ existing as community reshaping the I in agapeic relation. Life together is the singing of the self outside itself.[26] Even as "God's freedom has bound itself, woven itself into the spiritual communion"[27] likewise, human freedom is taken captive, circumscribed by the concreteness of human sociality, enacted time and again in responsibility for and fellowship with the other.

Anticipating the well-known phrase of the prison documents, "Jesus as the one for others," Bonhoeffer wrote as early as his habilitation thesis, "Herein other persons become Christ for us in what they both demand and promise, in their existential impositions upon us from outside."[28] Being in Christ is not just living alongside other people of whom we think as Christ for us, but it is being the new I with others in Christ. This being with others in Christ cannot be confused with particular strategies of evangelism, nor must it be construed in any sort of confessional imperialism (such as "anonymous Christian"). Rather, from the perspective of the I in Christ, the other is to be accepted and cared for, not only because I see Christ in the other or because the other mirrors and reflects Christ—not even because I confess that Christ is one for the other. Rather, from the perspective of the I in Christ, the other is to be accepted and cared for because Christ's love transforms the self in new and radically unanticipated expressions of compassion and mercy.[29] This is agape love in its basic sense.

Therefore, we can see Bonhoeffer as proposing a christological redescription of the claims of transcendental intersubjectivity, including its dialogical constructions. His task involves the inner rethinking of this philosophical tradition so that otherness and plurivocity are not reduced to self-mediation; rather, plurivocity depends on the mediation of Christ as the one who inaugurates the intermediation between I and other. Significantly, this task does not entail the sophomoric debunking of Hegelian dialectic but a revision of the dialectical logic with the intention of sustaining the independence—indeed the interdependence—of the self and the other in a christological relation. A description of the self is given in the promise of Bonhoeffer's theology which holds at once the transcendental subject *as genesis* and the relational self-becoming of the individual I *as completed end* in the project of transformed selfhood.

I claim that the task outlined by Theunissen best belongs to theology and that Bonhoeffer's thought and life offer essential groundwork for such a challenging conceptual work. The person originates in the integral self of the I (of the I=I) and yet extends beyond itself in christological relation. The other person as such does not pattern this movement, but it is Jesus Christ who calls the person away from the presumptions of subjective constitution into fellowship with others. The new I in Christ does not proceed forth with the intention of recontaining the self in identity; it goes out to the other not to return as a recovered I but to remain as an extended or distended self, always more than the I, and always with an other who is really other, while still remaining the I that it is.

Scharlemann's Acoluthetic Reason

In his book *The Reason of Following: Christology and the Ecstatic I,* Robert Scharlemann has attempted to show that christology, beyond its articulation of a confession of faith, also demonstrates a form of reason with characteristics of its own. Since it is the case that in every form of reason there is a certain configuration of the self's relation to its other, christological reflection needs to direct itself toward the uncovering of that mode of reason contained in the experience of following after. Theology's age-old obsession with the problem of the two natures of Jesus Christ has been pursued at the expense of explicating a conception of selfhood contained in the logic of christology. As such, Scharlemann develops a phenomenology of "acoluthetic" reason by attending to the way the self comes to itself by being outside itself in the ecstasis of following after. This project has important consequences for my work of thinking through Bonhoeffer's conception of the new being in Christ.

Scharlemann has three main concerns in his book: to understand the universality of the self contained in the saying or thinking of the I; to understand the being of the self that appears in the connection demonstrated by the copula between the "I" and the particular person, and to understand the capacity of the self to be outside itself in ecstatic relation. I will focus on the last.

Acoluthetic or *christological reason* is defined as "that form of reason in which the I of selfhood is exstantial; the inwardness of the self is confronted with itself outwardly."[30] Scharlemann claims that it is critical to recognize this relation not as one of an I to a Thou or an it, but of the I to itself: the essential trait of this relation is that "it involves an ecstatic possibility of the ego."[31] The call to the disciple to follow the master is simultaneously the call of the self to be one's self. Scharlemann argues that genuine discipleship is shaped exclusively by freedom, but freedom is a product of autonomy alone. None other than the I itself can elicit such autonomy for, as he says, "we follow one whom we can never address as 'thou' but can hear as the 'I' of our own peace or wholeness."[32] The following of the disciple after the lord is not an expression of the one obedient to the other but of the "follower's coming to be an 'I' in the fullness of being I."[33]

Therefore, when Jesus says, "If anyone will come after me, let him take up his cross and follow me" (Mark 8:34) or "If any man would come after me, let him deny himself and take up his cross daily and follow me" (Luke 9:23), we are to understand the voice of Jesus not as an alien authority, that is, not as the subjection of the ego of the disciple to the ego of the lord, but rather "as the power by which the I comes to itself."[34] To be sure, Scharlemann's reading at this point can be taken to mean that the call of Jesus bids the disciple to come to the veritable source of life, therein to be whole and free. However, he adds, "The 'Follow me!' calls the hearers to disengage themselves from the cares of being in the world."[35] That they are to go out and proclaim the Good News of the risen Christ, shaking the dust off their sandals when the proclamation falls on deaf ears and living apart from the conventions of the everyday, means that they exist "only as ones who speak and hear a peace in and with the words" they know as truth.[36] This situation suggests to Scharlemann the elimination of all traces of heteronomy—of any conceivable obedience to a concrete other—and the victorious advent of autonomy as the heart of salvation. The call of the "I am" of Jesus is the summons to the follower to come to itself as an I; the disciple "becomes autonomous through following."[37]

In rejecting all aspects of obedience to an other, Scharlemann makes a peculiar distinction between the *christological relation*, wherein the I comes to itself through *self-reception*, and *agapeic relation*, wherein the I comes to itself through *self-giving*. This distinction is problematic. Although the two possibilities are complementary, Scharlemann claims that the latter is not the christological, precisely because in the latter the self comes to be its own in the other. Although agape love is "the relation in which the self can give itself up here in its own location and find itself in its location in another person," this relation evades acoluthetic reason proper inasmuch as it is primarily positioned in the heteronomous difference of the Thou. It seems that in Scharlemann's christological relation, the other has no business in the affairs of the I, even though in both self-reception and self-giving there is an appearance of the exstantial I.

Similarly, Scharlemann draws a distinction between *ethical* and *christological relation* and between *aesthetic* and *christological reason*. I turn first to the former distinction. In ethical reason, the one encountering me is a subjectivity other than my own; in christological reason, that which I am presented in relation is a subjectivity that *is* my own. The latter is a relation *not* of respect, as one finds in moral or ethical action, but of ecstasis. Scharlemann says, "[The] 'I' of which one is otherwise aware only inwardly and as different from the world and everything in it is now presented not as 'you' or an it but as an *ego extra me*."[38] In ethical relation the operative activity is respect inasmuch as the I which is there in the other who encounters me and whom I encounter is not my own. In christological relation, by contrast, the I which is presented to me is the same as (not simply analogous to) the I that is my own. Thus, in christological relation the authority of the Christ must be the authority of the self to take over itself—of the identity of the I and the I. Anything else would approximate an authority that represses one's own freedom and will.[39] To be sure, the disciples recognize in Jesus the longing of their deepest selves. However, Scharlemann radically individualizes this recognition when he says, "He is not for them a 'thou,' as he would be in ethical relation, but 'I'; he is their 'I am,' and their following him is their coming to themselves."[40] There is only the emergence of christological authority, and the activity of acoluthetic reason, when "the other in the relation is identical with the I of self and is recognized as such."[41]

Although the implications of Scharlemann's description of acoluthetic reason for a social ontology of life together appear bleak, he attempts to protect his view against the criticism that it concludes in a kind of monadological solitariness. Hence, he argues that acoluthetic reason ought not be construed so as to view the self as coming to itself within itself alone. There is an extrinsicality of the self that follows after; there is an alterating intentionality in acoluthetic reason. But Scharlemann's cryptic qualification does not adequately hold off the force of the criticism. He says, "Instead, the freedom of the self as I is constituted within and without, immanently and exstantially, so that the plenitude of the I as I includes its ecstasis as well as its being in place."[42] In the final analysis, it is only *within the I* that the I can be so constituted "within and without." Even though he invokes Tillich's notion of the cross as self-negating symbol to account for the necessary disappearance of the other in christological relation, in fact, the other *as other* never appears in Scharlemann's description. The social sphere does not enter into the experience of following after; or if it does, it appears as a single moment that must give way to a final and univocal self-constitution. The question to Scharlemann in conversation with Bonhoeffer is whether he means that there occurs in acoluthetic reason a correspondence between the master's call (who remains always the master) and the disciple's following after (which enables her or him to be a disciple) or that the call itself is enacted inside the total structure of the I.

That the exstantial subject of christological relation does not elicit, nor is moved by, any concrete social act, compels one to press Scharlemann on what he means by "the other." Moreover, that *personal encounter* of Jesus Christ is repositioned to an interior dynamic of subjectivity makes the question even more urgent.[43] *Who is Scharlemann's other? Where is the other? Is an other really there?*

The further distinction between aesthetic and christological reason confirms the urgency of these questions. Aesthetic reason, even more than ethical, is closer to christological reason in the way it comports the self toward itself. In aesthetic activity there is an identification of the self and its own I in the form of aesthetic representation. One of Scharlemann's examples of aesthetic experience is worth mentioning. If a person "admires" or "is entranced" by such a renowned work as the Mona Lisa, the person experiences a kind of self-losing or "self-transporting" into the very time and place of the painting itself. Herewith, the person forgets himself or herself as one who resides outside that world and, for a moment, the aesthetic receiver encounters his own I in the work of art. "The ecstasis of the occurrence lies in this dislocation or translocation of the subjectivity of the self."[44] Absolute identification is not essential here, for even an approximation of aesthetic self-forgetfulness is adequate as an account of aesthetic reason. Scharlemann muses, "When, say, beholding Matisse's Pianist and Checker Players, we find ourselves just for a moment in that room listening to the silent piano playing and oblivious of ourselves in our empirical surroundings."[45]

How does the aesthetic experience differ from the ecstasis proper to acoluthetic relation? Primarily it differs in respect to the self-awareness of the subject. In christological reason, the self is presented with its own I in the I's other. But the I does not herein forget its own being in the identification; rather the I is made "all the more conscious" of itself in the experience. Scharlemann says, "Instead of letting the self forget its being 'I' here, it enables the self to come to itself."[46] On the other hand, aesthetic reason projects the being of the I into the representation without assurance of any reunification. "The aesthetic identification allows the self to find itself in another without the need to return to itself here; the christological identification presents the self to itself outside itself and also returns itself to its being an I of its own here."[47] Christological reason, then, unlike aesthetic or ethical, is not forgetful, but is mindful of self. Further, christological reason, like aesthetic reason, is a relation of subject to subject, but unlike aesthetic reason, is not an "oblivion" of the "I" here. Acoluthetic reason is, in short, that form of reason in which "the inward I is related to the exstantial I through the authority (*exousia*) that enables the following."[48]

If there is an other there, an other who stands concretely apart from me, this one serves only as an instrumental means for my own self-possession. If there is an other there, for whom I care and to whom I show compassion and mercy, I can never reach it in Scharlemann's description of christological relation. As he claims, in christological relation the other of the I is really the I itself, "the introjection of the self's own ownness."[49] "Each of them, the projecting and the introjecting, is equally originating subjecthood, and each of them is with equal originality the singularity and absoluteness of the I as such."[50]

As far as I can tell, there is no biblical, historical, theological, or experiential warrant for this narrow definition of discipleship. Is there any evidence in the Gospel narratives or in the documents of the apostolic community that fosters a conception of discipleship that both constricts following after to this singular introjection of the self within itself and eviscerates discipleship of its ethical and social dynamic? Moreover, the divisions between christological, aesthetic, and ethical reason are inadequate to the task of thinking about the constitution of the new being in Christ.

Bonhoeffer's genius is to provide a way of proceeding beyond the alternatives of Scharlemann's systematic presentation of forms of reason. Implicit in Bonhoeffer's theology is the claim that christological relation contains truths found in the forms of ethical, aesthetic, and acoluthetic reason, without being identical to any of the three. In this way, his description refigures *acoluthetic reason* by means of the following structure: the new I in Christ does not venture forth in a gesture of trying to recontain itself as identity, but in being called out in simple obedience, the *exstantial I does not return* as a recovered or consummated I, but it remains, extended in life with others, always more than the I. The truth of *aesthetic reason*, the self finding itself in the other without recontainment in its own I, and the truth of acoluthetic reason, the introjection of the self within and without in the experience of self-identification, are brought together in the notion of the overabundant self: the self remains itself by being more than itself in life with others. The return of the self to itself is not the identification of I=I, but the union of self and other in fellowship mediated by Christ. The self forgotten can herein mean the same as the self over-abundant, if by overabundance we mean not limitlessness but ek-stasis as a following after and a being-for and with the other.

Similarly, Bonhoeffer's christological relation combines the truth of *ethical* reason to the extent to which the other remains apart from me in its constitutive difference, and the other *person* who encounters me is really the other one there, even while we partake together in the one reality of Christ. In Bonhoeffer's christological relation, the other person is bound to my own freedom and will; thus, I cannot abandon my responsibility to the other person without simultaneously abandoning the integrity of following after Jesus Christ. As Irenaeus eloquently explained in *Against Heresies*, "For to yield assent to God, and to follow His Word, and to love Him above all, and one's neighbor as one's self (now man is neighbor to man), and to abstain from every evil deed, and all other things of a like nature . . . do reveal one and the same God."[51] Following after assumes radically concrete form, because it is shaped by the concreteness of God's coming to humanity in Jesus Christ.[52] Following after goes out to the other, for the humanity of the human I consists in the fact that another one is really there for me.[53]

Even more problematic with Scharlemann's notion of acoluthetic reason is its lack of intelligible content, that is, discernible moral and theological content. Who is this one who calls? Presumably it is anyone or anything who or which enables the I to become what it is in its singular here-and-now-ness. Scharlemann writes, "Not only the man Jesus, but anyone, can then be the exstantial I; any other can not only elicit respect as a free human being but also enable the will as a Christ."[54] There is no standard, beyond the principle of autonomous individuation, by which an illegitimate call could be distinguished from a legitimate call. The self-negating symbol of the cross, which Tillich utilizes as the motor of iconoclasm, Scharlemann subordinates to the experience of completed selfhood. In Scharlemann's appropriation, the symbol disappears because the self exhausts the usefulness of the symbol in the process of arriving at its own wholeness, not because it is the nature of the symbol itself (God's radical transcendence, or the protestant principle of dialectical negation) to always look away from itself and subvert its own claim to authority. Scharlemann says, "Having come to themselves through the following, they are able on their own to be the ones they are."[55]

In my view, Scharlemann's acoluthetic reason more closely resembles a pathology of faith than an expression of genuine discipleship. The introjection of the self within and without suggests the internalization of psychic excess in which the I is obstructed on its way to and from the concrete other; the I's openness is internally checked in a state of intermittent lethargy and anxiety. The consequences of this view for a course of action are not promising: on the one hand, quietism and resignation, on the other hand, uncritical obeisance to notions or persons capable of (at least momentarily) affirming my own "I am"; on the one hand, indifference and aloofness, on the other hand, idiosyncratic aggression and self-assertion.

According to Bonhoeffer, the reason of following is particular to the identity of the one who summons the I outside itself. The criterion is not what the self should become in the call, but *the one who calls* the person to obedience; and that one is not the I but in every case the not-I, the counter-Logos, the Christ. As Bonhoeffer explains in no uncertain terms:

> When the Counter-Logos appears in history, no longer as an idea, but as "Word" become flesh, there is no longer any possibility of assimilating him into the existing order of the human logos. The only real question which now remains is: "Who are you? Speak for yourself!" The question, "Who are you?", is the question of dethroned and distraught reason; but it is also the question of faith: "Who are you? Are you God himself?" This is the question with which christology is concerned. Christ is the Counter-Logos. Classification is no longer a possibility, because the existence of this Logos spells the end of the human logos. Only the question, "Who are you?", will do. The phenomenon is opened up only by this. He answers only to the question, "Who?"[56]

The call which enables the I to come to itself in life with others is the call of Jesus Christ.

Being There for Others: Trinitarian Self-Becoming

What is Bonhoeffer's view of christological relation? It is the taking shape of the overabundant I, of the self reshaped in Jesus Christ, signifying the conversion of the person from adamic self-identification of the real to christic mediation in life with others. The overabundant self is the person transformed by the God whose own love has overflowed, is overflowing, and always will overflow in the giving of the Son to save humanity. For it is the Father's gift of the Son to humanity that enables humanity to be the people it is intended to be, a people who in a common history with God are likewise reconciled to each other and to themselves as individuals.

Christological relation *gathers* outside; conversion, or *metanoia*, is not an activity that occurs within the cycles of the ego but a gracious miracle energizing the person (in the words of the prison writings) to be "caught up into" the messianic event of life together. Bonhoeffer enumerates the forms of this ecstatic activity in resolutely nonconceptual terms; in table fellowship with strangers, in attending to the sick, in fellowship with the weak and the suffering—in gathering with the ones outside.[57] He writes, "It is not the religious act that makes the Christian, but participation in the sufferings of God in earthly life."[58] The religious act always entails partiality or compartmentalization; faith, on the other hand, "involves the whole of one's life."[59] In other words, "Jesus calls men, not to a new religion, but to life."[60]

In the end, the place of the christological relation and the source of the self converge in the "being there for others." "Encounter with Jesus Christ. The experience that a transformation of all human life is given in the fact that 'Jesus is there only for others.'"[61] The self becomes itself in Christ, for Christ exists as the luminescence of agapeic togetherness. In life for and with others, the person becomes what he or she is intended to be by becoming more than what he or she is in overabundant love. This is not empty rhetoric or mere moral admonition but a way of conceiving the deepest transformation of what it means to be human. The new being in Christ, as Eberhard Jüngel has said in a similar context, "leads to a new and highly differentiated unity of the I with itself, a unity which has been opened up from inside."[62] In being opened up from the inside, the self is not a crater of God's great and violent judgment nor the archimedean point of all world-constitution, but it is an overabundance being now reshaped from self-enclosure to openness for life, creation, and fellowship. As a result, faithfulness is in its essence a togetherness with Jesus Christ, and therefrom a being caught up into life together with others. In Saint Paul's words, "For just as the sufferings of Christ flow over into our lives, so also through Christ our comfort overflows" (II Cor. 1:5). In this manner, the movement of the solitary I into life with others is animated by the ecstatic character of faith.

Bonhoeffer's description of the "new humanity" and its new patterns of agapeic relations shares many similar traits with the notion of justification in Martin Luther's "Freedom of a Christian." In this epochal manifesto of 1520, Luther delineates freedom from the requirements of the law in faith as the condition for the disposition of joyful sacrifice. "Love by its very nature is ready to serve and be subject to him who is Lord," he writes.[63] Importantly, faith's effects are more than dispositional; they are first of all structural. The new I does not respond to the other as across the distance of difference and ethical aggression but out of the spontaneity of its own reshaping. The new I, that is, who I am in Christ as opposed to who I am in Adam, "lives only for others and not for itself," precisely because faith extends the self outward. In the words of the Protestant scholastics, faith consists in *fides directa—actus directus*. "We conclude," Luther says, "that a Christian lives not in himself, but in Christ and in his neighbor."[64] In Bonhoeffer's phrasing, "God in human form, not . . . in the conceptual forms of the absolute, metaphysical, infinite, etc . . . but 'the man for others' . . . the man who lives out of the transcendent."[65]

Therefore, a positive, reconstructive thesis underlies this description. Faith which always enters *into* a person is what turns that person toward the outside. For Luther, it is God's Word which enters the individual and first distinguishes the "inner person" from the "outer." The "portal" of existence and the unity of the person are to be sought where a word is encountered through which one is rendered human, where a word "by turning one inward also brings one out of oneself."[66] The inner person is turned outward by the arresting Word, and in the event of this turning is turned away from the I to the other. As Jüngel says, "When the gospel addressing [the individual] summons him to 'surrender' himself to Jesus Christ 'and to trust in him anew,' then the inner man must be designed precisely for the purpose of going out of himself in order thus—with another!—to become a new man. The inner man exists in that change from within toward the outside. For this reason he can be turned away from himself."[67]

Similarly, for Bonhoeffer, christological relation allows the inner person to be called out of itself so as to become reshaped in togetherness, thus bursting all preoccupation with the winning of self-having and autonomy. In christological relation the other comes nearer to me than I have ever been able to be to myself, and in this way the other brings me to myself in a completely new way, so that I come to myself "from the furthermost distance."[68] In Saint Augustine's words, "But you were more inward than my most inward part and higher than the highest element within me."[69]

Luther imagines the tangibility of this "going outside oneself" as circumscribed in the hearing of the Word—the inner person is *called* out of itself in kerygmatic proclamation. Unbelief compresses the self into an interior servitude wherein the person cannot leave himself, "exactly for the reason that he remains only in himself, as though he were an outer man inwardly."[70] But since God shows himself in faith to be not only *for himself* but also *for us*, and not only *for us* but *in us*, then, as Luther says, we are outside ourselves. Jüngel writes, "For in essence humanity is the creature addressed by God and insofar sojourns with itself together with the Word addressing it and in the event of this sojourn is also taken out of itself."[71] In sojourning with God, the self sojourns with itself out of itself into the world reconciled to God. As the guarantor of faith, Jesus Christ fashions the intersection between the inner person and the outer self.

Bonhoeffer's conception of the self summons Luther's anatomy of the new being on the matter of the I overabounding in faith. The source of this transformed self involves neither the purely interior self not the purely social self but the reconstitution of the interior I as turned outward. The movement of the I as genesis to its christological self-becoming is not one of the former's decimation or disappearance. On the contrary, something happens *in and to the I* that anticipates and precedes its recentering in relation. As Jüngel puts it, "We can only really go beyond our self-relation if we relate to something over against us which is not immanent to our self-relation."[72] For Bonhoeffer, it is the presence of Christ as community that enacts the metanoia of the new being.

However, one important difference between Bonhoeffer and Luther must be noted. Bonhoeffer's heavy suspicion of inwardness compels him to drop the theologically and metaphorically cumbersome task of explicating the grammar of the inner and outer spheres. In emphasizing the axiom "Christ existing as community" as the principal agent of the call to the outside, he also avoids reducing the event of God's grace to the acoustic and individualistic call of proclamation. Bonhoeffer opposes any thinking in two spheres for the reason that it profanes the one reality interconnected through and mediated by Christ. He claims that the inner-outer distinction can produce theological convolutions which complicate what, in the final analysis, might be a situation so simple as: "Follow after," *nachfolge*, be with others as the losing, giving and finding of yourself.

However, the inner-outer distinction is opposed not only on theological but also on psychological grounds. In Tegel prison Bonhoeffer often appeared to his fellow inmates as strong and confident, a man of deliberate courage and piety. Yet when reading the prison papers we recognize that Bonhoeffer, contrary to appearances, often felt frightened, weak, and apprehensive. In a poetic reflection "Who am I?" he considers the dichotomy of ostensible surface and depth.[73]

Who am I? They often tell me
I would step from my cell's confinement
calmly, cheerfully, firmly,
like a squire from his country-house.

Who am I? They often tell me
I would talk to my warders
freely and friendly and clearly,
as though it were mine to command.

Who am I? They also tell me
I would bear the days of misfortune
Equably, smilingly, proudly,
like one accustomed to win.

Am I really all that which other people tell of?
Or am I only what I know of myself,
Restless and longing and sick, like a bird in a cage,
struggling for breath, as though hands were compassing my throat,
yearning for colors, for flowers, for the voices of birds,
thirsting for words of kindness, for neighborliness,
trembling with anger at despotisms and petty humiliation,
tossing in expectation of great events,
powerlessly trembling for friends at an infinite distance,
weary and empty at praying, at thinking, at making,
faint, and ready to say farewell to it all? . . .

Who am I? They mock me, these lonely questions of mind.
Whoever I am, thou knowest, O God, I am thine.[74]

Bonhoeffer resists the suggestion that the genuine self is the hidden self and the outer a mask to which the inner self is related as a fall from an original source.[75] Rather, he says, "Whoever I am, thou knowest, O God, I am thine."[76] Who "I am" is not finally my own possession; who "I am" is not an "I know" but an "I am known"—a "thou knowest," and perhaps concomitantly an "I am being known" in the christic intermediation of the other person there.

However, the question must be addressed whether Bonhoeffer's christological description of selfhood wears thin through the relentless force of its own logic. That is, does his description need a clearer and deeper trinitarian context? Does he emphasize the promeity of God's presence in the world at the expense of God's aseity? Would his discussion of "Jesus as the one for others" have richer theological substance were it positioned more prominently in the context of trinitarian discourse?

As I have shown throughout this book, Bonhoeffer attends with great intensity to revelation's secondary objectivity, namely, to the form of God's being for the world in the concrete presence of Jesus Christ. It is not necessary, and certainly not warranted by the content of Bonhoeffer's writings, to think of this concentration as contradictory of Barth's project of explicating the trinitarian identity of God. Bonhoeffer stated as early as *Sanctorum Communio* that only from the proposition "God comes from God" can the proposition "God comes to humanity" proceed. Conversely, the proposition "God comes to humanity" can be understood as a way of speaking about the proposition "God comes to God," to be sure not out of necessity but out of the overabundance of God's grace. In *God's coming to God to humanity*, God does not cease to be God, nor does God empty himself of his divinity. God is his own origin, but in coming to God as the goal of God's being, God comes to his other in humanity, again not out of necessity but through the overabundance of God's grace. The goal of God's coming to God is not the same as the origin, but it is in every way equal to the origin. Thus, who God is is the movement from origin to goal within the everlasting identity of God's being God. As Jürgen Moltmann explains, "This movement in God is made possible and determined by the fact that 'in the depth of that life emerges the divine mystery, the inner suffering thirst of the Godhead, its inner longing for its 'Others,' which for God is capable of being the object of the highest, most boundless love.' In his heart God has this passionate longing, not just for any, random 'Other' but for 'his' Other—that is, for the one who is the 'Other' for him himself. And that is man, his image."[77] God's togetherness with the world is at the same time an expression of God's being God; who God is is God's *being himself and being with the world.*

Bonhoeffer's thinking through the depths of worldliness is then a way of thinking through the depths of God's being God. By no means does it entail a monopoly or a rejection of the primary trinitarian task, but it is nonetheless part and parcel of that task. Bonhoeffer's project should be conceived as complementary with Barth's massive trinitarian theology, to be sure, with varying nuances and emphases, but nonetheless sharing the common concern of understanding the self-witness of the living God in Jesus of Nazareth and the relationship of humanity to that self-witness—of thinking after the God who has given himself to humanity as an expression of his own loving character.

What, then, is the implication of assuming a trinitarian context for understanding Bonhoeffer's christological description of the self? I propose the following. Just as God's love cannot be contained in the immanence of his self-relations but overflows toward humanity in the loving event of the Son, so the love of Christ overflows the new being of the self. The structure of being a self is transformed; love is that event in which an I no longer exists for itself but exists in connection to an other person on the way toward becoming a we, and in this sense the I becomes truly an I. In the event of love, humanity corresponds to the "God who has come to the world in both the most intensive and most extensive ways."[78] Everything that exists exists because this one event has become real: the everlasting miracle of God's saving love in Jesus Christ.

On the basis of this trinitarian presupposition, Bonhoeffer sketches the contours of the overabundant I. Christological relation returns us to our full humanity, albeit one chastened and fallible, which we had forsaken in the isolation of self-praise and self-constitution. Lest history's severe lessons fade from memory, Bonhoeffer cautions against romantic or nostalgic construals of this new identity. He says, "Our earthly song is bound to God's revealing Word in Jesus Christ. It is the simple song of the children of this earth who have been called to be God's children . . . not enraptured, but sober, grateful, reverent, addressed steadily to God's revealed Word."[79] Life together in Christ does not propel the person beyond the world into some grotesque distortion of human desire and limitation—as nowhere more clearly exemplified than in the Nazi's hideous obsessions with purity and uniformity. Life together in Christ enables the person to live life in the midst of suffering and dissonance, delight and joy—to be simply human. Hence Bonhoeffer writes in his letter of 5 December 1943, "My thoughts and feelings seem to be getting more and more like the Old Testament, and in recent months I have been reading the Old Testament much more than the New."[80] In prison he discovered again what he had so elegantly described in his earliest theological writings, that "it is only when one loves life and the world so much that without them everything would be gone, that one can believe in the resurrection and a new world."[81] There is no way of escape from the sufferings and responsibilities of the world, for the Christian "must drink the earthly cup to the dregs, and only in his doing so is the crucified and risen Lord with him, and he crucified and risen with Christ."[82] In Jesus Christ God has said Yes and Amen to all creation, and the divine Yes and Amen is "the firm ground on which we stand."[83]

Therefore, the trinitarian self-becoming of the individual I is not a turning back to that I that, as the transcendental source of the real, stands at its center.[84] That is, the overabundant I does not constitute a looking-back in the sense of an "authenticating repetition"

or "an unfolding of the still implicated beginning."[85] If that were the
case, the self which I am given by the other would become itself "the
true world midpoint."[86] Rather, the new being emerges in and out
of togetherness. But since the overabundant self must nonetheless
be in some sense a looking back to the beginning, the person looks
to Christ as to a beginning that precedes the subjective constitution
of the world. Jesus Christ as life together activates the living consciousness of the other as neighbor, enabling the self to have found
once again an origin that was obscured when the I indulged itself in
"that 'solitude' out of which it constitutes the world as its own."[87]
And so, near the end, Bonhoeffer can think even of a togetherness
that extends beyond the silencing of his own I: "Brother, when the
sun turns pale for me, live for me."

NOTES

Preface

1. Karl Barth, *Church Dogmatics* II/1, tr. G. W. Bromiley and Harold Knight (Edinburgh: T & T Clark, 1957), p. 16.

2. Heinrich Ott, *Reality and Faith*, tr. Alex Morrison (Philadelphia: Fortress Press, 1972.

3. Larry Rasmussen, *Dietrich Bonhoeffer: Reality and Resistance* (Nashville: Abingdon, 1972).

4. Hans Frei, *Types of Christian Theology*, ed. George Hunsinger and William C. Placher (New Haven: Yale University Press, 1992), p. 159.

5. Frei, *Types of Christian Theology*, p. 159.

6. Four notable exceptions are Andre Dumas, *Dietrich Bonhoeffer: Theologian of Reality*, tr., Robert McAffee Brown (New York: Macmillan, 1971); Clifford James Green, *The Sociality of Christ and Humanity: Dietrich Bonhoeffer's Early Theology, 1927–1933* (Missoula, Mont.: Scholars Press, 1975); Wayne Whitson Floyd, Jr., *Theology and the Dialectics of Otherness: On Reading Bonhoeffer and Adorno* (Lanham, Md.: University Press of America, 1988); and Hans-Richard Reuter, "Nachwort," in *Akt und Sein* (Munich: Christian Kaiser, 1988), pp. 163–85.

7. Eberhard Bethge, *Dietrich Bonhoeffer: Theologian, Christian, Contemporary*, tr. Erich Mosbacher et al. (New York: Harper & Row, 1970), p. 36.

8. Eberhard Bethge, *Dietrich Bonhoeffer: Theologe, Christ, Zeitgenosse* (Munich: Christian Kaiser, 1983), p. 101. (This information is not included in the English edition.)

9. For example, *Christ the Center*, tr. Edwin H. Robertson (New York: Harper & Row, 1978), originally published in 1960 from the 1933 lectures at Berlin; *Creation and Fall*, tr. John Fletcher (New York: Macmillan, 1959), originally published in 1937 from the 1933 lectures at Berlin; *Dietrich Bonhoeffers Hegel-Seminar 1933*, ed. Ilse Tödt (Munich: Christian Kaiser, 1988); "Grundfragen einer christlichen Ethik," *Gesammelte Schriften*, ed. Eberhard Bethge, vol. 5 (Munich: Christian Kaiser, 1972), pp. 156–79; "Die Geschichte der systematischen Theologie des 20. Jahrhunderts 1931/32,"

Gesammelte Schriften, vol. 5, pp. 181–226; "Das Wesen der Kirche," 1932, *Gesammelte Schriften,* vol. 5, pp. 227–74; "Gibt es einer christliche Ethik?" 1932, *Gesammelte Schriften,* vol. 5, pp. 275–99; "Jüngste Theologie," 1932– 1933, *Gesammelte Schriften,* vol. 5, pp. 300–339; "Probleme einer theologischen Anthropologie," 1932–1933, *Gesammelte Schriften,* vol. 5, pp. 340–58.

Chapter 1

1. Eberhard Bethge, *Dietrich Bonhoeffer: Theologian, Christian, Contemporary,* tr. Eric Mosbacher et al. (New York: Harper & Row, 1970), p. 50.
2. Quoted in Bethge, *Dietrich Bonhoeffer,* p. 50.
3. Quoted in Bethge, *Dietrich Bonhoeffer,* p. 50.
4. Bethge, *Dietrich Bonhoeffer,* pp. 50–51.
5. Martin H. Rumscheidt, "Doing Theology as if Nothing Had Happened: Developments in the Theology of Karl Barth from 1919 to 1933," *St. Luke's Journal of Theology* 30/1 (December 1986), p. 13.
6. Rumscheidt, "Doing Theology as if Nothing Had Happened," p. 275 (my emphasis).
7. Karl Barth, "Biblical Questions, Insights and Vistas," in Eberhard Jüngel, ed., *Karl Barth: A Theological Legacy* (Philadelphia: Westminster Press, 1986), pp. 59–60.
8. Karl Barth, *The Word of God and the Word of Man,* tr. Douglas Horton (Gloucester, Mass.: Peter Smith, 1978), p. 80.
9. Bethge, *Dietrich Bonhoeffer,* p. 60.
10. Barth, "Biblical Questions, Insights and Vistas," p. 52.
11. Bethge, *Dietrich Bonhoeffer,* p. 52.
12. Bethge, *Dietrich Bonhoeffer,* p. 52.
13. Bethge describes the young theologian in New York: "Bonhoeffer found it hard to suppress his feeling of European superiority when he was confronted daily with the American unconcern with what to him were the genuine problems of theology. He regarded what he heard, not as theology, but as religious philosophy, long since out-dated, until it occurred to him that he should study its premises. But when the students burst into loud laughter at quotations from Luther's *De servo arbitrio,* which struck them as funny, he again lost patience. . . . His teachers were dismayed when he based his work on the theology of revelation, the doctrine of justification or eschatology instead of on so-called realities. Niebuhr and Baillie in particular took trouble annotating the difficult and demanding essays written by their German guest. Baillie noted the German predilection for impossible associations of ideas such as 'revelation in hiddenness.' 'Is this not a perverse expression?' he wrote" (pp. 116, 118).
14. Bethge, *Dietrich Bonhoeffer,* p. 117f.
15. Dietrich Bonhoeffer, "The Theology of Crisis," 1966, *Gesammelte Schriften,* vol. 3, p. 111.

16. Bonhoeffer, *Gesammelte Schriften*, vol. 3, p. 123.

17. Bonhoeffer quoted in Bethge, *Dietrich Bonhoeffer*, p. 132.

18. Bonhoeffer quoted in Bethge, *Dietrich Bonhoeffer*, p. 132.

19. Bonhoeffer, *Gesammelte Schriften*, vol. 1, p. 19.

20. Dietrich Bonhoeffer, *A Testament to Freedom* (San Francisco: Harper, 1990), p. 412.

21. Bonhoeffer, *A Testament to Freedom*, p. 412.

22. Bonhoeffer, *A Testament to Freedom*, p. 412.

23. In a letter of 13 May 1942, Bonhoeffer mentioned to Barth that he was reading the galleys of *Church Dogmatics* II/2. Earlier in the fall of 1936 in a letter from Finkenwalde Seminary, Bonhoeffer had expressed reservations about Barth's idea of justification. Bonhoeffer's apprehension, John Godsey tells us, concerned whether Barth's "great emphasis on God's justifying work *for* us in Christ had caused him to neglect Christ's sanctifying work *in* us as we respond through a life of concrete discipleship" (John Godsey, "Barth and Bonhoeffer: The Basic Difference," *Quarterly Review* 7 (Spring 1987), p. 15.

24. Bonhoeffer, "Letter to Karl Barth," 17 May 1942, cited in Godsey, "Barth and Bonhoeffer," p. 16.

25. Godsey, "Barth and Bonhoeffer," p. 17.

26. More exhaustive accounts of the relationship have been developed by a number of writers. The first source, of course, is Bethge's biography. Paul Lehman has written an idiosyncratic but sometimes helpful article on the relationship. He focuses on the *capax-incapax* difference and the differences between their views of the concreteness of revelation ("The Concreteness of Theology: Reflections on the Conversation Between Barth and Bonhoeffer," in *Footnotes to a Theology: The Karl Barth Colloquium of 1972*, ed. H. Martin Rumscheidt [La Corporation pour la Publication des Etudes Academiques en Religion au Canada, 1974]). As I discuss later in the chapter, Godsey's article treats the problem in a more systematic way by comparing Barth's *theologia gloriae*, the affirmation of "the graciousness of God's action in Christ," to Bonhoeffer's *theologia crucis*, the affirmation of "the costliness of God's grace in Christ" ("Barth and Bonhoeffer," pp. 9–27).

27. By all accounts Bonhoeffer had read most of Barth's works from the 1920s. As previously stated, he also knew the first four parts of the *Church Dogmatics*. Although we have no record of his reaction to Barth's doctrine of election, we have considerable reaction to Barth's ethics in the II/2 volume (see Larry Rasmussen, "A Question of Method," in *New Studies in Bonhoeffer's Ethics*, ed. William J. Peck [Lewiston, N.Y.: Edwin Mellen Press, 1987]).

28. Dietrich Bonhoeffer, *Act and Being* (New York: Octagon Books, 1983), p. 26.

29. Hans-Richard Reuter, "Nachwort," in *Akt und Sein* (Munich: Christian Kaiser, 1988), unpublished translation by Jeff Owen Prudhomme, p. 4.

30. In medieval scholastic thought, to conceive of God as act (*actus*

purus) meant to think of God as nothing other than pure being. For Aquinas, the designation of God as *actus purus* was a translation of the Greek term for actuality (*energeia*). But as pure actuality, God was not thought in contradiction to the concept of being; rather, pure actuality was in conflict only with the notion of potency as an unactualized possibility. As pure act, God was to be understood as the first being (*primum ens*) in the sense of first mover, inasmuch as God contained "no unactualized possibilities for whose actualization he would have been dependent on some other being" (Reuter, "Nachwort," p. 165).

31. Reuter, "Nachwort," pp. 5–6.

32. Brünstad quoted in Bonhoeffer, *Act and Being*, p. 38.

33. Brünstad quoted in Bonhoeffer, *Act and Being*, p. 40.

34. Bonhoeffer, *Act and Being*, p. 42.

35. Bonhoeffer, *Act and Being*, p. 81.

36. Barth, *Church Dogmatics* II/1, tr. T. H. L. Parker et al. (Edinburgh: T & T Clark, 1957), p. 264.

37. Karl Barth, *The Epistle to the Romans*, tr. Edwyn C. Hoskyns (New York: Oxford University Press, 1968), p. 149.

38. Bonhoeffer, *Act and Being*, p. 80.

39. Bonhoeffer, *Act and Being*, p. 82.

40. Regin Prenter, "Dietrich Bonhoeffer and Karl Barth's Positivism of Revelation," in *World Come of Age*, ed. R. G. Smith (Philadelphia: Fortress Press, 1967), p. 106.

41. Cf. Robert E. Cushman, *Faith Seeking Understanding* (Durham, N.C.: Duke University Press, 1981), pp. 103–22.

42. Barth, *Epistle to the Romans*, p. 92.

43. Bonhoeffer, *Act and Being*, p. 113.

44. Bonhoeffer, *Act and Being*, p. 122.

45. Bonhoeffer, *Act and Being*, p. 121.

46. Bonhoeffer, *Act and Being*, p. 92.

47. Bonhoeffer, *Act and Being*, p. 102.

48. Barth, *Epistle to the Romans*, quoted in Bonhoeffer, *Akt und Sein*, p. 94.

49. Barth, *Epistle to the Romans*, p. 269.

50. Barth, *Epistle to the Romans*, p. 149.

51. Barth, *Epistle to the Romans*, p. 149.

52. Bonhoeffer, *Act and Being*, p. 95.

53. Bonhoeffer, *Act and Being*, p. 96.

54. Bonhoeffer, *Act and Being* (with my variations in translation), p. 90.

55. Bonhoeffer, *Act and Being*, p. 90.

56. Barth, *Church Dogmatics* II/1, p. 306.

57. Bonhoeffer, *Act and Being*, p. 123.

58. Bonhoeffer, *Act and Being*, p. 123.

59. Bonhoeffer, *Act and Being*, p. 92.

60. Hans Urs von Balthasar, *The Theology of Karl Barth*, tr. John Drury (Garden City, N.Y.: Anchor Books, 1972), p. 97.

61. Bethge, *Dietrich Bonhoeffer*, p. 137. Bonhoeffer writes, "Barth's book on Anselm has given me great pleasure [but] . . . in terms of substance nothing has grown less questionable, of course" (137).

62. Barth, *Epistle to the Romans*, p. 38.

63. Barth, *Epistle to the Romans*, p. 29.

64. This way of phrasing the issue is taken from Robert Scharlemann, course lectures on Protestant theology in the twentieth century, University of Virginia, 25 September 1985.

65. The specific act of God in Jesus Christ is the exclusive ground of the analogy; therefore, "both the ontic and the epistemic analogies have their presupposition in the free grace of God" (Hans Frei, "The Doctrine of Revelation in the Thought of Karl Barth, 1909 to 1922," Ph.D. diss., Yale University, 1956).

66. Barth, *Church Dogmatics* II/1, p. 181.

67. Barth, *Church Dogmatics* II/1, p. 181.

68. Cf. Eberhard Jüngel, *The Doctrine of the Trinity: God's Being Is in Becoming*, tr. Horton Harris (Edinburgh: Scottish Academic Press, 1966), p. 61.

69. Jüngel, *Doctrine of the Trinity*, p. 62.

70. Jüngel, *Doctrine of the Trinity*, p. 63.

71. Barth, *Church Dogmatics* II/1, p. 262.

72. Jüngel, *Doctrine of the Trinity*, p. 65.

73. Barth, *Church Dogmatics* II/1, p. 267.

74. Jüngel, *Doctrine of the Trinity*, pp. 66–68.

75. Barth quoted in Jüngel, *Doctrine of God*, p. 67.

76. Barth, *Church Dogmatics* II/1, p. 500.

77. Barth, *Church Dogmatics* II/1, p. 306.

78. Barth, *Church Dogmatics* II/1, p. 503.

79. Barth, *Church Dogmatics* II/1, p. 313.

80. Barth, *Church Dogmatics* II/1, p. 264.

81. Barth, *Church Dogmatics* II/1, p. 314.

82. Barth, *Church Dogmatics* II/1, p. 314.

83. Barth, *Church Dogmatics* II/1, p. 315.

84. Barth, *Church Dogmatics* II/1, p. 317.

85. Barth, *Church Dogmatics* II/1, p. 317.

86. Barth, *Church Dogmatics* II/1, p. 317.

87. Barth, *Church Dogmatics* II/1, p. 317.

88. Dietrich Bonhoeffer, *Letters and Papers from Prison* (New York: Macmillan, 1972), p. 286.

89. Bonhoeffer, *Letters and Papers from Prison*, p. 286.

90. Bonhoeffer, *Letters and Papers from Prison*, p. 286.

91. That is, Barth's critique of religion in the second edition of *The Epistle*

to the Romans (1922) involves the sharp claim that religion and law do not lead us to God. "The divine possibility of religion can never be changed into a human possibility" (p. 184). The question of whether religion provides the presupposition of and the precondition for the positive relation between God and humankind is to be answered in the negative (Ernst Feil, *The Theology of Dietrich Bonhoeffer*, tr. Martin Rumscheidt [Philadelphia: Fortress Press, 1985], p. 164). Religion is limited by the cross; it tears us apart and separates us from God. In *Church Dogmatics* II/1 religion is described as part of the dialectic of law and grace; the dialectic of revelation and religion leads to true religion. Faith is related to religion as gospel is to law.

92. Bonhoeffer, *Letters and Papers from Prison*, p. 287.

93. One remarkable example of this is Barth's 1958 "Letter to a Pastor in the German Democratic Republic," in which he connects the bleak situation of political repression under communism with the judgment of God. He says: "[The totalitarian state] in all its characteristics can be but God's instrument, inescapably fulfilling a function in his plan. The judicial function of a rod of discipline? Yes, even this function. This power would not have gained control over you had it not been for all the sins of past leaders and people in society, state, and church. You are assuredly undergoing a painful process of purification and fiery refining, such as the Western world also will not escape sooner or later in some form, perhaps at the hands of Asia and Africa. But who sits in judgment? . . . God above all things! Sovereign even over the legalistic totalitarianism of your state! . . . "Totalitarianism" also, in a way, is the grace of the gospel which we all are to proclaim, free grace, truly divine and truly human, claiming every man wholly for itself. To a degree the Communist state might be interpreted and understood as an image of grace—to be sure a grossly distorted and darkened image. Indeed, grace is all-embracing, totalitarian" ("Letter to a Pastor in the German Democratic Republic," in *How to Serve God in a Marxist Land*, ed. Robert McAffee Brown [New York: Association Press, 1959], pp. 54–58). According to Barth, the theological axiom of lordship which he invoked in the 1930s as a means of resisting National Socialism was not pertinent to the situation of the 1950s, since the Communist state was not properly speaking on behalf of God. At worst, communism was Christian heresy, an internal Christian dispute.

94. Dietrich Bonhoeffer, *Ethics*, tr. Neville Horton Smith (New York: Macmillan, 1965), p. 201.

95. Bonhoeffer, *Ethics*, p. 201. Only in light of Christ as the reconciliation of God and world can we make sense of Bonhoeffer's perennially unsettling words at Tegel prison, "Before God and with God we live without God. God lets himself be pushed out of the world on the cross." When God is spoken of in this way, "the godlessness of the world is not . . . concealed, but rather, revealed, and thus exposed to an unexpected light" (*Letters and Papers from Prison*, p. 362).

96. Bonhoeffer, *Letters and Papers from Prison*, p. 362.

97. Bonhoeffer, *Ethics*, p. 361.

98. Barth, *Church Dogmatics* II/1, p. 58.

99. Barth, *Church Dogmatics* II/1, p. 58.

100. Barth, *Church Dogmatics* I/2, tr. A. T. Thompson and Harold Knight (Edinburgh: T & T Clark, 1956), p. 63. In the preface to *Church Dogmatics* I/1, tr. G. W. Bromiley (Edinburgh: T & T Clark, 1936), Barth makes the point clearly: "For I actually beieve that a better church dogmatics (even apart from all ethical utility) might actually make a more important and weightier contribution even to questons and tasks such as German liberation, than most of the well-intentioned material which so many, even among theologians, think they can and should produce when they dilettantishly take up such questions and tasks" (Barth quoted in Friedrich-Wilhelm Marquardt, "Socialism in the Theology of Karl Barth," in *Karl Barth and Radical Politics*, ed. and tr. George Hunsinger [Philadelphia: Westminster Press, 1976], p. 68).

101. Barth, *Church Dogmatics* I/2, p. 68.

102. Barth, *Church Dogmatics* I/2, p. 68.

103. Barth, *Church Dogmatics* I/2, p. 68 (my emphasis).

104. Barth, *Church Dogmatics* I/2, p. 68.

105. Barth, *Church Dogmatics* I/2, p. 423.

106. George Hunsinger says, "The history of every human being is seen [by Barth] as included in that of Jesus. The history of Jesus is taken as the center which establishes, unifies, and incorporates a differentiated whole in which the history of each human being as such is included. This act of universal inclusion is his accomplishment and achievement" (*How to Read Karl Barth: The Shape of His Theology* [New York: Oxford University Press, 1991], p. 108).

107. Hans Frei writes, "There is then a way of talking about the presence of Christ that is, for the Christian, not appropriate to the description of Christ's relation to the believer. It is that of talking about Christ's presence before talking about his identity, of trying directly and concretely in our talk to grasp the presence of Christ. What is grasped is empty space—the shadow of our own craving for full and perpetual presence" (*The Identity of Jesus Christ: The Hermeneutical Basis of Dogmatic Theology* [Philadelphia: Fortress Press, 1975], p. 34).

108. Eberhard Jüngel, *God as the Mystery of the World*, tr. Darrell L. Guder (Grand Rapids, Mich.: Eerdmans, 1983), p. 388.

109. Reuter, "Nachwort," pp. 28–29.

110. Karl Barth, "Letter to a Pastor in the German Democratic Republic," pp. 54–58.

111. Barth, *Church Dogmatics* II/1, p. 270.

112. Barth, *Church Dogmatics* II/1, p. 271.

113. Bonhoeffer, *Act and Being*, p. 94.

114. Jüngel, *God as the Mystery of the World*, p. 378.

115. Hunsinger, *How to Read Karl Barth*, p. 120.

116. Karl Barth, "From a Letter to Superintendent Herrenbrück," in *World Come of Age*, ed. R. G. Smith (Philadelphia: Fortress Press, 1967), p. 90.

117. Barth, "From a Letter to Superintendent Herrenbrück," p. 90.

118. Karl Barth, "Letter to Eberhard Bethge, in *Fragments Grace and Gay*, ed. Martin Rumscheidt (London: Collins, 1971), p. 121.

119. Karl Barth, *Letters 1961–1968*, tr. Geoffrey W. Bromiley, ed. Jürgen Fangmeier and Hinrich Stoevesandt (Grand Rapids, Mich.: Eerdmans, 1981), p. 252.

120. Barth quoted in Hunsinger, *How to Read Karl Barth*, p. 256.

121. Barth quoted in Hunsinger, *How to Read Karl Barth*, p. 256.

122. Hunsinger, *How to Read Karl Barth*, p. 256.

123. Hunsinger, *How to Read Karl Barth*, p. 257.

124. Hunsinger, *How to Read Karl Barth*, p. 257.

125. Barth, *Church Dogmatics* IV/3, tr. G. W. Bromiley (Edinburgh: T & T Clark, 1961), p. 117.

126. Barth, *Church Dogmatics* IV/3, p. 119.

127. Barth, *Church Dogmatics* IV/3, p. 119.

128. Barth, *Church Dogmatics* IV/3, p. 148.

129. Barth, *Church Dogmatics* IV/3, pp. 149–50.

130. Barth, *Church Dogmatics* IV/1, tr. G. W. Bromiley (Edinburgh: T & T Clark, 1956), p. 7.

131. Barth, *Church Dogmatics* IV/1, p. 7.

132. Barth, *Church Dogmatics* IV/1, p. 7.

133. Barth, *Church Dogmatics* IV/1, p. 7.

134. Barth, *Church Dogmatics* IV/1, p. 9.

135. In particular, see *Church Dogmatics* III/1, tr. J. W. Edwards et al. (Edinburgh: T & T Clark, 1953), pp. 194ff.; II/4, tr. A. T. Mackey (Edinburgh: T & T Clark, 1961), pp. 14–25; and IV/2, tr. G. W. Bromiley (Edinburgh: T & T Clark, 1958), pp. 533–53.

136. Barth, *Church Dogmatics* IV/2, p. 533.

137. Godsey, "Barth and Bonhoeffer," p. 25.

138. Godsey, "Barth and Bonhoeffer," p. 25.

139. Godsey, "Barth and Bonhoeffer," p. 25.

140. Godsey, "Barth and Bonhoeffer," p. 26.

141. Barth quoted in Godsey, "Barth and Bonhoeffer," p. 26.

142. Godsey, "Barth and Bonhoeffer," p. 27.

143. Bonhoeffer quoted in Godsey, "Barth and Bonhoeffer," p. 27.

144. Cf. J. N. D. Kelly, *Early Christian Doctrines* (New York: Harper, 1960), p. 173.

145. Bonhoeffer, *Ethics*, p. 198.

146. Hunsinger, *How to Read Karl Barth*, p. 141.

147. Barth quoted in Hunsinger, *How to Read Karl Barth*, p. 141.

148. Barth, *Church Dogmatics* II/1, p. 16.

149. Barth, *Church Dogmatics* II/1, p. 16.

150. Barth, *Church Dogmatics* II/1, p. 16.

151. Barth, *Church Dogmatics* II/1, p. 16.

152. Barth, *Church Dogmatics* II/1, p. 49.

153. Barth, *Church Dogmatics* II/1, p. 50

154. Referring to Bonhoeffer as a Barthian is problematic. Wilhelm Niesel in an otherwise superficial review of *Akt und Sein* in the literary supplement of *Reformierte Kirchenzeitung* (March 1931) suggests what I think is a reasonable way of talking about Bonhoeffer in releation to Barth: "We wished to draw attention to [Bonhoeffer's] work only because it contains many very good individual observations and shows how much a pupil of Seeberg's has learnt from Gogarten and Barth." A pupil of Seeberg's indeed; Bonhoeffer never gives up certain sympathies with the liberal theology advanced at Berlin to the extent that he wants to bring the liberal emphasis of revelation's social concreteness into the larger paradigm shift advanced by Barth.

155. Dietrich Bonhoeffer, "What Is a Christian Ethic?" in *No Rusty Swords: Letters, Lectures and Notes 1928–1936*, tr. John Bowden and Edwin Robertson (New York: Harper & Row, 1965), p. 47.

Chapter 2

1. See John Smith, "The Significance of Karl Barth's Thought for the Relationship between Philosophy and Theology," *Union Seminary Quarterly Review* 28 (1972), pp. 15–30.

2. Karl Barth, *Credo*, quoted in S. W. Sykes, "Introduction," in *The Way of Theology in Karl Barth*, ed. H. Martin Rumscheidt (Allison Park, Pa.: Pickwick Publications, 1986), p. 7.

3. Barth, *Credo*, quoted in Sykes, "Introduction," p. 7.

4. I have in mind Richard Rorty's formulation of this term in "Beyond Realism and Anti-Realism: Heidegger, Fine, Davidson, and Derrida," in *Wo Steht analytische Philosophie Heute*, ed. Ludwig Nagl and Richard Heinrich (Vienna: R. Oldenbourg Verlag, 1986).

5. William Nicholls, *Systematic and Philosophical Theology* (Middlesex: Penguin Books, 1971), p. 86.

6. Karl Barth, "The Word of God and the Task of the Ministry," in *The Word of God and the Word of Man*, tr. Douglas Horton (Gloucester, Mass.: Peter Smith, 1978), p. 197

7. Barth, "The Word of God and the Task of the Ministry," p. 192.

8. Barth, "The Word of God and the Task of the Ministry," p. 192.

9. Barth, "The Word of God and the Task of the Ministry," p. 192.

10. Barth, "The Word of God and the Task of the Ministry," p. 192.

11. Barth, "The Word of God and the Task of the Ministry," p. 192.

12. Barth, "The Word of God and the Task of the Ministry," p. 194.

13. Karl Barth, *The Humanity of God*, tr. Thomas Wieser and John Newton Thomas (Atlanta: John Knox Press, 1978), p. 14.

14. Robert Scharlemann refers to Wilfried Härle's article, "Der Aufruf der 93 Intellektuellen und Karl Barths Bruch mit der liberalen Theologie" (*Zeitschrift für Theologie und Kirche* 72/2 [1974], pp. 207–24), as a case in

which critical investigation of Barth's reflection uncovered more of a "transfigured memory" than a historical fact ("Publishing in Scholarly Journals: Advising Junior Colleagues," *Bulletin of the Council on the Graduate Study of Religion* 15, 3 [June 1984], pp. 73–76).

15. Barth, *The Humanity of God*, p. 19.

16. Barth, *The Humanity of God*, p. 20.

17. Karl Barth, *The Theology of Schleiermacher*, tr. Geoffrey W. Bromiley (Grand Rapids, Mich.: Eerdmans, 1982), p. 16.

18. Richard R. Niebuhr, *Schleiermacher on Christ and Religion* (New York: Scribner's, 1964), p. 121.

19. Barth, *The Theology of Schleiermacher*, p. 216.

20. Rudolf Bultmann in *Karl Barth–Rudolf Bultmann Letters, 1922–1966*, tr. Geoffrey W. Bromiley (Grand Rapids, Mich.: Eerdmans, 1981), p. 38.

21. Bultmann, *Barth-Bultmann Letters*, p. 38.

22. Bultmann, *Barth-Bultmann Letters*, p. 38.

23. Bultmann, *Barth-Bultmann Letters*, p. 39.

24. Bultmann, *Barth-Bultmann Letters*, p. 39. One cannot help recalling Barth's frequent admonition to friends and students that the most industrious way to begin the day is with the Bible and the morning newspaper.

25. Barth, *Barth-Bultmann Letters*, p. 40.

26. Barth, *Barth-Bultmann Letters*, p. 41.

27. Barth, *Barth-Bultmann Letters*, p. 41.

28. Barth, *Barth-Bultmann Letters*, p. 41.

29. Barth, *Barth-Bultmann Letters*, p. 41.

30. Barth, *Barth-Bultmann Letters*, p. 42.

31. See Martin H. Rumscheidt, "Doing Theology as if Nothing Had Happened: Developments in the Theology of Karl Barth from 1919 to 1933," *St. Luke's Journal of Theology* 30/1 (December 1986), pp. 7–19.

32. Karl Barth, "Fate and Idea in Theology" in *The Way of Theology in Karl Barth*, p. 26.

33. Barth, "Fate and Idea," p. 26.

34. Barth's point resonates with Calvin's counsel in the *Institutes of the Christian Religion*: "What good is it to profess with Epicures some sort of God who has cast aside the care of the world only to amuse himself in idleness? What help is it, in short, to know a God with whom we have nothing to do?" (John Calvin, *Institutes of the Christian Religion*, tr. Ford Lewis Battles [Philadelphia: Westminster Press, 1960], I.2.2., p. 41).

35. Barth, "Fate and Idea," p. 27.

36. Joseph McClellend writes, "An uncritical stress on the statement 'God is' leads to an objectivity which posits a necessary relationship between beings and Being, a heteronomous relationship that binds us *velite nolite* to God as Fate" ("Philosophy and Theology—A Family Affair [Karl and Heinrich Barth]," in *Footnotes to a Theology: The Karl Barth Colloquium of 1972*, ed. Martin M. Rumscheidt [The Corporation for the Publication of Academic Studies in Religion in Canada, 1974], p. 35).

37. Barth, "Fate and Idea," p. 33.

38. Barth, "Fate and Idea," p. 36.

39. Barth, "Fate and Idea," p. 36.

40. Barth, "Fate and Idea," p. 37.

41. Barth, "Fate and Idea," p. 39.

42. Barth, "Fate and Idea," p. 44.

43. Barth, "Fate and Idea," p. 49.

44. Barth, "Fate and Idea," p. 49.

45. In a letter to the Swiss poet Carl Zuckmayer, Barth tells the story of a young Canadian theological student who interviewed him one afternoon in his Basel office. During the conversation the student asked Barth with great earnestness what role reason played in his theology. Quickly Barth retorted, "I use it!" (*A Late Friendship: The Letters of Karl Barth and Carl Zuckmayer*, tr. Geoffrey W. Bromiley (Grand Rapids, Mich.: Eerdmans, 1982), p. 49.

46. Barth, "Fate and Idea," p. 50.

47. Barth, "Fate and Idea," p. 50.

48. Barth, "Fate and Idea," p. 53.

49. Barth, "Fate and Idea," p. 53.

50. Barth, "Fate and Idea," p. 53.

51. Barth, "Fate and Idea," p. 52.

52. Barth, "Fate and Idea," p. 57.

53. Barth, "Fate and Idea," pp. 31–32.

54. Barth, "Fate and Idea," p. 31.

55. Barth, "Fate and Idea," p. 31.

56. Karl Barth, "The First Commandment as an Axiom of Theology," in *The Way of Theology in Karl Barth*, p. 63.

57. Barth, "The First Commandment," p. 64.

58. Barth, "The First Commandment," p. 67.

59. Barth, "The First Commandment," p. 67.

60. Barth, "The First Commandment," p. 67.

61. Barth, "The First Commandment," p. 71.

62. Barth, "The First Commandment," p. 70.

63. Barth, "The First Commandment," p. 70.

64. Barth, "The First Commandment," p. 72.

65. Barth, "The First Commandment," p. 74.

66. Barth, "The First Commandment," p. 75.

67. Barth, *The Humanity of God*, p. 45.

68. Karl Barth, "Philosophy and Theology," *The Way of Theology in Karl Barth*, ed. Martin M. Rumscheidt (Allison Park, Penn.: Pickwick Publications, 1986), p. 80.

69. Barth, "Philosophy and Theology," p. 80.

70. Barth, "Philosophy and Theology," p. 81.

71. Barth, "Philosophy and Theology," p. 81.

72. Barth, "Philosophy and Theology," p. 81.

73. Barth, "Philosophy and Theology," p. 82.

74. Barth, "Philosophy and Theology," p. 82.

75. Barth, "Philosophy and Theology," p. 87.

76. Barth, "Philosophy and Theology," p. 88.

77. Barth, "Philosophy and Theology," p. 89.

78. Barth, "Philosophy and Theology," p. 89.

79. Barth, "Philosophy and Theology," p. 89.

80. Barth, "Philosophy and Theology," p. 93.

81. Barth, "Fate and Idea," p. 50.

82. Karl Barth, "Wo ist nun dein Gott?" cited in Eberhard Jüngel, *Karl Barth: A Theological Legacy*, trans. Garrett E. Paul (Philadelphia: Westminster Press, 1986), p. 95.

83. Hans Urs von Balthasar, *The Theology of Karl Barth*, tr. John Drury (Garden City, N.Y.: Anchor Books, 1972), p. 81.

84. Luther, from Hägglund, *Theologie und Philosophie bei Luther*, in Stephen Ozment, *The Age of Reform 1250–1550: An Intellectual and Religious History of Late Medieval and Reformation Europe* (New Haven: Yale University Press, 1980), p. 238.

85. Rorty, "Beyond Realism and Anti-Realism," p. 4.

86. Rorty, "Beyond Realism and Anti-Realism," p. 4.

87. Rorty, "Beyond Realism and Anti-Realism," p. 4.

88. Rorty, "Beyond Realism and Anti-Realism," p. 12.

89. Rorty, "Beyond Realism and Anti-Realism," p. 12.

90. Rorty, "Beyond Realism and Anti-Realism," p. 12.

91. Rorty, "Beyond Realism and Anti-Realism," p. 12.

92. Rorty, "Beyond Realism and Anti-Realism," p. 12.

93. Richard Rorty, *Contingency, Irony and Solidarity* (Cambridge: Cambridge University Press, 1989), p. 6.

94. Rorty, "Beyond Realism and Anti-Realism," p. 20.

95. Barth, *Church Dogmatics* I/1, in Franklin Sherman, "Act and Being," in *The Place of Bonhoeffer: Problems and Possibilities in His Thought*, ed. Martin E. Marty (New York: Association Press, 1962), p. 106.

Chapter 3

1. Dietrich Bonhoeffer, *Act and Being* (New York: Octagon Books, 1983), p. 15.

2. Bonhoeffer, *Act and Being*, p. 70.

3. Bonhoeffer conceives "genuine" transcendental philosophy as the mode of thinking in reference to something transcendental, to that which is the condition of the possibility of the experience of the self itself, which is not reducible to the self-identity of the I. It is the knowing of onself as directed to that which is in every case the not-I. Kant's "original design" illustrated the character of the act of knowledge as fundamentally directed toward that which transcends the entity: act is an ever-changing "in-bezug-auf," an *intentional-*

ity toward, a pure extension and reference. A "genuine" ontological philosophy demonstrates the priority of being over consciousness. Bonhoeffer quotes
Micholai Hartmann to acknowledge that ontology's task is that of illuminat-
ing the reality of being outside of consciousness and of arguing that "the object of knowledge has a relation to this being, however it is not identical with
this entity" (quoted in *Akt und Sein* [Munich: Christian Kaiser, 1988], p. 53).
A genuine ontology is critical of transcendental thought, "for being, which
indeed is also being-there ("Dasein") and thought-being ("Denksein") transcends the given, the entity" (*Act and Being*, p. 54). Although there are themes
from both traditions which Bonhoeffer appropriates for theological purposes,
he questions the theological value of philosophical phenomenology. While
focusing on phenomena and their essents rather than on concrete human being
and its existence, phenomenology assumes that human being already contains
within itself the modalities of essential vision; consciousness has priority over
being. Unlike a pure ontology, phenomenology understands its task as the
recovery of what is essentially deposited *in mind* and not as the discovery of
a larger, extrinsic grid of concerns. Although *noesis* is directed to *noema*, the
noetic-noematic parallel structure resides immanently in consciousness.

4. Bonhoeffer, *Act and Being*, p. 72.

5. Bonhoeffer, *Act and Being*, p. 70.

6. Dietrich Bonhoeffer, *Sanctorum Communio*, tr. Ronald Gregor Smith
(London: Collins, 1963), p. 28.

7. Bonhoeffer, *Sanctorum Communio* (Kaiser), p. 29. On this matter
Barth simply said, "There never has actually been a *philosophia christiana*,
for if it was *philosophia* it was not *christiana*, and if it was *christiana* it was
not *philosophia*" (*Church Dogmatics* I/1, tr. G. W. Bromiley [Edinburgh:
T & T Clark, 1936], p. 6).

8. Eberhard Jüngel, *God as the Mystery of the World*, tr. Darrell L. Guder
(Grand Rapids, Mich.: Eerdman's, 1983), p. 390.

9. Bonhoeffer, *Akt und Sein*, p. 12; "das Anliegen des echten Transzen-
dentalismus wie das der echten Ontologie in einem 'kirchlichen Denken' zur
Einheit zu bringen."

10. Bonhoeffer quoted in Hans-Richard Reuter, "Nachwort," in *Akt und
Sein* (Munich: Christian Kaiser, 1988), unpublished translation by Jeff Owen
Prudhomme, p. 25.

11. Gottlieb Fichte, *The Science of Logic*, ed. and tr. John Lachs and Peter
Heath (Cambridge: Cambridge University Press, 1982), p. 93.

12. Jacques Derrida, *Writing and Difference*, tr. Alan Bass (Chicago:
University of Chicago Press, 1978); *Dissemination*, tr. Barbara Johnson (Chi-
cago: University of Chicago Press, 1981); *Margins of Philosophy*, tr. Alan Bass
(Chicago: University of Chicago Press, 1982).

13. Jacques Derrida, *Writing and Difference*, p. 279.

14. This is perhaps another way of stating a remark made by Camille
Paglia, "Is there anything *more* affected, aggressive, and relentlessly concrete

than a Parisian intellectual behind his/her turgid text?" (*Sexual Personae* [New York: Vintage Books, 1991], p. 34).

15. See "Structure, Sign and Play in the Discourse of the Human Sciences," in *Writing and Difference*, pp. 278—93.

16. Jacques Derrida, "The Laws of Reflection: Nelson Mandela, in Admiration," in *For Nelson Mandela*, ed. Jacques Derrida and Mustapha Tlili [New York: Seaver Books, 1987], pp. 11–42.

17. Bonhoeffer, *Act and Being*, p. 71.

18. Paul Tillich, "Philosophy and Theology," *The Protestant Era*, tr. James Luther Adams [Chicago: University of Chicago Press, 1957], p. 83.

19. Tillich, "Philosophy and Theology," p. 83.

20. Tillich, "Philosophy and Theology," p. 84.

21. Tillich, "Philosophy and Theology," p. 84.

22. Tillich, "Philosophy and Theology," p. 85.

23. Paul Tillich, *Systematic Theology*, vol. 1 [Chicago: University of Chicago Press, 1951], p. 24.

24. Tillich, *Systematic Theology*, vol. 1, p. 24.

25. Tillich, "Philosophy and Theology," p. 10.

26. Tillich, *Systematic Theology*, vol. 1, p. 24.

27. Tillich, *Systematic Theology*, vol. 1, p. 24.

28. Tillich, "Philosophy and Theology, p. 88.

29. Paul Tillich, *Dynamics of Faith* [New York: Harper & Brothers, 1958], p 1.

30. Tillich, "Philosophy and Theology," p. 88.

31. Tillich, "Philosophy and Theology," p. 90.

32. Tillich, "Philosophy and Theology," p. 90.

33. Tillich, *Systematic Theology*, vol. 1, p. 25.

34. Tillich, "Philosophy and Theology," p. 92.

35. Tillich, *Systematic Theology*, vol. 1, p. 69.

36. Tillich, *Systematic Theology*, vol. 1, p. 69.

37. Tillich, "Philosophy and Theology," p. 87.

38. Tillich, *Systematic Theology*, vol. 1, p. 69.

39. Dietrich Bonhoeffer, "Die Geschichte der systematischen Theologie des 20. Jahrhunderts 1931/32," *Gesammelte Schriften*, vol. 5 [Munich: Christian Kaiser, 1972], p. 219.

40. Bonhoeffer, "Die systematische Theologie des 20. Jh.," p. 220.

41. Bonhoeffer, "Die systematische Theologie des 20. Jh.," p. 219.

42. Bonhoeffer, "Die systematische Theologie des 20. Jh.," p. 219.

43. Bonhoeffer, "Die systematische Theologie des 20. Jh.," p. 220.

44. Bonhoeffer, "Die systematische Theologie des 20. Jh.," p. 226.

Chapter 4

1. Dietrich Bonhoeffer, *Sanctorum Communio*, tr. Ronald Gregor Smith [London: Collins, 1963], p. 13.

2. Bonhoeffer, *Sanctorum Communio*, p. 13.

3. Bonhoeffer, *Sanctorum Communio*, p. 38.

4. Bonhoeffer, *Sanctorum Communio*, p. 38.

5. See Clifford Green's classic study of the early Bonhoeffer, *The Sociality of Christ and Humanity: Dietrich Bonhoeffer's Early Theology, 1927–1933* (Missoula, Mont.: Scholars Press, 1975).

6. Emmanuel Levinas, "Martin Buber and the Theory of Knowledge," in *The Levinas Reader*, ed. Sean Hand (Oxford: Basil Blackwell, 1989), p. 63.

7. Bonhoeffer, *Sanctorum Communio*, p. 28.

8. Bonhoeffer, *Sanctorum Communio*, p. 28.

9. Bonhoeffer, *Sanctorum Communio*, p. 28.

10. Levinas, *Totality and Infinity*, p. 36.

11. Levinas, *Totality and Infinity*, p. 37.

12. Levinas, *Totality and Infinity*, p. 40.

13. Hegel in Jean Hyppolite, *Genesis and Structure of Hegel's Phenomenology of Spirit*, tr. Samuel Cherniak and John Heckman (Evanston, Ill.: Northwestern University Press, 1974), p. 580.

14. Bonhoeffer, *Sanctorum Communio*, p. 26.

15. Bonhoeffer, *Sanctorum Communio*, p. 26.

16. Dietrich Bonhoeffer, "The Inaugural Lecture: Man in Contemporary Philosophy and Theology," in *No Rusty Swords: Letters, Lectures and Notes 1928–1936*, tr. John Bowden and Edwin Robertson (New York: Harper & Row, 1965), pp. 50–55.

17. Dietrich Bonhoeffer, *Christ the Center*, tr. Edwin H. Robertson (New York: Harper & Row, 1983), p. 29.

18. Bonhoeffer, *Sanctorum Communio*, p. 29.

19. Bonhoeffer, *Sanctorum Communio*, p. 28.

20. Michael Theunissen, *The Other: Studies in the Social Ontology of Husserl, Heidegger, Sartre and Buber*, tr. Christopher Macann (Cambridge: MIT Press, 1984), p. 161.

21. Theunissen, *The Other*, p. 162.

22. Bonhoeffer, *Sanctorum Communio*, p. 34.

23. Bonhoeffer, *Sanctorum Communio*, p. 35.

24. "The character of a Thou is in fact the form in which the divine is experienced; every human Thou has its character from the divine Thou" (*Sanctorum Communio*, p. 36). The difference of God and I is the absolutely original relation which is analogously resident in the difference of I and human Other (*analogia relationis*). As the principal analogue, the former is the condition of the possibility of the latter. "The other person presents us with the same problem of cognition as does God himself. My real relation to the other is oriented on my relation to God" (*Sanctorum Communio*, p. 36). The divine Thou is luminescent in the human Thou—and the human other exists only insofar as God makes it thus.

25. Bonhoeffer, *Sanctorum Communio*, p. 36.

26. Bonhoeffer, *Sanctorum Communio*, p. 46.

27. Bonhoeffer, *Sanctorum Communio*, p. 46.

28. For an insightful modern treatment of the Trinity which offers a corrective of this kind of shortsightedness, see John J. O'Donnell, S.J., *The Mystery of the Triune God* (New York: Paulist Press, 1989). See also L. Gregory Jones's consructive attempt to ameliorate the problem in the discourse of moral theology in *Transformed Judgment: Toward a Trinitarian Account of the Moral Life* (Notre Dame: University of Notre Dame Press, 1990).

29. Bonhoeffer, *Sanctorum Communio*, p. 105.

30. Bonhoeffer, *Sanctorum Communio*, p. 105.

31. Bonhoeffer, *Sanctorum Communio*, p. 105.

32. Bonhoeffer, *Sanctorum Communio*, p. 105.

33. Bonhoeffer, *Sanctorum Communio*, p. 116.

34. Bonhoeffer, *Sanctorum Communio*, p. 37.

35. Bonhoeffer, *Sanctorum Communio*, p. 106.

36. Bonhoeffer, *Sanctorum Communio*, p. 106.

37. Bonhoeffer, *Sanctorum Communio*, p. 106.

38. Bonhoeffer, *Sanctorum Communio*, p. 119.

39. Bonhoeffer, *Sanctorum Communio*, p. 123.

40. Martin Buber, *I and Thou*, tr. Walter Kaufmann (New York: Scribner's, 1970), p. 89. There is no indication that Bonhoeffer ever read Buber. The extraordinary situation of the philosophers of dialogue is that their working in virtual ignorance of each other did not affect the synchronicity of their investigations (cf. Theunissen, "Postscript," in *The Other*).

41. Buber, *I and Thou*, p. 69.

42. Buber quoted in Theunissen, *The Other*, p. 277.

43. Buber quoted in Theunissen, *The Other*, p. 286.

44. Buber, *I and Thou*, p. 62.

45. Buber, *I and Thou*, p. 71.

46. Ernst Feil, *The Theology of Dietrich Bonhoeffer*, tr. Martin Rumscheidt (Philadelphia: Fortress Press, 1985), pp. 61–64.

47. Feil, *The Theology of Dietrich Bonhoeffer*, p. 62.

48. Bonhoeffer, *Sanctorum Communio*, p. 127.

49. Bonhoeffer, *Sanctorum Communio*, p. 129.

50. Bonhoeffer, *Sanctorum Communio*, p. 129.

51. Theunissen, *The Other*, p. 363.

52. Theunissen, *The Other*, p. 363.

53. Theunissen, *The Other*, p. 363.

54. Theunissen, *The Other*, p. 367.

55. Theunissen, *The Other*, p. 369.

56. Levinas, "Martin Buber and the Theory of Knowledge," pp. 59–74.

57. Bonhoeffer, *Act and Being*, p. 88 (my emphasis).

58. Bonhoeffer, *Act and Being*, p. 89.

59. Levinas, "Martin Buber and the Theory of Knowledge," p. 69.

60. Levinas, "Martin Buber and the Theory of Knowledge," p. 70.

Chapter 5

1. Karl Barth, *Protestant Theology in the Nineteenth Century*, tr. Brian Cozens, Herbert Hartwell et al. (Valley Forge, N.Y.: Judson Press, 1959), p. 396. Jacques Derrida registers his respect of Hegel in similar terms when he writes, "We will never be finished with the reading or rereading of Hegel, and, in a certain way, I do nothing other than attempt to explain myself on this point" (quoted in Mark C. Taylor, "Introduction," in *Deconstruction in Context*, ed. Mark C. Taylor [Chicago: University of Chicago Press, 1986], p. 1).

2. Barth, *Protestant Theology*, p. 283.

3. Richard Rorty, *Contingency, Irony and Solidarity* (Cambridge: Cambridge Univerrsity Press, 1989), p. 78.

4. G. W. F. Hegel, *The Phenomenology of Mind*, tr. J. B. Baillie (New York: Harper Torchbooks, 1967), p. 804.

5. Rorty, *Contingency, Irony and Solidarity*, p. 78.

6. Barth, *Protestant Theology*, p. 296.

7. Barth, *Protestant Theology*, p. 303.

8. Barth, *Protestant Theology*, p. 286.

9. Barth states, "When God manifests himself the philosopher of religion has already understood him in the preliminaries of this act, and he already has the level in his hand which he has only to depress to advance from God's act of revealing to the higher level of God being manifest, in which every given thing, all duality, is annulled, all speaking and listening has lost its object and been transformed again into pure knowing, the knowing of the human subject, as it originally proceeded from him" (*Protestant Thought*, p. 303).

10. Although Bonhoeffer refers occasionally to the *Philosophy of Right* and the *Encyclopedia*, his critique is primarily engaged with Hegel's *Phenomenology of Spirit* and the *Lectures on the Philosophy of Religion*.

11. Bonhoeffer's theological anthropological description of human being as a being-for others can seem trivial when deracinated from its christological soil. When this happens the ethical dimension of his theology appears monochronic and thin; being-for others begins to sound like ethical religion, a nice thing to do perhaps but not radical in the total breadth of personal transformation. Bonhoeffer's engagement with Hegel's thought may be seen as one reason why such exclusively ethical interpretations of being-for others are superficial: Hegel compelled Bonhoeffer to consider nothing less than the ontological and structural reconfiguration of the person in fellowship with God. Despite the differences between the two thinkers, there is strong agreement on the point that life with God involves the most basic transformations of the self.

12. Hans Küng writes, "The *Phenomenology* attempts to present the doctrine of a comprehensive reconciliation of God and man which will be at one and the same time radically modern and radically Christian" (*The In-*

carnation of God: An Introduction to Hegel's Theological Thought as Prolegomena to a Future Christology, tr. J. R. Stephenson [Edinburgh: T & T Clark, 1987], p. 224).

13. Raymond Keith Williamson, *Introduction to Hegel's Philosophy of Religion* (Albany: State University of New York Press, 1984), p. 173.

14. Williamson, *Introduction to Hegel's Philosophy of Religion*, p. 128.

15. Hegel, *Phenomenology of Mind*, p. 152.

16. Hegel, *Phenomenology of Mind*, p. 153.

17. Hegel, *Phenomenology of Spirit*, tr. A. V. Miller (Oxford: Oxford University Press, 1977), p. 66. I make use of both the Baillie and the Miller translations of *Phänomenologie des Geistes*.

18. Williamson, *Introduction to Hegel's Philosophy of Religion*, p. 177.

19. Charles Taylor, *Hegel* (Cambridge: Cambridge University Press, 1975), p. 142.

20. Hegel, *Phenomenology of Mind*, p. 218.

21. Hegel, *Phenomenology of Mind*, p. 229.

22. Hegel, *Phenomenology of Spirit*, p. 110.

23. Hegel, *Phenomenology of Spirit*, p. 476.

24. Hegel quoted in Eberhard Jüngel, *God as the Mystery of the World*, tr. Darrell L. Guder (Grand Rapids, Mich.: Eerdmans, 1983), p. 87.

25. Hegel quoted in Jüngel, *God as the Mystery of the World*, p. 87.

26. Hegel quoted in Bernard M. G. Reardon, *Religion in the Age of Romanticism* (Cambridge: Cambridge University Press, 1985), p. 72.

27. Hegel, *Phenomenology of Mind*, p. 780.

28. Hegel, *Phenomenology of Mind*, p. 780.

29. G. W. F. Hegel, *Lectures on the Philosophy of Religion*, tr. R. F. Brown, P. C. Hodgson, and J. M. Steward, ed. Peter C. Hodgson (Berkeley: University of California Press, 1985), vol. 3, p. 140.

30. Hegel, *Lectures on the Philosophy of Religion*, vol. 3, pp. 211–23.

31. Hegel, *Lectures on the Philosophy of Religion*, vol. 3, p. 237.

32. Hegel, *Phenomenology of Spirit*, p. 477. One such cognitive representation would be Kant's categorical imperative. Cf. Hegel, "The Spirit of Christianity and Its Fate," in *Early Thological Writings*, tr. T. M. Knox (Philadelphia: University of Pennsylvania Press, 1971).

33. Hegel, *Lectures on the Philosophy of Religion*, vol. 3, p. 237.

34. Hegel, *Lectures on the Philosophy of Religion*, vol. 3, p. 237.

35. Hegel, *Phenomenology of Mind*, p. 783.

36. Jean Hyppolite, *Genesis and Structure of Hegel's Phenomenology of Spirit*, tr. Samuel Cherniak and John Heckman (Evanston, Ill.: Northwestern University Press, 1974), p. 603.

37. Hyppolite, *Genesis*, p. 603.

38. Hegel, *Lectures on the Philosophy of Religion*, vol. 3, p. 346.

39. Dietrich Bonhoeffer, *Sanctorum Communio*, tr. Ronald Gregor Smith (London: Collins, 1963), p. 28.

40. Bonhoeffer, *Sanctorum Communio*, p. 28.

41. Bonhoeffer, *Sanctorum Communio*, p. 36.

42. The phrase is Wayne Floyd's; see his *Theology and the Dialectics of Otherness: On Reading Bonhoeffer and Adorno* (Lanham, Md.: University Press of America, 1988), p. xi.

43. Bonhoeffer, *Sanctorum Communio*, p. 37.

44. Taylor, *Hegel*, p. 71.

45. William Desmond, *Dessire, Dialectics and Otherness* (New Haven: Yale University Press, 1988), p. 6.

46. Merold Westphal, *History and Truth in Hegel's Phenomenology* (Atlantic Highlands, N.J.: Humanities Press International, 1979), p. 213.

47. Hegel quoted in Westphal, *History and Truth in Hegel's Phenomenology*, p. 213.

48. Taylor, *Hegel*, p. 107.

49. Taylor, *Hegel*, p. 107.

50. Hegel quoted in Taylor, *Hegel*, p. 108.

51. William Desmond, *Philosophy and Its Others* (Albany: State University of New York Press, 1990), p. 4.

52. Desmond, *Philosophy and Its Others*, p. 4.

53. Hegel, *Phenomenology of Spirit*, p. 10.

54. In fact, in *Act and Being* Bonhoeffer advances very much the same critique as Desmond. "If in original transcendentalism mind was in tension between transcendent poles and was thus irrevocably their co-ordinate, henceforth the movement of the mind is purely self-illumined, which is to say that in principle it has come to rest. The mind's forth-proceeding from itself ensues only under the conditions of its being by itself" (*Act and Being* [New York: Octagon Books, 1983], p. 27).

55. Ilse Tödt, ed., *Dietrich Bonhoeffer's Hegel-Seminar 1933* (Munich: Christian Kaiser, 1988), p. 10.

56. Lehel quoted in Tödt, *Dietrich Bonhoeffer's Hegel-Seminar 1933*, p. 10.

57. Hegel quoted in Williamson, *Introduction to Hegel's Philosophy of Religion*, p. 175.

58. Williamson, *Introduction to Hegel's Philosophy of Religion*, p. 175.

59. Hegel, *The Philosophy of Religion*, vol. 3, 106–7. This citation is taken from the earlier translation by E. B. Speirs and J. Burden Sanderson (London: Kegan Paul, Trench, Trübner & Co., 1895).

60. Hegel, *Lectures on the Philosophy of Religion*, vol. 3, p. 65.

61. Hegel, *Lectures on the Philosophy of Religion*, vol. 3, p. 327.

62. Hegel, *Phenomenology of Spirit*, p. 14.

63. Hegel quoted in Jüngel, *God as the Mystery of the World*, p. 74.

64. G. W. F. Hegel, *Faith and Knowledge*, tr. W. Cerf and H. S. Harris (Albany: State University of New York Press, 1977), p. 190.

65. Jüngel, *God as the Mystery of the World*, p. 78.

66. Hegel, *Lectures on the Philosophy of Religion*, vol. 3, p. 125.

67. Hegel, *Lectures on the Philosophy of Religion*, vol. 3, p. 125.

68. Hegel, *Lectures on the Philosophy of Religion*, vol. 3, p. 125.

69. Hegel, *Lectures on the Philosophy of Religion*, vol. 3, p. 132.

70. Hegel, *Lectures on the Philosophy of Religion*, vol. 3, p. 132.

71. Thus, the *analogia entis* is correct to show the affinity between God and creation but mistaken to the extent that it fails to emphasize the necessity of Christ for the analogy's efficacy. Let me make a few comments about Bonhoeffer's use of analogy.

In *Act and Being* he commends the Thomistic continuity between the *statu corruptionis* and the *status gratiae* (the unity of becoming and being "in tension") as a helpful way to move beyond the discontinuity of the "old Adam" and the "new being." With the continuity of one's own possession of "being" ("Seinsverhaltens"), the person as characterized in the analogy of being is also guaranteed continuity in relation to the being of God, so that human being, whether in Adam or in Christ, can be certain of its connectedness with God.

Nevertheless, the anthropology implicit herein exaggerates the continuity between God and humanity in the description of a *general* state of nature and thus fails to emphasize human being as always already located either in a being-in Adam or a being-in Christ. Bonhoeffer explicates this objection to the *analogia entis* in terms of a problem which arises in thinking of the relation between the human and the divine side of the analogy and the attendant idea of God. Bonhoeffer's point here is intriguing and easily overlooked in reading the text. It involves the following steps. (1) The *analogia entis* is based on the analogy of being a creature. The Thomistic doctrine of being is valid for the being of humankind as creature, to the extent that human being is determined essentially through creatureliness (*Act and Being*, p. 68). This is the general statement which demonstrates the continuity of the mode of being in both *status corruptionis* and *status gratiae*. Both the human side and the divine side of the analogy are assured continuity in light of the general creaturely orientation of the analogy. With the continuity of his own self-condition ("des eigenen Selbstverhaltens"), human being is guaranteed through the *analogia entis* a continuity of the being-condition of God ("des Seinsverhaltens Gottes"), so that human being, whether in the original state in Adam or in Christ, is always secured in its analogy to God. (2) Human being, however, is never a general description but a concrete one of being already either in Adam or in Christ; human being is only toward God in grace (in community) or in guilt (in individual isolation). (3) With the removal of the human side, that the analogy is based on a description of the creatureliness of human being, we lose also the divine side of the analogy, that there is a continuity on the divine side. What is problematic in the analogy of being is the compromise of the particularity of the person by the pre-formation of divine attributes in the concept of analogous being. The freedom and specificity of revelation (God's comporting himself to the world in grace, judgment, fellowship, etc.) are relegated to a general theory of divine being.

72. Dietrich Bonhoeffer, *Christ the Center*, tr. Edwin H. Robertson (New York: Harper & Row, 1983), p. 62.

73. Dietrich Bonhoeffer, *Creation and Fall*, tr. John Fletcher (New York: Macmillan, 1959), p. 36.

74. Bonhoeffer, *Creation and Fall*, p. 36.

75. Bonhoeffer, *Creation and Fall*, p. 37.

76. Bonhoeffer, *Creation and Fall*, p. 37.

77. Bonhoeffer, *Creation and Fall*, p. 55.

78. Dietrich Bonhoeffer, *Life Together*, tr. John W. Doberstein (New York: Harper, 1954), p. 24.

79. Bonhoeffer, *Life Together*, p. 36.

80. George Hunsinger, *How to Read Karl Barth: The Shape of His Theology* (New York: Oxford University Press, 1991), p. 109.

81. Dietrich Bonhoeffer, *Ethics*, tr. Neville Horton Smith (New York: Macmillan, 1965), p. 57.

82. Desmond, *Philosophy and Its Others*, pp. 1–61.

83. Bonhoeffer, *Ethics*, p. 74.

84. Hegel, *Lectures on the Philosophy of Religion*, vol. 3, p. 62.

85. Bonhoeffer, *Akt und Sein* (Munich: Christian Kaiser, 1988), p. 94.

86. Hegel, *Philosophy of Religion*, vol. 3, pp. 64–65.

87. Hegel, *Philosophy of Religion*, vol. 2, p. 109 (old edition).

88. Jüngel, *God as the Mystery of the World*, p. 94.

89. Jüngel, *God as the Mystery of the World*, p. 95.

90. Jüngel, *God as the Mystery of the World*, p. 95.

91. Soren Kierkegaard, *Fear and Trembling*, tr. Alastair Hannay (New York: Penguin, 1985), p. 61.

92. Bonhoeffer, *Sanctorum Communio*, p. 127.

93. Karl Barth, *Church Dogmatics* I/2, tr. G. T. Thompson and Harold Knight (Edinburgh: T & T Clark, 1956), p. 280.

94. Barth, *Church Dogmatics* I/2, p. 280.

95. Bonhoeffer, *Act and Being*, p. 92.

96. Bonhoeffer, *Act and Being*, p. 93.

97. Bonhoeffer, *Act and Being*, p. 136.

98. Bonhoeffer, *Act and Being*, p. 92.

99. Bonhoeffer, *Act and Being*, p. 136.

100. Bonhoeffer, *Act and Being*, p. 93.

101. Bonhoeffer, *Ethics*, p. 202.

102. Bonhoeffer, *Ethics*, p. 202.

103. Bonhoeffer, *Ethics*, p. 202.

104. Bonhoeffer, *Life Together*, p. 116.

105. Reardon, *Religion in the Age of Romanticism*, p. 85.

106. Reardon, *Religion in the Age of Romanticism*, p. 84.

107. Hegel, *Philosophy of Religion*, vol. 3, p. 326.

108. Bonhoeffer, *Ethics*, p. 205.

109. Bonhoeffer, *Life Together*, p. 20.

110. Bonhoeffer, *Ethics*, p. 139.

111. Bonhoeffer, *Ethics*, p. 194.

112. Bonhoeffer, *Ethics*, p. 197.

113. Bonhoeffer, *Ethics*, p. 197.

114. Bonhoeffer, *Ethics*, p. 198.

115. Bonhoeffer, *Ethics*, p. 197.

116. Karl Rahner, *Concise Theological Dictionary*, p. 17.

117. Irenaeus, *Against Heresies*, ed. Alexander Roberts and James Donaldson (Grand Rapids, Mich.: Eerdmans, 1989), p. 443.

118. Rahner, *Concise Theological Dictionary*, p. 17.

119. J. N. D. Kelly, *Early Christian Doctrines* (New York: Harper, 1960), p. 173.

120. Kelly, *Early Christian Doctrines*, p. 173.

121. Dietrich Bonhoeffer, *Letters and Papers from Prison* (New York: Macmillan, 1972), p. 170.

122. Bonhoeffer, *Letters and Papers from Prison*, p. 170.

123. Bonhoeffer, *Letters and Papers from Prison*, p. 170.

124. Bonhoeffer, *Ethics*, pp. 198–99.

125. Bonhoeffer, *Ethics*, p. 34.

126. Bonhoeffer, *Ethics*, p. 34.

127. Bonhoeffer, *Ethics*, p. 34.

128. Bonhoeffer, *Act and Being*, p. 181.

129. Dietrich Bonhoeffer, *The Cost of Discipleship*, tr. Reginald H. Fuller (New York: Macmillan, 1963), p. 62.

130. Bonhoeffer, *The Cost of Discipleship*, p. 62.

131. Bonhoeffer, *The Cost of Discipleship*, p. 71.

132. Andre Dumas, *Dietrich Bonhoeffer: Theologian of Reality*, tr. Robert McAfee Brown (New York: Macmillan, 1971), pp. 124–25.

133. Dumas, *Dietrich Bonhoeffer*, p. 139.

134. Bonhoeffer, *Ethics*, p. 35.

135. Bonhoeffer, *Ethics*, p. 55.

136. Eberhard Jüngel quoted in Hans Küng, *The Incarnation of God: An Introduction to Hegel's Theological Thought as Prolegomena to a Future Christology*, tr. J. R. Stephenson (Edinburgh: T & T Clark, 1987), p. 552.

137. Of course, there are resonances of Hegel in Bonhoeffer's proposal. In the "Tübingen Essay" of 1793 Hegel protests the arid scholasticism of his Lutheranism by distinguishing between subjective and objective (or positive) religion. The former is alive in the "inwardness of our being" and "active in our outward behavior" (484); the latter is derivative and abstract—it is "cold reflection." While the distinction is interesting for comparative-critical purposes, Bonhoeffer resists Hegel's turn to subjectivity ("The Tübingen Essay of 1793," in H. S. Harris, *Hegel's Development: Toward the Sunlight, 1770–1801* (Oxford: Clarendon Press, 1972). Also, Hegel's early essay on the positivity of Christianity (1795) delineates morality, that is, Kantian ethics, as the essential content of the religion of Jesus, a religion which immedi-

ately lost its originary freedom to the authoritarian bondage of personality, intuition, and doctrine. While there might be loose structural affinities with Bonhoeffer's program, the capabilities of the autonomous moral agent have no room in his theology. More to the point of Bonhoeffer's critique is Hegel's later view that "ethical life is the most genuine cultus" (*Lectures on the Philosophy of Religion*, Appendix, p. 451, 1831). Peter Hodgson remarks, "That is, when the subjective appropriation of reconcilation that occurs in the cultus takes on objective, ethical structure or substance, the true and universal actualization of divine-human reconcilation is achieved" (p. 451). This point is deserving of greater treatment. However, one noteworthy qualification in ascribing Hegel's view to Bonhoeffer is that Hegel investigates this correlation in terms of the *orders* or creation which represent organic extensions of the cultus. Further, Bonhoeffer is not equating community with ethical life. Ethics as formation is not primarily about the person's conformity to Christ—although the active conformation to Christ is not relinquished—but about Christ's becoming real and taking form in the person (see Robin Lovin, "Biographical Context," in *New Studies in Bonhoeffer's Ethics*, ed. William J. Peck [Lewiston, N.Y.: Edwin Mellen Press, 1987], p. 205). In other words, formation amplifies new possibilities of conformation. Bonhoeffer says, "Ethics as formation, then, means the bold endeavor to speak about the way in which the form of Jesus Christ takes form in our world, in a manner which is neither abstract nor casuistic, neither programmatic nor purely speculative. Concrete judgments and decisions will have to be ventured here" (*Ethics*, p. 79).

138. Jörg Rades, "Bonhoeffer and Hegel from *Sanctorum Communio* to the Hegel Seminar with Some Perspectives from Later Works," unpublished manuscript, p. 25.

139. Bonhoeffer, *Act and Being*, p. 169.

140. Hans-Jürgen Abromeit explains, "Bonhoeffer stresses so greatly the personal being of Jesus Christ as a living encounter that this cannot be expressed correctly in conceptual structures, but only in the demand of obedience" (*Das Geheimnis Christi* [Neukirchen-Vluyn: Neukirchener Verlag, 1991], p. 28).

141. Dietrich Bonhoeffer, "Die Geschichte der systematischen Theologie des 20. Jahrhunderts 1931/32," in *Gesammelte Schriften*, vol. 5 (München: Christian Kaiser, 1972), p. 226 (my emphasis).

Chapter 6

1. Eberhard Bethge, *Dietrich Bonhoeffer: Theologian, Christian, Contemporary*, tr. Eric Mosbacher et al. (New York: Harper & Row, 1970), p. 58.

2. Bethge, *Dietrich Bonhoeffer*, p. 94.

3. Bethge, *Dietrich Bonhoeffer*, p. 118. The last received extended treatment in Bonhoeffer's seminar presentation, "The Theology of Crisis and Its Attitude Toward Philosophy and Science," and in the essay "Concerning the

Christian Idea of God," which Baillie persuaded Bonhoeffer to publish in *The Journal of Religion.*

4. Bethge, *Dietrich Bonhoeffer*, p. 97.

5. Robert P. Scharlemann makes only a suggestive connection between the two but the suggestion opens up considerable room for reflection. Scharlemann writes, "Dietrich Bonhoeffer's habilitation thesis, entitled *Akt und Sein*, was discernibly influenced by the early Heidegger and is one of the first indications of how the attempt might be made [to destrue the history of ontology]" (*Inscriptions and Reflections: Essays in Philosophical Theology* [Charlottesville: University Press of Virginia, 1989] p. 30).

6. J. J. Mehta, *Martin Heidegger: The Way and the Vision* (Honolulu: University of Hawaii Press, 1967), p. 26.

7. See, for example, *The Later Heidegger and Theology*, ed. James M. Robinson and John B. Cobb, Jr. (New York: Harper & Row, 1963).

8. Jeff Owen Prudhomme, "The Relation of Ontological and Theological Reflection in the Thought of Martin Heidegger," Ph.D. diss., University of Virginia, 1991.

9. Prudhomme, "Ontological and Theological Reflection in the Thought of Martin Heidegger," p. 139.

10. Martin Heidegger, *Being and Time*, tr. John Macquarrie and Edward Robinson (New York: Harper & Row, 1962), p. 331/379. All subsequent references to *Being and Time* are indicated in the body of the text with German pagination first and English second.

11. Otto Pöggeler, *Martin Heidegger's Path of Thinking* (Atlantic Highlands, N.J.: Humanities Press, 1989), p. 41.

12. Ernst Feil, *The Theology of Dietrich Bonhoeffer*, tr. Martin Rumscheidt (Philadlphia: Fortress Press, 1985), p. 32.

13. Dietrich Bonhoeffer, *Act and Being* (New York: Octagon Books, 1983), p. 28.

14. Bonhoeffer, *Act and Being*, p. 28.

15. Heidegger, *Being and Time*, quoted in Bonhoeffer, *Act and Being*, p. 62.

16. Bonhoeffer, *Act and Being*, p. 62.

17. George Kovacs, *The Question of God in Heidegger's Phenomenology* (Evanston, Ill.: Northwestern University Press, 1990), p. 83.

18. Bonhoeffer, *Act and Being*, p. 63.

19. Bonhoeffer, *Act and Being*, p. 64.

20. Bonhoeffer, *Act and Being*, p. 65.

21. Bonhoeffer, *Act and Being*, p. 65.

22. Kovacs, *The Question of God in Heidegger's Phenomenology*, p. 9.

23. Cf. Kovacs, *The Question of God in Heidegger's Phenomenology*, p. xix.

24. Kovacs, *The Question of God in Heidegger's Phenomenology*, p. 48.

25. Kovacs, *The Question of God in Heidegger's Phenomenology*, p. 48.

26. Dietrich Bonhoeffer, *Christ the Center*, tr. Edwin H. Robertson (New York: Harper & Row, 1978), p. 30.

27. Bonhoeffer, *Christ the Center*, p. 31.

28. Pöggeler, *Martin Heidegger's Path of Thinking*, p. 41.

29. Heidegger quoted in Kovacs, *The Question of God in Heidegger's Phenomenology*, p. 97.

30. Dietrich Bonhoeffer, "Man in Contemporary Theology and Philosophy," in *No Rusty Swords: Letters, Lectures and Notes 1928–1936*, tr. John Bowden and Edwin Robertson (New York: Harper & Row, 1965), p. 38.

31. Kovacs, *The Question of God in Heidegger's Phenomenology*, p. 103.

32. Bonhoeffer, "Man in Contemporary Philosophy and Theology," p. 57.

33. Bonhoeffer, "Man in Contemporary Philosophy and Theology," p. 57.

34. Bonhoeffer, "Man in Contemporary Philosophy and Theology," p. 57.

35. Bonhoeffer, "Man in Contemporary Philosophy and Theology," p. 57.

36. Bonhoeffer, "Man in Contemporary Philosophy and Theology," p. 57.

37. Jürgen Habermas, *The Philosophical Discourse of Modernity*, tr. Frederick Lawrence (Cambridge: MIT Press, 1987), p. 150. Habermas writes, "Heidegger passes beyond the horizon of the philosophy of consciousness only to stay in the shadows."

38. Bonhoeffer, "Man in Contemporary Philosophy and Theology," p. 60.

39. Bonhoeffer, "Man in Contemporary Philosophy and Theology," p. 61.

40. Hans Frei, *The Identity of Jesus Christ: The Hermeneutical Basis of Dogmatic Theology* (Philadelphia: Fortress Press, 1975). Talk of presence before identity, as of potentiality over reality, may mean, as Frei writes, "the total diffusion of Jesus into our presence so that he no longer has any presence of his own" (p. 34). Frei's conclusion is pertinent to Bonhoeffer's misgivings about the category of potentiality: "The cost of being contemporaneous with him would then be, it seems, that he no longer *owns* his own presence or, if he does, that we cannot apprehend or comprehend that fact" (p. 34).

41. Bonhoeffer, "Man in Contemporary Philosophy and Theology," p. 64.

42. Or, in Barth's words, "God is the new, [the] incomparable. . . . He cannot be grasped, brought under management, and put to use" (Karl Barth, "Biblical Insights and Vistas," *The Word of God and the Word of Man*, tr. Douglas Horton [Gloucester, Mass.: Peter Smith, 1978], p. 74).

43. Bonhoeffer, "Man in Contemporary Philosophy and Theology," p. 65.

44. Bonhoeffer, "Man in Contemporary Philosophy and Theology," p. 65.

45. Hans-Richard Reuter, "Nachwort," in *Akt und Sein* (Munich: Christian Kaiser, 1988), unpublished translation by Jeffrey Prudhomme, p. 30.

46. Reuter, "Nachwort," *Akt und Sein*, p. 30. The only precondition Bonhoeffer admits for self-understanding and for understanding God is the resolute decision to follow after in obedience in the service of the truth. However, this is not a condition which establishes itself apart from revelation; rather, following-after is the response to the calling of costly grace, the

call of Christ. "Discipleship is not an offer man makes to Christ. It is only the call which creates the situation" (Dietrich Bonhoeffer, *The Cost of Discipleship*, tr. R. H. Fuller [New York: Macmillan, 1963], p. 68). Obedience does not isolate the person from the community but instead represents the ethical form of our life together with God.

47. Karl Barth, *The Epistle to the Romans*, tr. Edwyn C. Hoskyns (New York: Oxford University Press, 1968), p. 149.

48. Bonhoeffer, *Act and Being*, p. 99.

49. Bonhoeffer, *Act and Being*, p. 108.

50. Bonhoeffer, *Act and Being*, p. 116.

51. Bonhoeffer, *Act and Being*, p. 132.

52. Eberhard Jüngel, *God as the Mystery of the World*, tr. Darrell L. Guder (Grand Rapids, Mich.: Eerdmans, 1983), p. 221.

53. Jüngel, *God as the Mystery of the World*, p. 221.

54. Bonhoeffer, *Act and Being*, p. 112.

55. Bonhoeffer, *Act and Being*, p. 113.

56. Jüngel, *God as the Mystery of the World*, p. 223.

57. In Jüngel, *God as the Mystery of the World*, p. 223.

58. Cf. John J. O'Donnell, S.J., *The Mystery of the Triune God* (New York: Paulist Press, 1989), p. 160.

59. Bonhoeffer, *Christ the Center*, p. 47.

60. O'Donnell, *The Mystery of the Triune God*, p. 161.

61. I am indebted to James J. Buckley for clarification on this notion of divine relinquishment as (more precisely put) divine re-enactment of aseity.

62. Bonhoeffer, *Act and Being*, p. 139.

63. Bonhoeffer, *Act and Being*, p. 160.

64. Bonhoeffer, *Act and Being*, p. 139.

65. Michael Theunissen, *The Other: Studies in the Social Ontology of Husserl, Heidegger, Sartre and Buber*, tr. Christopher Macann (Cambridge: MIT Press, 1984), p. 175.

66. Theunissen, *The Other*, p. 179.

67. Theunissen, *The Other*, p. 179.

68. Theunissen, *The Other*, p. 183.

69. Theunissen, *The Other*, p. 184. He writes, "'The They itself belongs to the Others,' and, indeed, in the strong sense, that being-with-one-another completely resolves one's Dasein into the mode of being of 'the Others.'"

70. Theunissen, *The Other*, p. 186.

71. Theunissen, *The Other*, p. 187.

72. Habermas argues that Heidegger's refusal to attend to the genuine depths of everyday discourse disables him from understanding the communicative and interlocutory practices of human community: "Heidegger enciphers the palpable distortions of everyday communicative practice into an impalpable destining of Being (*Seinsgeschick*) administered by philosophers. At the same time, he cuts off the possibility of any deciphering by the fact that he shoves aside the defective everyday practice of mutual under-

standing as a calculation-oriented practice of self-maintenance—oblivious of Being and [thus] vulgar—and deprives the dirempted ethical totality of the lifeworld of any essential interest" (*Philosophical Discourse of Modernity*, p. 139).

73. Kovacs, *The Question of God in Heidegger's Phenomenology*, p. 75.

74. Theunissen, *The Other*, p. 190.

75. Theunissen, *The Other*, p. 190. As Theodor Adorno has argued, the insistence on total self-sufficiency gives way to the extreme confirmation of selfhood; "it becomes an Ur-image of defiance in self-abnegation" (*The Jargon of Authenticity* [Evanston, Ill.: Northwestern University Press, 1973], p. 152).

76. Habermas, *Philosophical Discourse of Modernity*, p. 149.

77. Habermas, *Philosophical Discourse of Modernity*, p. 150.

78. Theunissen, *The Other*, p. 191.

79. Theunissen, *The Other*, pp. 191–92.

80. Therefore, when Heidegger talks of the possibility of becoming "authentically bound together" ("eine eigentliche Verbundenheit") through a devotion of Dasein to a common activity, he describes an ontic state of affairs, which in no way restores a primordial sense of being-with to the ontological structures of Dasein.

81. Theunissen, *The Other*, p. 192.

82. Bonhoeffer, *Christ the Center*, p. 112.

83. This language appropriates Eberhard Jüngel's description in *God as the Mystery of the World* of God's giving himself to life and death for the sake of life.

84. Dietrich Bonhoeffer, *Sanctorum Communio*, tr. Ronald Gregor Smith (London: Collins, 1963), p. 128.

85. Bonhoeffer, *Act and Being*, p. 134.

86. Bonhoeffer, *Act and Being*, p. 109.

87. Bonhoeffer, *Christ the Center*, p. 47.

88. Habermas, *Philosophical Discourse of Modernity*, p. 140.

89. Habermas, *Philosophical Discourse of Modernity*, p. 140.

90. Trent Schroyer, "Foreword," in Adorno, *The Jargon of Authenticity*, p. xvii.

91. Theunissen, *The Other*, p. 379.

Chapter 7

1. Dietrich Bonhoeffer, *Lettters and Papers from Prison*, tr. Reginald Fuller et al., ed. Eberhard Bethge (New York: Macmillan, 1972), p. 312.

2. Bonhoeffer, *Lettters and Papers from Prison*, pp. 33–35.

3. Bonhoeffer, *Letters and Papers from Prison*, p. 35. Hans-Richard Reuter's speculative comment on the prison metaphor is apropos of these bleak impressions: "It may be ventured, whether Bonhoeffer with his battle against the solipsistic claim of autonomy on the part of subjectivity did not

deal with an assault of despair, which he himself experienced as a representative of just this autonomous form of consciousness and which is to be evaluated as the subjective factor in a merciless deconstruction of all philosophical self-understandings" ("Nachwort," in *Akt und Sein* [Munich: Christian Kaiser, 1988], unpublished translation by Jeffrey Owen Prudhomme, p. 30).

4. Dietrich Bonhoeffer, *Act and Being* (New York: Octagon Books, 1983), p. 158.

5. Bonhoeffer, *Act and Being*, p. 158.

6. Eberhard Jüngel, *Theological Essays*, tr. J. B. Webster (Edinburgh: T & T Clark, 1989), p. 134.

7. Jüngel, *Theological Essays*, p. 134.

8. Bonhoeffer, *Letters and Papers from Prison*, p. 105.

9. Bonhoeffer, *Letters and Papers from Prison*, p. 381.

10. Bonhoeffer, *Act and Being*, p. 169.

11. Rainer Maria Rilke, "Lament," in *The Selected Poetry of Rainer Maria Rilke*, tr. Stephen Mitchell (New York: Vintage International, 1989), p. 9.

12. Dietrich Bonhoeffer, "What Is a Christian Ethic?" in *No Rusty Swords: Letters, Lectures and Notes 1928–1936*, tr. John Bowden and Edwin Robinson (New York: Harper & Row, 1965), p. 44.

13. Bonhoeffer, *No Rusty Swords*, p. 44.

14. Bonhoeffer, *A Testament to Freedom: The Essential Writings of Dietrich Bonhoeffer* (San Francisco: Harper & Row, 1970), p. 367.

15. Bonhoeffer, *A Testament to Freedom*, p. 367.

16. Dietrich Bonhoeffer, *No Rusty Swords*, p. 44.

17. Eberhard Bethge, *Dietrich Bonhoeffer: Theologian, Christian, Contemporary*, tr. Eric Mosbacher et al. (New York: Harper & Row, 1970), p. 90.

18. Bethge, *Dietrich Bonhoeffer*, p. 92.

19. Bonhoeffer, *No Rusty Swords*, p. 44.

20. In *The Cost of Discipleship* Bonhoeffer writes, "And what does the [biblical] text inform us about the content of discipleship? Follow me, run along behind me! . . . To follow in his steps is something which is void of all content. It gives no intelligible programme for a way of life, no goal or ideal to strive after. It is not a cause which human calculation might deem worthy of our devotion, even the devotion of ourselves. . . . At the call, Levi leaves all that he has—but not because he thinks that he might be doing something worth while, but simply for the sake of the call. Otherwise he cannot follow in the steps of Jesus. This act on Levi's part has not the slightest value in itself, it is quite devoid of significance and unworthy of consideration. . . . Beside Jesus nothing has any significance" (*The Cost of Discipleship*, tr. Reginald H. Fuller [New York: Macmillan, 1963], pp. 62–63).

21. How does this work out in nontheological practice? At the risk of diverting our focus in a different direction, let me offer the following example. The question might be asked whether there is a conflict with the thought that the self comes to itself in life with others and the psychoanalytic claim

that the self has to reckon with its own interiority and private drama before it can attain wholeness, recover the capacity to relate to others, and attain a sense of satisfaction with one's life. Does there exist here an unresolvable contradiction? If not, how can the apparent contradiction be resolved? To begin, the fact that the self comes to itself in life with others, does not, as I have said, impede the affirmation of the individual. It simply holds that the individual cannot achieve completeness of self by recourse to the power of the self alone, but it instead awaits and anticipates breakthrough (*Durchbruch*) as the event that empowers the self to turn outward and to be what it is by being more than the I. In this manner, breakthrough can assume the form of the other person, that is, my neighbor, my child, my lover, my enemy. Breakthrough can also occur as the breakthrough of the other of the self to itself; the recollection of past events hitherto hidden from consciousness, or the disclosure of new levels of experience, unexpected feelings of compassion, anger, lust, kindness, and the like. I take this kind of breakthrough to be in part what Paul Tillich means when he says, "Vitality is the power of creating beyond oneself without losing oneself." Both of these types in Bonhoeffer's view are grounded in the breaking-in of the living God in Jesus Christ. The last does not negate the first two but establishes the context in which they become meaningful.

22. Michael Theunissen, *The Other: Studies in the Social Ontology of Husserl, Heidegger, Sartre and Buber*, tr. Christopher Macann (Cambridge: MIT Press, 1984), pp. 366–69.

23. Theunissen, *The Other*, p. 365.

24. Theunissen, *The Other*, p. 22.

25. Theunissen, *The Other*, p. 367.

26. See William Desmond's intriguing discussion on philosophical mindfulness and the alterating event of song in "Being Mindful: Thought Singing Its Other" in his *Philosophy and Its Others* (Albany: State University of New York Press, 1990), pp. 259–311.

27. Bonhoeffer, *Act and Being*, p. 122.

28. Bonhoeffer, *Act and Being*, p. 124.

29. Perhaps pneumatology is the proper means to understand this subjective alteration; however, Bonhoeffer's theology is sorely lacking in a developed notion of the spirit, and thus, this task must be deterred to future considerations.

30. Robert Scharlemann, *The Reason of Following: Christology and the Ecstatic I* (Chicago: University of Chicago Press, 1991), p. 116.

31. Scharlemann, *The Reason of Following*, p. 116.

32. Scharlemann, *The Reason of Following*, p. 34.

33. Scharlemann, *The Reason of Following*, p. 34.

34. Scharlemann, *The Reason of Following*, p. 31.

35. Scharlemann, *The Reason of Following*, p. 30.

36. Scharlemann, *The Reason of Following*, pp. 30–31.

37. Scharlemann, *The Reason of Following*, p. 36.

38. Scharlemann, *The Reason of Following*, p. 116.

39. Scharlemann, *The Reason of Following*, p. 117.

40. Scharlemann, *The Reason of Following*, p. 117.

41. Scharlemann, *The Reason of Following*, p. 117.

42. Scharlemann, *The Reason of Following*, p. 119.

43. Scharlemann writes, The Christ, who at the start is there in another over against 'me' although identical with 'my' being, is at the end no longer there because he has returned to the state of inwardness" (*The Reason of Following*, p. 119). Further: "The Christ-figure differs, therefore, from other human beings by being the one who reflects the very inwardness of the self. . . . If there were no Christ-figure in the world, the 'I' of the here-and-now would be a point of view from which everything is viewed and understood but could not itself be seen or understood" (p. 158).

44. Scharlemann, *The Reason of Following*, p. 121.

45. Scharlemann, *The Reason of Following*, p. 123.

46. Scharlemann, *The Reason of Following*, p. 122.

47. Scharlemann, *The Reason of Following*, p. 122.

48. Scharlemann, *The Reason of Following*, pp. 123–24.

49. Scharlemann, *The Reason of Following*, p. 100.

50. Scharlemann, *The Reason of Following*, p. 100.

51. Irenaeus, *Against Heresies*, ed. Alexander Roberts and James Donaldson (Grand Rapids, Mich.: Eerdmans, 1989), p. 478.

52. Put differently, but with similar concern, Eberhard Jüngel argues persuasively that the being of God is a being who "explodes" the very alternatives of presence and absence (*God as the Mystery of the World*, tr. Darrell L. Guder [Grand Rapids, Mich.: Eerdmans, 1983], p. 62).

53. Eberhard Jüngel, "Humanity in Correspondence with God," in *Theological Essays*, p. 134.

54. Scharlemann, *The Reason of Following*, p. 120.

55. Scharlemann, *The Reason of Following*, p. 119.

56. Dietrich Bonhoeffer, *Christ the Center*, tr. Edwin H. Robertson (New York: Harper & Row, 1978), p. 30.

57. Bonhoeffer, *Letters and Papers from Prison*, p. 362.

58. Bonhoeffer, *Letters and Papers from Prison*, p. 361.

59. Bonhoeffer, *Letters and Papers from Prison*, p. 362.

60. Bonhoeffer, *Letters and Papers from Prison*, p. 362.

61. Bonhoeffer, *Letters and Papers from Prison*, p. 381.

62. Jüngel, *God as the Mystery of the World*, p. 324.

63. Martin Luther, "The Freedom of a Christian," in *Martin Luther: Selections from his Writings*, ed. John Dillenberger (Garden City, N.Y.: Anchor Books, 1961), p. 80.

64. Luther, "The Freedom of a Christian," p. 80.

65. Bonhoeffer, *Letters and Papers from Prison*, pp. 381–82.

66. Eberhard Jüngel, *The Freedom of a Christian*, tr. Roy A. Harrisville (Minneapolis: Augsburg Press, 1988), p. 56.

67. Jüngel, *The Freedom of a Christian*, p. 63.

68. Jüngel, *God as the Mystery of the World*, p. 324.

69. Augustine, *The Confessions*, tr. Henry Chadwick (Oxford: Oxford University Press, 1991), p. 43.

70. Jüngel, *The Freedom of a Christian*, p. 75.

71. Jüngel, *The Freedom of a Christian*, p. 65.

72. Jüngel, "Humanity in Correspondence with God," p. 134.

73. I am indebted for this point to Norman Lilligaard. "Reservations About the Hermeneutics of Suspicion," unpublished NEH paper, Fordham University, July 1990.

74. Bonhoeffer, *Letters and Papers from Prison*, pp. 347–48.

75. Lilligaard, "Reservations About the Hermeneutics of Suspicion," p. 6.

76. Bonhoeffer, *Letters and Papers from Prison*, p. 348.

77. Jürgen Moltmann, *The Trinity and the Kingdom*, tr. Margaret Kohl (San Francisco: HarperCollins, 1991), pp. 45–47.

78. Jüngel, *God as the Mystery of the World*, p. 392.

79. Dietrich Bonhoeffer, *Life Together*, tr. John W. Doberstein (New York: Harper, 1954), p. 58.

80. Bonhoeffer, *Letters and Papers from Prison*, p. 157.

81. Bonhoeffer, *Letters and Papers from Prison*, p. 157.

82. Bonhoeffer, *Letters and Papers from Prison*, p. 337.

83. Bonhoeffer, *Letters and Papers from Prison*, p. 391.

84. Theunissen, *The Other*, p. 379.

85. Theunissen, *The Other*, p. 379.

86. Theunissen, *The Other*, p. 319.

87. Theunissen, *The Other*, p. 379.

INDEX